Getting By
on
$100,000 a Year

AND OTHER SAD TALES

Andrew Tobias

SIMON AND SCHUSTER · NEW YORK

Designed by Eve Metz
Manufactured in the United States of America
1 2 3 4 5 6 7 8 9 10

The material in this book has originally appeared in *Esquire,
Institutional Investor, Money, New York Magazine,* and *Playboy,* in
slightly different form.

Library of Congress Cataloging in Publication Data

Tobias, Andrew P
    Getting by on $100,000 a year and other sad tales

    1. Finance, Personal.   2. Business.   3. United States—
Economic conditions—1971–   I. Title.

FOR
CLAY FELKER,
SHELDON ZALAZNICK
AND
BYRON DOBELL
—WITH THANKS

CONTENTS

INTRODUCTION
Why We're Getting Poorer;
What We Could Do About It

There are two ways of becoming poorer: You can be paid less, or you can be paid more and have it *buy* less. Since there is no evidence that any self-respecting American will sit still for a cut in pay, we go the second route—inflation.

But why must we become poorer at all?

There are several ways of looking at this.

To begin with, picture a tropical island with luscious bread-fruits hanging from every branch, toasting in the sun. It is a small island, but there are only 400 of us on it, so there are more breadfruits than we know what to do with. We're rich. Now picture 4,000 people on the same small island, reaching for the same breadfruits. Number one, there are fewer to go around; number two, you've got to build ladders to reach most of them; number three, the island is becoming littered with breadfruit crumbs. Things get worse and worse as the population gradually expands to 40,000. Welcome to a poor, littered tropical paradise.

Or picture Portage and Trumbull counties, Ohio, where I have an interest in seventeen recently drilled oil and gas wells and where I am, presumably, reaping windfall profits.

All told, it cost the partnership $2.25 million to drill these wells, which is very cheap when you think of what it costs to drill up in the Arctic or off the coast of Australia—but very expensive when you consider how oil used to come bubbling out of the ground *on its own* in some areas of Texas and Oklahoma, particularly in the movies. When you drill in Trumbull and Portage counties, Ohio, you are almost guaranteed to hit the Clinton sand formation, which runs beneath much of the eastern part of the state. The Clinton sand formation oozes, but does not gush, oil and gas. All seventeen of our wells hit the formation, and all began to ooze.

So emaciated have the breadfruit trees become, at least in Ohio, that our seventeen wells in the month of June produced an average of two and a half barrels of oil apiece per day. Drip, drip, drip. America, meanwhile, was burning oil at the rate of 21 million barrels a day. You have heard of "a drop in the bucket"? Every so often, one of our buckets fills up and a truck comes by to empty it.

Let me say that our general partners are not idiots—nor swindlers, masochists, nor, so far as I know, hexed. They weren't looking for *bad* places to drill. They weren't looking for *dumb* places to drill. And yet here we are, dripping our little hearts out to make the difference between an America that turns the lights out when leaving the room and an America that, in many households, is still unwilling to make that sacrifice. I don't think of my oil as the batch in the tank of a speeding ambulance. I see it as the batch chauffeurs use to keep the motor running, air conditioning going, and windows rolled up when it is 70 degrees outside and they have two hours to kill while their passengers are in watching *A Chorus Line*. Mine is the oil that generates the electricity it takes to heat the water that's left running while the nation shaves.

When Americans first began pursuing happiness, there were fewer than 3 million of them on the continent. Their automotive and air conditioning needs were minimal. After 200 years of rapidly growing consumption—200 years of chipping away at enormous but finite resources—the United States remains rich and vast enough to support comfortably 220 million people . . . but the breadfruits are getting harder to reach. Each year, we consume prodigious quantities of nonrenewable resources, leaving less and less for the still greater consumption we contemplate for the following year. (The resources do not simply disappear after we consume them—would that they did. They become pollution and garbage that are themselves becoming increasingly difficult and expensive to dispose of.)

There is a little less left each year to split up and more of us among whom to split it. In 1850, the average U.S. square mile, chock-full of resources and virtually pristine, supported fewer than eight people. By 1910, that mile was shared among 31 of us. And today, even with the addition of Alaska, we come packed 62 to the somewhat depleted, substantially polluted mile. That's still a wonderfully low population density, and we are still wonderfully rich; but on a resources per capita basis, we do indeed become poorer each year.

For a long time, this did not seem to be the case. It did not *seem* as if resources were growing scarcer, because our skill at extracting them was improving. Also, we could reach around the globe pretty much at will, with little competition, for whatever resources we lacked at home. But technological improvement no longer outpaces rising costs—of labor, of protecting the environment, of "digging ever deeper"—and the world is no longer ours alone to exploit. This is not a new idea, by any means, but one that a great many people prefer not to grasp.

If we focus on oil, our worst problem, it is not hard to see how we are becoming poorer. As recently as 1972, oil imports cost us less than $5 billion. Seven years later—1979—our tab for imported oil is $65 billion. We are transferring that much wealth *annually* to the oil-exporting nations. How much is $65 billion? It is, for one thing, $295 for every one of us, or $1,180 for a family of four. The bill is not presented directly, of course, but each of us pays it. It is as if someone came around to the head of the household and said, "Well, you owe us one thousand one hundred eighty dollars this year for oil that used to cost you practically nothing—how do you want to pay it? In a deduction from your salary?"

"You must be joking."

"A withdrawal from your savings account?"

"Get outta here."

"Well, then—in higher taxes?"

"Hell, no! Who are you, anyway?"

"Never mind that. Okay. What we'll do is just raise the price of everything—particularly fuel, but everything else as well —so that your pay and your savings are *worth* one thousand one hundred eighty dollars less."

How much is $65 billion? At $400 an ounce, it is all the gold in Fort Knox ($58 billion) and then some—and that would just pay for 1979. In 1980, with another $65 billion bill to pay, we could transfer ownership of 32.5 million acres of $2,000-an-acre farmland—approximately the entire state of Iowa. Of course, we wouldn't actually ship them the land, just ownership of it. They would employ us to till their soil and then sell us the harvest. In 1981, they could have Wisconsin. In 1982, we could trade our entire steel industry for part of the oil we will be importing and give them Sears and A&P for the rest. (Oops—A&P is no longer ours to give; controlling interest belongs to the Germans.) In 1983, based on current market values, we could pay the bill by giving them IBM, RCA, and General Motors, plus the copyrights to all our motion pictures.

As we grow poorer and poorer.

Of course, because the $65 billion is diffused—a few pennies on each head of lettuce, a dime or two on each gallon of gas, a penny or two on each postage stamp—the transfer of wealth is not so dramatic. It slips by us practically unnoticed. But whether you diffuse it or just give them Iowa, it still comes to $65 billion—*a year.* Unless the price goes up. And *still* more than half the country continues to disbelieve the "energy crisis." For the luxury of driving cars that average only fourteen miles to the gallon, for the luxury of scoffing at calls to keep summer thermostats at 78 degrees, we are *hemorrhaging.*

We get paid more dollars, but they are worth less. According to the Union Bank of Switzerland, Americans are now less rich, based on per capita gross national product (admittedly a materialistic measure), than the Swiss, the Kuwaitis, the

Danes, the Swedes, the West Germans, the Belgians, and the Norwegians. "Europe on $5 a day," indeed!

One way we could grow richer even while resources are becoming scarcer would be to work harder. Right? But at least until recently—and this is not necessarily a bad thing, of course—the long-term trend in this country has been just the reverse. We've been starting work later in life, quitting earlier, and living longer. Working fewer years to support longer lives. Working five days a week instead of six. Where the average worker in 1925 might have spent something like 60 percent of all the days of his life on the job, the corresponding figure today would be more like 40 percent. In *material* terms at least, such trends tend to impoverish rather than enrich.

The way to grow richer even though we work less and even while resources become scarcer is to be more productive.

WASHINGTON, July 30 [1979] (Reuters)—Productivity in the United States, a key factor in the inflation rate, suffered its sharpest drop in more than five years during the second quarter of 1979, the Labor Department reported today. . . . As productivity falls, it increases the cost of producing goods and services and increases inflation.

And inflation makes us poorer.

Productivity increases have been anemic in recent years. Why?

In large measure, this has been the price—much of it worth paying—of "government regulation." The goods and services we buy may *look* the same as they used to, but actually they were produced more cleanly, more safely, and less noisily by workers who have had more equal opportunity (not to mention federal urinal standards). What's more, we've saved the snail darter. These improvements are worthwhile in most cases— but dear. By some estimates, the cost of government regulation comes to $100 billion a year. And, like the oil import bill, it is largely a *new* bill that until this past decade we never had to pay before. (Congress doesn't call them "bills" for nothing.)

Rather than raise taxes to pay *this* enormous bill—$1,800 a year for a family of four—we've raised prices.

Instead of spending to make factories more productive, we've spent to clean them up. But it's cost us. From the front page of *The New York Times:*

WASHINGTON, Aug. 12—The average American is likely to see his standard of living drastically reduced in the 1980's unless productivity growth is accelerated, the Joint Economic Committee, a Congressional body, warned today.

Crucial to productivity is capital investment (people get more done with tools than without them), and in this regard, inflation creates a vicious circle. Because inflation is so pervasive, people feel foolish saving—so they spend. Or in some cases, they "save" not in banks or stocks or bonds but in gold or diamonds—which is fine for the South African and Soviet economies but does less than nothing at all for our own. Even our new high interest rates, unheard of in the 1950s and '60s, have done little to encourage saving—but much to discourage capital investment.

While in the short term it may be smart for individuals to "play the inflation game" by spending rather than saving—a dubious proposition at best—it is as fundamental as one of Aesop's fables that in the long run an individual or a nation that saves little will be less wealthy than an individual or a nation that saves a lot. Wealth is "built up"—not squandered. The Japanese save 25 percent of their disposable income (to our 5 percent), whistle on their way to work (five and a half days a week), and as a result, even without benefit of resources (they are packed 799 to the square mile), the Japanese have been prospering. (They and the Germans have the added advantage of not having to "waste" nearly so much of their wealth on such nonproductive expenditures as large military establishments.)

It doesn't matter what economic system you have. As Lenin has lately been quoted—with some urgency—in the Soviet

press: "In the final analysis, productivity is the most important, most crucial thing for the success of the new social
order."

Incidentally, Ivan has his own problems. The Soviets spend
an even larger proportion of their wealth than we do in the
nonproductive military sector; they have substantially less incentive to work hard and innovatively; and it is now widely
predicted that Russia, like the United States before it, will
soon see domestic demand for oil overtake domestic supply.
Russia, too, will be competing to buy Iraqi crude.

So. Our resources are dwindling; the bill for oil imports
alone is $65 billion a year and climbing; productivity is fall-
ing. We're getting poorer. To paraphrase Karl Malden (although Karl Marx might be more appropriate): What *will* we
do? What *will* we do?

The preferred cliché is that "there are no simple solutions."
What is just the tiniest bit frustrating, however, is that—to a
large extent, anyway—there *are*.

The average car on the road in America today gets fourteen
miles to the gallon. What if someone were to invent a car that
got 30 or even 40 miles to the gallon? In five or six years, by
gradually replacing inefficient cars with efficient ones, we
could about double the fuel efficiency of our fleet. The average car could get 28 miles to the gallon instead of fourteen,
thereby cutting gasoline usage in half. Bingo. Our cars would
be smaller and less zippy—a sacrifice—but we would cut our
oil imports nearly in half, as well. And our auto emissions. Our
balance of trade deficit might be wiped out altogether.

Congress has mandated that the fleet of 1985 model cars
Detroit will put on the road average 27½ miles to the gallon,
but that is not really the way to get at the problem. First, it's
insufficient. If the average 1985 model gets 27½ miles to the
gallon, the average of *all* cars on the road will be appreciably
less. Second, the way to make the country more fuel efficient
is not to mandate standards, not to ban ads for big cars, not to
stamp CAUTION: THE ENERGY SECRETARY HAS DETERMINED

. . . prominently on big fenders, but to make us *want* to be more fuel efficient. Appeals to patriotism have very little effect in this regard. What seem to work much better are appeals to self-interest.

If Congress mandated a $1-a-gallon federal tax to be placed on gasoline in 25-cent-a-year steps over the next four years, people would have the prospect, when they went to pick out their next new car, of paying $2 to $3 for a gallon of gas in the not too distant future. This seemingly unreal prospect—which is already *fact* throughout Europe—would do amazing things in the nation's auto showrooms. Forget "the moral equivalent of war"—it would be the moral equivalent of "every man for himself in a desperate struggle to conserve gas." The average fuel efficiency of the American automobile would jump from fourteen miles a gallon like a nervous burglar at the sound of a doorbell. *Nothing* can provide an incentive to conserve fuel like making it more expensive.

And yet—expressed as a cost per mile rather than as a cost per gallon—the average motorist would actually not be paying much more than he does now. At 85 cents and fourteen miles to the gallon today, it costs six cents to drive a mile. At $2 and 28 miles per gallon—never mind the *40 miles per gallon* some current models get—it would cost seven cents.

We are not talking about taking fewer trips or driving shorter distances or car pooling, all of which would save still more gas if anyone chose to do them. Those things involve sacrifice. The only sacrifice I am suggesting is the sacrifice of driving in a smaller car with less pickup. A real sacrifice, to be sure . . . a sacrifice some people would decide not to make (they could still buy bigger cars) . . . but a sacrifice that would save the country $30 billion or so a year. Or $40 billion or $50 billion a year, depending on where the price of oil goes. (It's not likely to go down.)

As for the obnoxious federal gasoline tax of $1 a gallon by 1984: The only way such a tax could or should be passed would be to guarantee, absolutely, that every penny collected be returned by lowering *other* taxes. (In addition, farmers and truckers would need a special break, as would poor people who drive a lot.) A $1-a-gallon gasoline tax would raise enough revenue to cut personal income taxes nearly *in half!* What a boon to productivity that would be!

The government would not be collecting more tax than it already does; it would simply be taxing different things. Shifting incentives. It would strongly *dis*courage the wasteful use of energy, because we are hemorrhaging, and strongly *en*courage work and saving and investment (through dramatically lower income taxes), because these are the things that make an economy and a people prosper.

Otherwise, we can kiss Iowa goodbye, and then Wisconsin, as we rapidly sink into economic mediocrity. It is astonishing how fast these things happen. One statistic: The total government, personal, and corporate debt in the United States climbed from $1.6 trillion in 1970 to over $4 trillion today. (One way to maintain your life-style when you're getting poorer is to borrow.)

The problem with economic mediocrity is not just that we have fewer toaster ovens per capita than we otherwise might have. Truth to tell, we may have enough already. The problem is at least as much a social one. When the pie is growing at 3 or 4 percent a year, it is not hard to apportion. Growth is the lubricant that eases many a potential conflict; it allows everyone to get a little more every year. When the pie stops growing, I can only have more if you have less. *You* in fact might be a good sport and accept less—but I know a few people who would not be so good-natured. More than ever, it will be the people in need who are pitted against the ones with power— not great for the social fabric.

Drastically cutting oil imports would permit us to keep enormous hunks of the pie for ourselves. It would also strengthen the dollar, thereby lessening inflation (imports would cost less). And it would relieve some of the pressure on the world market for oil, lowering the price of the remaining oil we would still have to import.

All things considered, we face an agonizing choice: Either we can continue to watch our economy go down the drain—

continue to see inflation rage and our wealth erode—or we can drive smaller cars. (Sure, other things would help, but the big leverage is in gasoline.)

The New York Times editorialized recently:

In a prudent society, the price of gas would equal its real cost. Motorists would pay for each gallon what it costs to replace it with synthetic fuel, plus a hefty tax for the intangible cost of continuing American dependence on foreign energy. Drivers could then decide how to adjust; presumably they would drive less, and buy more efficient cars. That more prudent world, in short, would be a lot like Western Europe, where gasoline now costs $2 to $3 a gallon, gas lines are unheard of and the average family sedan gets 35 miles a gallon.

Yet five years of acrimonious national debate have brought Americans no closer to the European solution.

We are either fools or masochists; I think a combination of both.

November 1979

I
Profiles
in Splurge

GETTING BY
ON
$100,000 A YEAR

(NO, IT'S NOT EASY—BUT IT CAN BE DONE!)

Things are rough all over. I have this little Filipino girl—
Lenisa—through the auspices of the Foster Parents Plan, who,
if she really exists (and if she doesn't, someone is making $18
a month writing me little crayon letters in Filipino), sleeps on
the floor of a toiletless hut. She thanks God and me in each
letter for my generosity, and I thank God I have running
water, Charmin, and a king-size bed with Magic Fingers.

Last night I had Stanley over for dinner. Stanley, an investment banker in his early thirties, has his own problems. And,
as he is a graduate of a well-known business school and a
resident of Manhattan's Upper East Side, you can imagine
they are rather more sophisticated than little Lenisa's. If he
were to outline them for me once a month, they would come
typed on an IBM Correcting Selectric II, "dictated but not
read," and signed for him in his absence by his secretary.
(Stanley travels a lot.)

Unlike Lenisa—whose letters, as translated, tend to be
quite straightforward ("I tell you that I passed the year of
studies. I tell you also that during the rainy season part of our
house fall down. Greetings and best wishes")—Stanley manages to retain a sense of humor about *his* problems. He's half
serious and half joking when he tells you, which is the first
thing he told me, "You know, it's incredible, but you just can't

live in this city on a hundred thousand dollars a year." (And here I thought $80,000 or $90,000 was all it would take.)

When I say Stanley was half joking, I don't mean he was *kidding*, simply that he recognized the absurdity of the situation—that on a six-figure income he could still have money problems. That he had, for example, to park his car down by the docks somewhere to save a measly $80 a month over what it would have cost him to park in his building.

It is an absurd situation that a fair proportion of the world's elite find themselves in, and one, I thought, worth exploring.

"You can't live on a hundred thousand a year?" I asked, pouring Stanley a Scotch. "How many kids have you got?"

"None that I know of," he smiled.

"Wife?"

"No wife."

"Alimony?"

He shook his head.

"Well, then, how can you possibly spend so much?"

The first $40,000 or so, I knew, he would immediately dismiss as the tax collector's share. (Technically, the federal, state, and city income taxes a New Yorker pays on $100,000, assuming a bare minimum of deductions, would be closer to $50,000, but Stanley's deductions are more robust.) The next $12,000 I assumed would be the annual rent on a $1,000-a-month luxury high-rise apartment, of which there are many in New York (one- and two-bedroom, mostly), but no: his rent is a mere $415 a month. He would like to move to a larger apartment, he says (or to buy one—a great tax shelter), but he can't afford to. This one, "rent stabilized" by New York's rent control laws, is too good a deal.

So—$40,000 for taxes, $5,000 for rent (plus another $1,000 for utilities, Christmas tips to the building staff, and home phone)—I was now fairly on tenterhooks to discover where the remaining $54,000 goes.

Ten thousand, he said, goes to the summer rental on Long Island.

"Just ten?" I asked. (Sarcasm is not my middle name, but could be.) "What—no tennis court?"

"No," he acknowledged sadly, and that meant having to maintain membership in the local tennis club ($500). Also, back in the city: a Princeton Club membership ($350), Racquet Club membership ($500), and New York Athletic Club membership ($650). Physically fit, socially impeccable, perpetually tan.

No, far from its having a tennis court or even a pool, Stanley said, considering the ice cubes in his Scotch, this was a relatively modest place in the Hamptons he got to use only about ten weekends a year, when he wasn't out of the country on business.

"Aha!" said I, seeing a way to breathe new life into his bank account, "why not share the house with a friend? You'd save five thousand dollars."

"When you make a hundred thousand dollars a year," he said, "you feel you don't want to share."

"Well, then, why not take a house in a somewhat less chic Hampton and save the five thousand that way?"

"When you are making—"

"But it's only fifteen minutes away!"

"Business," Stanley explained. "You've got to be there for business. You've got to run in the right circles if you want to do the big deals. It's the old self-fulfilling prophecy." You can't play with the high rollers, in other words, if you're out in the lobby feeding the slots.

We tabled discussion of the summer place, began hacking up a slab of *pâté de campagne*, and moved on to transportation. One has to get *out* to a summer place, does one not?

It was toward this end that Stanley bought the Mercedes-Benz he can't afford to garage for $120 a month and takes the subway to retrieve. Being constrained by fairly conventional office hours, however, he found driving out to the Hamptons to entail a great deal of idling in traffic and disappointingly little 110-mile-an-hour cruising (of which his motorcar is effortlessly capable, given the proper stretch of road). Hence the seaplane he wound up taking to the beach as often as not ($40 each way). His girl friend, who was able to get out of the city early, sometimes even on Thursday, would take the car and meet Stanley at the plane.

His girl friend, it developed—and those preceding and contemporaneous with her—represents a fair portion of Stanley's fiscal dilemma. A night out in New York mounts up: $35 or $50 for theater tickets (unless they are scalped, in which case they are $50 *each*), $15 for cabs, $60 for dinner, and perhaps $30 at Regine's or Studio 54. Because, Stanley explained, if you like to date dazzling women, as he does, such an evening is not the Big Night Out—it is the *typical* night out.

"I used to think," he said, palm outstretched to stay the objection he could see forming on my lips, "that these gals would love to skip all that glitz and glamour and just come over in blue jeans for a quiet evening by the fire—is that what you were going to say?" It was. "Well," he concluded, "they don't."

So you've got the unreimbursed $150 nights out. Once or twice a week: $7,500 or $15,000 a year. And, largely for business reasons, you have the cocaine, which Stanley estimates runs him another $3,000 per annum. ("Listen, if the stuff is going around, every so often you've got to reciprocate with some of your own.") A legitimate business expense, he maintains, but one he declines to itemize on his tax return.

Now, even after we add these and other incidentals—steak for the freezer for those occasional nights home alone, tapes for the Betamax, $228 a year for cable TV and Home Box Office (not that he ever gets much chance to watch it), the weekends in St. Croix, the maid, the $100 Andre Oliver sweaters (that is as much as Stanley will spend for a sweater, even though Andre Oliver offers another style at $250), the obligatory charitable and political contributions—even after all this, he does have *some* money left over. But that goes toward his retirement. He wants to save at least $25,000 a year, in one form or another (tax-sheltered oil and gas deals are the current form), because he wants to become rich. This is very clearly the *point* of being an investment banker, after all, whatever subsidiary satisfactions the career may provide. And you can hardly become rich—after starting with nothing but debts to a variety of classy educational institutions—if you don't put at least $25,000 a year away. After twenty years, assuming you've been adroit enough to make your money grow fast enough after taxes to keep up with inflation, you will have put away the equivalent of half a million 1978 dollars. And something tells me Stanley doesn't want to wait twenty years to be worth half a million. Such a sum may go a long way in St. Paul, Minnesota—or the Philippines—but in Beverly Hills, Palm Beach, or Belgravia it is the price of a nice big house, with enough left over to remodel the kitchen—maybe.

Stanley knows this. He knows he should be putting more than $25,000 into those oil partnerships, and he also knows he's not putting away even that much. Poor Stanley.

Stanley is probably one of the million most privileged human beings on earth. And yet, whatever it says about social justice or human nature—or, simply, the human comedy—to this very special, extraordinarily fortunate group, the problems *are* real.

"No joke!" a normally lighthearted friend of mine interrupted with real feeling when I told him the topic of my story. If there was humor in the notion of "getting by" on $100,000 a year, he didn't see it. A commuter, he pays, among other things, federal income tax, Social Security tax, Pennsylvania income tax, New York State nonresident income tax, New York City nonresident income tax, sales tax, county tax, township tax, and school tax, the last three being billed as one and amounting to a modest $2,200 per annum. To Lenisa, whose family's entire electrical consumption consists of the power to run two 25-watt light bulbs, this commuter's life might seem inordinately complicated, not to mention lavish (just getting to and from work requires a car, a train, a subway, an elevator, and approximately $3,000 a year). But to my friend, it is a struggle just to afford the life his middle-class parents seemed to manage with relative ease. They had bought a house in a similar exurb for $28,000 thirty years ago, and it came with fifteen acres of property and a 5 percent mortgage. Sleep-in help cost next to nothing. *His* house, 25 years later, had cost five times as much, sat on a third as much property, and cost 8.5 percent to finance. And there was no longer such a thing as sleep-in help—or if there was, he didn't know anyone who could afford it. A new roof this year cost him $6,000. To earn that extra, unexpected $6,000, after tax, he had to earn an extra $14,000 before tax. Next year he will probably have to paint.

There is inflation—just when we were getting used to $10 ties, Saks started charging $15 and, for some, $30. There is the inflation *tax*—the effect of putting a larger and larger proportion of your income into the highest tax brackets. There is the illusion effect—your income *seems* so large you assume you can afford things you really can't. And there is the credit trap —you buy them anyway, on time (with your income, you can borrow a fortune). Add to this the ratchet effect (a luxury, once sampled, becomes a necessary comfort incorporated into all future budgets) and the self-deception effect (if I'm smart enough to be earning $100,000 a year, surely I'm smart enough to earn more), and you have the six-part formula for high-income anxiety.

"I'm taking seventy-five or eighty thousand dollars in after-tax money out of the business each year," says a Tennessee real estate developer who pays little or nothing in taxes because of the way his real estate ventures are structured. "It is the equivalent of—what? maybe a hundred twenty-five thousand dollars a year before tax, or even more—*and I don't make it on that!* It's unbelievable, but I don't." To make up the deficit, he goes deeper in debt. His personal debt is now into six figures, secured by his real estate interests. He didn't want to sell off any of the real estate until recently, he says, because he anticipated divorce proceedings and "wanted to keep a low profile on what I may have been worth, in case it got nasty." (It did not: alimony was set at $15,000 a year; he got to keep, and provide for, the three children.)

Before ticking off his personal expenses (which totaled $11,000 more than the $80,000 he was taking out of the business), he ticked off some of the perks he and his partners *don't* have to pay for personally: $1.5 million of life insurance, each; complete medical insurance, down to the last penny; golf and tennis club memberships (they own the club); horses (maintained to show off properties to prospective buyers); a 40-foot boat (which, before allowing for the captain, costs about $10,000 a year to pay off and maintain); season tickets to sporting events; one automobile apiece; business lunches and dinners.

He says that at the end of the year, after he's sold off some property to pay back the bank, he will go through his personal expenses to bring them into some sort of balance. "There's no question there are places to cut," he says (thinking, perhaps, of the day his ex-wife—*in one day,* at wholesale, no less—went through $1,000 at the pro shop). "But that doesn't mean that there's any provision for the kids' college, or for a savings account. I'm assuming that my savings are my share of the real estate values in the business—and that's an advantage most people don't have. If I had to face the full realities of life at, say, a hundred twenty-five a year before tax—but without the perks and without the equity I'm building in the business—I'd be crying more blues than I am now."

Finally we have an unmarried woman, a movie executive, who might be making $100,000 a year if she were a man, but who is nonetheless doing quite well—$72,000. The difference is not $28,000 as one might at first conclude but—after tax—$12,600.

"The interesting thing to me," she explains, "is that I have so much paid for by the studio—my car, my insurance, and virtually all food and entertainment—and I'm *still* broke. It makes me nervous. I don't know where it all goes." She has no savings account. She worries that her checks may bounce. "Literally! I remember being in New York, stocking up on the Pierre Michel shampoo I buy there—one hundred nine dollars' worth—and calling my secretary back in L.A. to be sure she had deposited my paycheck, so the hundred-nine-dollar check wouldn't bounce."

So what are we to make of these sad cases? That the rich deserve a tax break? Hardly—although it surely would be encouraging to see a token decrease in the maximum federal tax rate on earned income, from 50 percent to say, 47.5 percent. (That way, before state taxes, anyway, high-income people would at least feel they are the majority shareholders in their lives, not just fifty-fifty partners.)

Or are we to think that these elite are somehow evil to be living so well—and complaining to boot—when billions live in squalor? Hardly—although I will confess to not having been bowled over by the amounts they budgeted to charitable giving. (Eighteen dollars a month through the Foster Parents Plan really *is* all it takes to make a difference in a family's life, pointless as that may seem given the size of the problem.)

The real bottom line, it seems to me, was provided by an unemployed friend I have quoted elsewhere, who explained to me: "You can live well if you're rich and you can live well if you're poor. But if you're poor, it's much cheaper."

May 1978

DO YOU SINCERELY WANT GLENN TURNER TO BE RICH?

If you spent an hour circling La Guardia with Glenn W. Turner and his dwarfs on one of his fleet of aircraft, there is an alarming chance that you would deplane an inspired man. It might have cost you $5,000, and it might be hard to explain to the wife just why you had decided to give up your steady job after all these years. But you would never again run short of mink oil and you would be in the good company of thousands of others who have gone the same route lately. Want their names? Check with the office of New York Attorney General Louis Lefkowitz. Planning a move to New Jersey or Connecticut? Don't worry; they have attorneys general, too.

I first met Glenn Turner when he came to Harvard Business School to address the Marketing Club. About five foot nine, stocky, with a full head of black hair and a handsome open face notwithstanding the harelip, Turner strode into Aldrich Hall wearing a bejeweled American flag and a gold bald eagle pin on the wide lapel of his yellow-striped three-piece suit. His shoes were made of unborn calf's skin, "hair side outside." The components of his wardrobe, including the full head of black hair, are all sold by Glenn W. Turner Enterprises.

In his nasal, ungrammatical Southern drawl Turner allowed as how he was a dumb country boy from Marion, South Carolina. The key to success in life isn't education, he told us, it's attitude. You've got to think positive. You're as good as you think you are. Trouble is, most people have been brainwashed into thinking they're not very good. If an eighth-grade dropout with a harelip can make it, *anybody* can! "I could have gotten where I am now faster with an education, but I'm doing all right," he said. "As long as I have a row of buttons on my desk and I can push one and get the right man with a college degree to tell me what to do, that's all I need. And pretty soon I'm gonna get one big button to push to get somebody else to figure out which little buttons to push." As for his harelip, which should be carried on his company's books (beneath trademarks and copyrights) as an intangible asset, Turner recalls his days as a door-to-door sewing machine salesman: "I see you're looking at my lip, ma'am," he would say to a prospect. "I guess you think I've got a harelip. To tell you the truth, it's something I put on every morning before I go to work so people will notice me. I can let you have one for a hundred dollars."

Turner described the "system" he had invented to allow "the little guy" to go into business for himself and earn in a month what he used to earn in a year. To start this system he set up Koscot Interplanetary, Inc., which would sell a full line of mink-oil-based "kosmetics." His uncle had had to co-sign a $5,000 note to get things rolling. Turner had gone broke three times before, and his credit was poor. Three times his car had been repossessed. "But every time it was a Cadillac. I always went down in style."

Turner's "system" had a certain elegant simplicity. For $5,000, Koscot would sell the little guy a "distributorship." The little guy, in turn, could then earn money in two ways: (a) hire a sales force to peddle Koscot kosmetics door-to-door; or (b) sign up other little guys at $5,000 a clip, retaining a $2,650 commission. Since there were no kosmetics in existence until Koscot was eight months old, the first little guy Turner enrolled, a nineteen-year-old cripple from Marion, Ohio, had an easy choice. He started selling distributorships at once and in no time earned $80,000. The 35 or so distributors he had enrolled could, in turn, also earn $80,000 if *they* signed up 35 more distributors each, who in turn . . . Assuming just one distributorship to a family, after five rounds of this chain-letter game every U.S. household would own a Koscot distributor-ship. Where would the last 51,296,875 little guys in find an-other 35 each to enroll, and thereby earn *their* $80,000? Perhaps that's why Turner called his company Koscot "Inter-planetary."

One of the aspiring M.B.A.'s in the audience suggested to Turner that by borrowing eight months' worth of distributor-ship fees in order to finance his company before there was any product available, he had made these distributors his bankers —unwitting bankers who were getting no interest on their money. Turner noted that these early distributors were not complaining.

Another student suggested it would be the later distributors —the overwhelming majority—who would be hurt in the same way that 95 percent of the participants in a chain-letter inevitably lose their money. Turner explained that chain let-ters are illegal because they involve no product, but that he was going to build the finest cosmetics business in the coun-try. Just because his business isn't run the way we're taught businesses should be run at Harvard, he said, sympathetically, we think something must be wrong with it. He told us we should come down to Orlando to see his plant and meet his people and make up our *own* minds. In fact, he said, rising to the challenge, "I'll fly you all down for a couple of days, all expenses paid."

Forty-two of us met at the Butler Aviation terminal some days later. There, dwarfing a Falcon Fan Jet belonging to the General Electric Company, was a twin-engine Convair 340, *circa* 1953, with "GlennAire" painted across the red-white-and-blue fuselage. Turner bought six of these from Delta, but does most of his own flying in one of his two Lear Jets, one of his puddle jumpers, or one of the helicopters made by a com-pany he owns jointly with his attorney, F. Lee Bailey. That's right, and Mr. Bailey would be flying down in *his* Lear to have dinner with us that night.

On board representing Turner Enterprises was a 33-year-old former mutual fund salesman named Dave Clarkson. Dave had invested $5,000 to become a distributor a year before and had already sold a dozen more distributorships before being asked to work on Turner's nine-man public relations staff in the Orlando office. Dave said there was a lot of money to be made in the "retail" end of the business (selling cosmetics) if you stuck with it, but that he was more interested in the "wholesale" end (selling distributorships). His dozen distributors, he said, weren't doing much retail business, either.

Koscot had agreed to limit the number of U.S. distributorships to 30,000 in order not to form an endless chain. With 26,000 distributorships already sold, the country was almost saturated. However, Turner had already cranked up a scheme called "Dare to Be Great," a self-motivation course that uses Turner as a model, and "Kash Is Best, Inc.," a cash-discount card, on the same principle. The last people into Koscot would be given the chance to be the first in on these new chains. "And it grows geometrically," Dave was saying. "That's the exciting thing about it."

"It's hard to understand such fabulous success," I said.

Dave smiled. "You don't have to understand it," he said, "just believe it."

"Down to your left you can see Koscot's new one point seven million dollar plant, paid for in cash. Four football fields could fit inside without touching any of the outer walls," the stewardess said. We landed. At the end of a red carpet that had been laid on the tarmac were the reigning Miss Orlando, crown and all, and Turner.

Disney World's EPCOT—Experimental Prototype for the Communities of Tommorrow—was the inspiration for the "cot" at the end of many of Turner's company names: "Kosmetics" for the communities of tomorrow—Koscot; "Fashcot" for wigs; "Transcot" for the trucking company that supplies their 325 satellite warehouses with product; "Emcot" for elegant minks; "Servcot" to allow customers to charge purchases on any of 250 cards; "Souncot" for records, including two platterfuls of Turner's philosophy—"Mr. Enthusiasm" and "You Can Better Your Best."

There is less to Turner's 70 companies than meets the eye. Most are either foreign distributorships, like Koscot of Canada, Mexico, the United Kingdom, and Italy; or they are in the "development stage," like Commuter Inns of America ("Oh, really?" we asked. "How many Inns have you gotcot?" "The first is planned for Orlando") and Vitacot ("The slogan on our vitamins will be 'Guaranteed to do nothing for you'—Turner told us—'Take 'em if you want 'em, don't if you don't.' There was a peanut salesman in Marion who advertised his peanuts were 'the worst in town.' People bought them to see if they really were. If they got a good bag, they kept buying; if they happened to get a bad bag, they didn't complain").

We pulled into the Koscot parking lot—passing a Transcot trailer that read, "This product made on the third planet from the sun." We were met by John and Greg Rice, 20-year-old twin dwarfs 33 inches tall. "How do you boys feel?" they were asked. "Like dimes in a bunch of nickels, Mr. Turner!" That night F. Lee Bailey explained how, near the end of a day in court, the judge might ask whether Bailey would prefer to adjourn or to present a short witness. Bailey would then produce one of these short witnesses to extol Turner, he said.

Tour time. The trophy room was crammed with all kinds of testimonials, including one in Braille. Turner had received an invitation to the Nixon inaugural. NASA had presented him with a five-foot missile model. He is one of five white men to be an honorary Creek Indian chief.

In the Emcot showroom we saw mink-topped golf tees (60 cents), mink neckties ($25), and mink-trimmed hot pants ($480). In the House of Glenn we could order suits or shoes or ties like Mr. Turner's, or $1.25 key chains with his photo encased in plastic. The manager, wearing a pink cowboy shirt, brightened when he heard we were from Harvard. He used to service the pool tables in the Harvard dorms, he said.

We saw the $21,000-a-month IBM 360-30 and the adjoining file room with its long banks of padlocked cabinets. We toured the huge spotless air-conditioned mechanized warehouse, complete with piped-in music. We asked about the two security guards and learned from Clark Stone, chief of security and Mr. Turner's personal bodyguard, that there were 32 men on the force. He described the new lead-lined executive offices that would prevent bugging—bugs had been found in the past.

We walked through the $700,000 wing being built for the international headquarters. Visitors will enter the large rotunda, ascend the spiral staircase that hangs above the fountain, and walk into the executive suite—unless Turner has pulled the control that electronically seals off this section of the building. Next to his new office—750 square feet with marble wall and fireplace (fireplace?)—Mr. Turner has a two-chair barber room, a private bedroom, a sauna, and a weight room—he can still press 200 pounds, though he hasn't had time to work out in years. No private bar, though. Turner doesn't drink or smoke.

Across the hall was Miss Kim Kollins's office. Three years ago she was a beautician. When we met her she had become assistant to the international vice chairman of the board of Koscot Interplanetary and manager of Fashcot. She believes in reincarnation. Having been a Greek princess last time, she ordered a $3,600 Grecian desk for her office. She also believes in astrology and bases her hiring policy on the stars. A Virgo herself, she has some very capable Capricorns assisting her. "You may think it's crazy, but by golly it works." Before we left, she told us, "Your analytical minds don't accept us because our way of business is different—it's a philosophy."

In most offices there was either a framed color photograph of Chairman Turner—the largest one I saw was three by five feet—or some gold eagles or American flags, or all three.

When we crowded into Turner's own office, I stood by a "Remember Me? Hello, I'm Your Flag" plaque, next to a narrow four-shelf bookcase. Among the titles I picked out: Maltz, *Psycho Cybernetics;* Stone, *The Success System That Never Fails;* Volumes I–VIII, *The Law of Success;* Billington, *God*

Is Great; Settel, *The Faith of Billy Graham;* Douglas, *How to Cultivate the Habit of Succeeding;* Hill, *Grow Rich with Peace of Mind;* and Rothblatt and Bailey, *Defending Business and White Collar Crimes.*

In the bus out to Mr. Turner's for dinner. Four years ago the Turners lived in a 27-foot house trailer. Their present $260,000 home is being replaced by a $1 million castle, which will have a $75,000 boathouse large enough for 150 guests. (Where does all this money come from? Cosmetics? Or from enticing people to pay thousands of dollars to join the chain?)

We gathered in the living room as the Koscot executives on the spiral staircase introduced themselves one by one and came down to join us. With each introduction, Mr. Turner, who was sitting on the floor next to me, would make some quip—as though showing his color slides. Laughter and applause evoked barking from the seeing-eye dog that belonged to Dick Mailman, whom Turner had taken from a $48-a-week job in a pizza parlor and made a $30,000-a-year Dare to Be Great executive. Tomorrow, we were told, Mr. Mailman was to get his first crack at flying a helicopter.

F. Lee Bailey, a faculty member of the American Institute of Hypnosis—and for a while a member of the executive committees of both Koscot and Dare to Be Great—was arrogant but captivating. He had been engaged by Turner in 1969, when it became clear that Turner needed more than the routine corporate counsel. Bailey said he went to work for Turner on a handshake and agreed to take nothing but expenses for the first year. Turner noted that expenses were pretty high for a lawyer who piloted a Lear Jet.

The title of Bailey's address, the highlight of the evening, was "Legal Ramifications of Unorthodox Business Practices." He told us he had never had a better client or, in many respects, a better friend. The first 30 days on the Turner case he spent visiting most of the attorneys general in the country and "left them sufficiently befuddled to slow down the litigation." He said that Koscot "relied on the good faith of its people as an internal control to frustrate the potential for misrepresen-

tation, which is definitely there." Referring to Koscot's moti-
vational techniques—such as groups of prospective investors
shouting, MMMMMONEY! in unison at "Golden Opportunity meetings"—he explained that "the need to be jacked up
is ever present at all levels of society. It's a form of quasi-
hypnosis." After the Crist Sisters, artists on the Souncot label,
played a couple of songs for us, we piled back into the bus,
chanted, MMMMMONEY! a few times, dared to be pooped,
and went to sleepcot.

Our first discussion the next morning was with Terrell
Jones, one of Mr. Turner's indescribably attired right-hand
men, widely acclaimed in the Turner organization for his 165
IQ. Jones started telling more colorful stories. Those in the
group who were anxious to learn such facts as sales volume,
cash flow, profitability, and the ratio of wholesale to retail
sales reminded him of Turner's promise to "open the books"
when we came down.

"I don't know the facts," Jones explained.

"Who does?"

"I don't know—someone on salary. Sometimes it pays to be
dumb. I thought you wanted to know about business; I didn't
know you wanted to know about facts."

On the chain-letter issue, Terrell said, "Our intent has always been to set up the retail. We've made a lot of mistakes
and it's costing us a lot of money to find the right system. . . .
We'll let somebody who's having trouble building his steady
retail get into Dare to Be Great and make some of the fast
money to help in the other."

Then we met the vice president of finance, a two-year vet-
eran of Bernie Cornfeld's IOS, and Harvard Business School
'70. He didn't know many facts, either, but he did allow that
1970 sales had been about $39 million, including the income
from "ten or fifteen thousand distributorships—say twenty-
five million." On its own, he said, the retail business was not
yet profitable.

After lunch we had our final meeting with Glenn Turner.
We watched the videotape of an interview he had had on one
of the networks:

"Most people work in the same job until they're sixty-five and get a gold watch," Turner said. "I have a gold watch. Know what it says on the back? 'To Glenn W. Turner, the greatest guy in the world, from Glenn W. Turner, the greatest guy in the world.' "

"Do you really have a watch like that?" the reporter asked.

"No."

"Mr. Turner, what would you do if you were mayor of New York?"

"I'd go inspire the governor to get more money and build new cities out West and move the people out there."

After the film we asked Turner why we hadn't been allowed to look at the books. "See, an idiot builds companies, an expert runs them. I don't get involved in the day-to-day affairs. I don't know what's going on in my companies. If my people won't give you facts, I have to go along and take their advice."

He said he knew a lot of us thought he had flown us down as a publicity stunt—but they were not planning any publicity. "You all won't believe why I brought you down here, but I'll tell you." He leaned toward us confidentially. "Just for the hell of it. I wanted you to see a business you know couldn't work, work. I get a kick out of it."

We were given "You Can Better Your Best" albums and Sir Koscot toiletries kits on the way back to the airport.

It is not hard to understand how rational analyses of Turner Enterprises tend to get muddled, especially among the unsophisticated lower-income groups to whom his efforts are largely directed—"persons in the $5,000 to $10,000 income bracket, the young, the gullible, the unemployed or other persons in desperate need of a source of income," as a deputy of Attorney General Lefkowitz put it. Turner is immensely likable and inspirational. His pitch and his motives *seem* genuine. The products are good—if you can find someone selling them.

Nevertheless, Turner's legal troubles are mounting. At last count F. Lee Bailey is up against 30 state attorneys general, the Federal Trade Commission, the Securities and Exchange

Commission, private suits, and perhaps soon the U.S. Attorney General, whose mail fraud investigative division is said to be quietly preparing a criminal suit. Earlier this month a Kansas district court flatly barred Koscot Interplanetary from doing any business in the state.

The highest court to reach a decision thus far is the Iowa Supreme Court. In November 1971, Justice Rawlings said, "Despite the thinly veiled cloak of respectability with which Koscot has attempted to clothe its pyramidal merchandise sales promotion scheme, the badge of fraud clearly shows through." And last month Justice Pashman of the Superior Court of New Jersey said, with respect to Dare to Be Great, "I must conclude . . . that defendant's operations are fraudulent. . . . The program attracts the unwary and preys upon their folly. It dooms them to failure from the very beginning and omits to apprise them of its unfeasibility."

Still, Turner Enterprises remains very much in business, with new enterprises popping up at a great rate. "The only way to stop them," one local state official told me, "is to put them away with criminal prosecution." *

February 1972

* By the time government authorities were finally able to close Turner down—but not put him away—Turner Enterprises had taken in more than $100 million, most of it in franchise fees.

THE APPRENTICESHIP OF FRANK YABLANS

A sampling of the cast, for flavor:

Charles Bronson, as Paul Kersey, is setting himself up to be mugged in the park. When the muggers approach (time after time), he blasts them.

Dino De Laurentiis has produced this movie, which he calls *Debt-a-Weeesh.* He has spent much of the week trying to get three full-page ads for its July 24 opening out of

Frank Yablans, our hero, or at least our central character, who is, make no mistake about it, president of Paramount Pictures. The name is ya-*BLAHNS.*

Rex Reed has seen Bronson plugging muggers in the park and thinks *Death Wish* is "terrific." Yablans quips that this means Rex must think the movie was produced by

Bob Evans, the head of Paramount's Hollywood studio, who is Frank Yablans's employee, close friend, equal partner, arch rival, nemesis, or imminent successor, depending on whom you've been talking with. Both he and Frank, like the Corleone boys, are vying for the approval of

The Mad Austrian, sequestered on the 42nd floor of the Gulf + Western Building, in the chairman's office—cradling a tomcat in the crook of his elbow, we like to think, with his back to the camera and his eye on the stock market. This man, Charlie Bluhdorn, ran Paramount single-handed for a while after Gulf + Western bought it in 1968; Frank Yablans, though he still talks with Charlie every day (and, we're told, does a sensational Bluhdorn imitation), has managed to beat the boss back to a largely supervisory role.

The Shark, co-starring with Richard Dreyfuss in another company's upcoming movie version of *Jaws,* figures into our own script only to the extent that his mechanical malfunctionings are apparently holding everyone up on Cape Cod well beyond schedule, which means that Dreyfuss won't be around to promote the opening of *The Apprenticeship of Duddy Kravitz.* Frank Yablans says his competitors would have been much better off if The Shark had swallowed The Dolphin (as in *Day of the*) and died of indigestion, and neither picture had been made.

Frank Yablans can be very funny, very charming, in a tough sort of way, when he wants to be. With me around, he wants to be. Maybe he should have me around more often.

CUT TO: A conversation I had with Ted Zephro, until last October one of Frank's right-hand men. "I wonder," I asked Zephro, "whether Frank acts natural with his staff when a reporter's around." (Who can, after all?) "Was he pleasant?" Zephro asked back. "Very." "Then that wasn't Frank."

CUT TO (this is how movie people talk—"cut to"): An executive staff meeting I was allowed to attend. Frank is in good form. As the meeting is breaking up, out in the hallway I overhear one of Frank's people asking another, "What's got into Frank? Why's he in such a good mood?"

Frank *can* be pleasant, *does* have a warm, boyish side—but he doesn't display it very often to people less powerful than he. Where some chiefs run their team of executives like a benign high school coach, from the sidelines, knowing the guys will perform because it would kill them to let him down, Frank runs his team like the star player, which he is, knowing his guys will perform because if they let him down, he would kill them. He is in on every play, down to details like schedules in Buffalo or whether to have comment cards at a sneak preview in Houston.

"Norman," he says to rotund, beleaguered, lovable Norman Weitman, general sales manager, who has just returned to a meeting with some statistics Frank wants, "are you planning to go down to Houston for the *Longest Yard* preview?"

"No."

"Well, plan on it."

"Okay," says Norman resignedly—picture Zero Mostel in the role—"I'll plan on it."

"Are there going to be comment cards at the screening?" Frank asks.

"Bob Aldrich [the director] doesn't want them," someone volunteers.

"Well, *I* want comment cards," Frank snarls.

"Okay, we'll have comment cards."

And so it goes. One minor movie mogul calls Frank "the head of distribution who also happens to be president of the company." But it works. Since taking over, Frank has simplified things. There are fewer executives, they work harder, they work together, and they work for him. He himself works entrepreneurial hours and is very good at what he does.

FADE IN: The executive conference room of Paramount Pictures on the 33rd floor of the Gulf + Western Building. A shiny white-and-blue sailfish, looking decidedly out of its element, arches across one long wall; opposite are two *Godfather* posters in cheap wooden frames. Frank is screening a sales film that will be used to introduce a new photographic process Paramount controls.

The sales film, very clever, runs for a few minutes showing how, with "Magicam," real-sized people can perform on doll-house-sized sets. The actor is actually photographed on an empty set, with one or two life-size props to give him his bearings; meanwhile, another camera superimposes the miniature set, in synch with the first camera. Also very clever. The idea is that miniature sets are cheaper to construct than real ones, and the Magicam process allows for special effects. Frank suggests they add a segment with a set of the Oval Office, and a Nixon impressionist making a speech. As he's talking, Frank says, a giant hand should reach down and discard one piece of furniture after another, and then, when the set is bare, remove the President as well. This improvement is agreed to.

MAGICAM EXECUTIVE, speaking to Frank as the film ends: We added this tag for you, sir. It's not on the other copies of the film.

ANNOUNCER ON FILM: Ladies and gentlemen, it is now my pleasure to introduce the president of Paramount, who wishes to relate his feelings about the Magicam process.

PURPORTED PRESIDENT OF PARAMOUNT (because, make no mistake, *Frank Yablans* is the president of Paramount), doing a full-scale Brando/*Godfather* imitation: My friends . . . I truly hope . . . that through this demonstration today . . . we have communicated to you . . . the fact . . . that Magicam is indeed a revolutionary innovation. . . . If, somehow . . . despite of our efforts . . . we have failed to convince you . . . then what can I say . . . except from the bottom of my heart . . . *f--- you!*

The Magicam executive hastily reiterates that this tag is not on the copies for outside distribution, but Frank loves it. "You have to use it! It's terrific! In the first place"—he laughs—"this has become Paramount's trademark: 'If you don't like it, *f--- you!*' "

Such is not the trademark of a weak company, and it must be no end of satisfaction to Frank that the weak company he took over in 1971 is now perhaps the strongest company in the movie business. This summer Paramount had more prints out in the field, they say, making more money, than any company has had since "the golden days of Hollywood." One-time TV rights to *The Godfather* were recently sold to NBC for $10 million, doubling the old TV record. *Godfather II* opens at Christmas. And beyond that there are hoped-for "giants" like *The Day of the Locust* (Easter), *The Last Tycoon* (about Thalberg's last days at MGM), *Marathon Man* (from William Goldman's not-yet-published novel), *Three Days of the Condor* (Redford), and even "Project X," which is the proposed "Walter Winchell Story," starring Bob Hope.

There will also be more bombs, of course, à la *Jonathan Livingston Seagull*. But at Paramount the profits on the Big Pictures have more than canceled out the occasional losers, in part because pictures are kept to relatively modest budgets.

Paramount profits grew to $38.7 million in 1973, or 22 percent of Gulf + Western's total, on sales of $277.5 million. This suggests that Frank has done a great job. (It doesn't prove it, mind you, but there is that suggestion.) It also puts him in a position of substantial power. He likes that.

What he doesn't like is all the publicity his friend and studio head, Bob Evans, has been getting. In the last month I've told several people that "I'm doing a piece on the president of Paramount Pictures." "Bob Evans?" they ask. So it has been extraordinarily easy to get Frank to agree to this story.

QUICK TAKE: Lunch at "21." Three of Frank's publicity honchos are pitching a *Newsweek* staffer who says Bob Evans is being considered for a *Newsweek* cover. The purpose of this caviar-and-champagne luncheon, courtesy of the shareholders of Gulf&Western, is to persuade him that Bob Evans doesn't *deserve* to be on the cover of *Newsweek*—Frank does. (Neither one, to date, has made it.) Le tab: $245.

FADE IN: Frank's northeast-corner office, magnificent view, gold *Godfather* Oscar sitting by the multi-buttoned phone. Frank has a button for each of his key people. When their phones buzz, they know it's he. Frank also has a button that automatically shuts the door to his office ("It must have been the wind"), another for the door to the adjoining private john, and, of course, a button for each of the drapes.

Frank is meeting with three Canadians whose *Apprenticeship of Duddy Kravitz* is opening in a few days. It is the story of a Jewish cab driver's son—Frank is himself a Jewish cab driver's son—who fights his way out of the ghetto and into a three-piece suit. He is insanely energetic, likable, and full of impish fun. But he is also fiercely motivated, selfish, conniving, ruthless, and calculating. He does what he has to do to get his way. Bob Evans is credited as having been the first of many to subtitle this film "The Frank Yablans Story."

The Canadians are asking Frank to downplay the fact that this is a Canadian film. Agreed. Frank is advising them to play down the Golden Bear award the film won at the Berlin Film

Festival—you don't want to give the film an *auteur* image, Frank says. Agreed. The Canadians want to know why the film is opening on a Wednesday. Because, Frank explains, he recently discovered that the original scheduling would have had four Paramount releases opening on the same day. He has ordered them spaced apart so that each will get more attention. Who at Paramount, the Canadians want to know, should they "lee-ayse" with? They should "lee-ayse" with him, Frank explains wryly, or else they won't get any answers. Frank pauses to read a note that is carried in to him and, annoyed, responds defiantly—"Tell him I will *not* be up 'in five minutes.' I will be up when I finish my meeting." CUT TO a tomcat being stroked in the crook of an unidentified elbow.

The Canadians are asking why *Duddy* (which rhymes with "goody") is opening at the Forum, a Broadway theater, as well as the Baronet. Aren't Broadway audiences less sophisticated than Third Avenue audiences? "That's bull----, That's *bull*----," says Frank, who estimates that opening-day gross at the Forum will be $5,400. Frank explains that when he opened *Chinatown* on Broadway along with Third Avenue, "my partner Bob Evans was sucking his thumb in the corner for a month." But—Frank pulls out the exact figures—Broadway outgrossed Third Avenue.

Frank buzzes.

"Yes, Frank?"

"Bring in the schedules on *Duddy Kravitz*."

Norman Weitman comes in with the schedules on *Duddy Kravitz*. Frank doesn't like them, and changes them. Norman had the schedules at the two theaters staggered, but Frank doesn't want the last show to start any later than 10:30 P.M., even if it means cutting back from six performances a day to five (which it does). It is too late to change the Sunday *Times* ad, but Monday's will be changed. (Anyone who used Sunday's ad and arrived to find the late show already half an hour gone will now understand why it would have done no good to complain "right on up to the president of the goddamned company, if I have to"—because it was the president of the goddamned company, if you can believe it, who adjusted the time half an hour.)

"How well will the film do?" the Canadians want to know. Frank, who has been relishing his older-wiser-and-vastly-more-powerful role in this meeting, tells them that "the film could do ten million." Dramatic pause. "Or it could do one million." He tells them, "Face it—it's a flawed film. It's a flawed film." He pauses just long enough for the blood to begin burning their cheeks—"but *every* film is flawed," he says. Relief. Frank says he has high hopes.

Finally, the Canadians hand Frank "a very hot property" they would like him to read. Without even looking at it, he tells them, "I've read it. I turned it down two months ago." But . . . but . . . And indeed Frank has read it: he's well plugged in, he knew what they'd be bringing him, and he does his homework.

But lest we come away quite as awed by Frank as the Canadians seemed to, it should be noted that the opening-day gross at the Forum, as it turned out, was not $5,400. It was $809. After running there ten days, *Duddy* was moved to the Little Carnegie, which, some say, plays to a more sophisticated audience.

If Frank isn't a certified oracle, he is nonetheless persuasive. And if he takes himself very seriously—he has political ambitions and is convinced that becoming a congressman would be "no problem"—he also has the ability to laugh at himself. "The thing I found so amazing," recalls Peter Maas, author of *Serpico*, of his first encounter with Frank, "is that I walked into his office determined that I wasn't going to go with what he wanted [a snake coiled around a nightstick on the cover of *Serpico*—Maas hates snakes]—but within five minutes I just didn't have any answers.

"We were eyeball to eyeball and I got the full force of his sales pitch. And he was killing me. He was telling me he knew how to sell, and he was selling *me!* I mean, I didn't know what to do. And what I usually do at moments like this is I shuffle my feet—and I happened to look down and I realized I was six inches lower than he was. You know that split-level office he has—I was so taken with the view, and with him, I didn't notice it at first. So I got up on his level, so he had to look up, and he said, 'Sometimes I'm not as tall as I appear.' Everybody laughed, including Frank, and that sort of broke the spell."

QUICK TAKE:

YABLANS: Does someone have the minutes of the last meeting where I said Norman Weitman's estimates are full of s---?

NORMAN: That's in the minutes of every meeting, Frank.

FADE IN: A day in mid-July. Last night Frank screened a film at home in Scarsdale, then stayed up until two A.M., he says, reading the Magicam status report. He has arrived at his office, via chauffeured limousine, at seven A.M., finished a three-hour breakfast meeting with "the chairman," and finds Dino De Laurentiis waiting for him on his way into the Magicam presentation. (After which there will be lunch at La Grenouille with David Merrick, an advertising/publicity meeting, a visit from his tailor, a business dinner, and, at home, another screening.)

"What the hell kind of shirt is that?" Frank demands playfully of one of his staff as he and Dino and I walk past into his office. "You look like the mayor of Puerto Rico." With me around, Frank is being charming again.

Dino and Frank begin playfully arguing about the gross on *Walking Tall*, a picture similar to *Death Wish*. Dino says it's grossed $40 million; Frank bets him $100 it is closer to $14 million, and produces a $100 bill. Dino unravels five twenties, which Frank deems marginally acceptable.

Buzz. "Barry, what's the latest gross on *Walking Tall?*"

The answer comes back, $14.3 million. Frank jumps up and down with delight (but doesn't bother to collect).

Dino is still pushing for three full pages for *Death Wish*. Frank says, "Dino, have I ever f----- you?"

"Som-a-time," Dino says, like a hurt child.

"Never! Come on, Dino, never!"

"You-a try," Dino offers, by way of compromise.

Frank holds firm at a full page Sunday, a half-page Wednesday (opening day), and then, if the reviews are good, a full-page review ad on Friday. (They stay up all night to put together these review ads.) Dino leaves, saying, "Frank fokk-a me every morning. Frank-a no work good unless he fokk-a me every morning."

Dino De Laurentiis, Europe's biggest producer-come-to-America, has made or presented nearly 600 films over the years and is worth tens of billions of lire. He got started, he has recalled, collecting discarded bottles on Capri, filling them with tap water, and labeling them something like "Capri's Famous Water of Life." He and Frank have an informal partnership which Frank describes this way: "There is no formula at all with Dino; it is project by project. I consider him under a moral obligation to come to me with everything he has, and I consider myself under a moral obligation to reject anything I don't like."

Will *Death Wish* inspire an actual vigilante to murder muggers? "Possibly," says Frank. Is there anyone who censors films for this kind of problem? "The responsibility is our own," says Frank. Has a script ever been turned down for "social-responsibility" reasons? "No."

And, while I am on the subject, a related one. I asked Charles Glenn, Frank's top marketing man, what Paramount would do if, hypothetically, it had an absolutely dreadful film the executives were convinced no one—but *no* one—would enjoy, but to which they thought they could draw enough people, through a catchy title, ads, etc., to recoup their investment. "We would release it," Glenn told me candidly.

This is a business, after all. The marketing department has been working up a list of areas where crime in the streets is highest, and will target special efforts on *Death Wish* there, hoping to stir up the kind of controversy that will get people to the box office.

CUT TO: Ted Zephro, who, as I've said, became Frank's right-hand man in the sales organization. Ted is in an exhibitor's office arguing about terms. (In this business, each deal is negotiated.) Ted has just kicked one of the office chairs through a partition to make his point. The exhibitor, cool as a canister, looks at Ted, raises his eyebrows and purses his lips, as if to appraise this performance, and says—"Not quite, but almost as good as Frank."

Frank came up this route, field sales, first with Warner, then Disney, then Filmways, and finally Paramount. He knows the size and feel and "house nut" (break-even) of every major theater in the country.

"Frank swore the day he arrived," says Zephro, "that he would become president of the company—and I just laughed. 'Play your cards right,' and all that stuff, he told me, 'and I'll take care of you.'" Less than two years later, Charlie Bluhdorn, who had hired him to captain through disasters like *Paint Your Wagon* and *Catch-22,* made Frank president.

"We got our money back on those films," Frank notes with satisfaction. As Zephro recalls: "Frank didn't allow anyone to see *Catch-22.* He was the only one who was gonna see it, right? So we're waiting for him outside the screening room and he comes out, and I swear to God, if he doesn't win an Academy Award, no one will. His eyes are glossy—I says, 'Frank, how's the picture?' He says, 'It touched me so much, I really can't even talk to you right now.' And he just walked off, like—like into the sunset. I think he wouldn't let anybody else see it because he knew it was a stiff, see? This is how smart the f---ing guy is. He got me and some of his other top guys so f---ing high on this picture that when we went out in the field, we killed, you know. We thought it was the coming of Christ, this picture. He makes up a policy for distribution terms on this film that's the roughest policy that was ever perpetrated on the exhibitors. He said he wanted to raise twelve million in front—never before done. I said, 'Frank, I'm not going to get these terms.' He says, 'Zeph, I'm depending on you.'"

Anyway, says Zephro, "We did raise eight million on the picture and made these deals. When I saw the picture I almost threw up. I told Frank and he says, 'Shut up, will ya—I know what I'm doing.' I says, 'What about the exhibitors?' He says, 'I know how to handle 'em. We're going to have another one coming down the line and they're going to have to pay for that one, too. And they'll stand in line for you.' And he ended up right, because the next picture we had was *Love Story,* right? And Frank went through the same goddamn thing—only this time he let us see the picture."

"One of the great problems in this business is collecting our film rentals," Frank explains. "So we evolved a program here of getting our money in advance. On *Catch-22* we got twelve and a half million before the picture was released. On *Godfather* we got fifteen million or sixteen million before the picture was even shot. They didn't pay, they didn't get the picture. It was that simple. On *Great Gatsby* we collected eighteen million prior to release, and on *Godfather Part II* we will collect thirty . . . two . . . million . . . dollars," he says with special emphasis, of which $5 million is already in—four months before release. "Now, that doesn't mean that if *Godfather II* bombs we're not going to have to give back some of that money, because it's not in our interest to bankrupt a theater—"

CUT TO: Ben Sack, who owns all the big Boston theaters, telling me that he predicts 40 percent of all the exhibitors will be bankrupt within six months or a year. "Exhibitors are being made the suckers of the industry," he says, "having to put up guarantees for movies that haven't even been made yet," and with new theaters costing three times what they used to.

CUT BACK TO FRANK, SAYING, "But what it does assure us is if we sell the picture to play twenty weeks, before that theater gets back any money it's going to have to play it twenty weeks. And in those twenty weeks we're going to earn quite close to whatever that money is, even if the film is a disappointment." What's more, explains Frank, "They're not going to get *Godfather II* until everything else is paid up, too, so they really can't defeat it. They may not be paying other companies," he smiles, "but they're paying Paramount."

If, on average, Paramount is getting its nearly $300 million annual revenues 90 days faster than a less well managed company would, then, with money going for 1 percent a month these days, Paramount's pretax profits are boosted $9 million by this policy.

The other Yablans innovation, beginning with *Catch-22* and perfected with *Gatsby*, is in hyping every last ounce of potential out of a selected few superfilms that are actually only mediocre. *Love Story*, for example, was, in Frank's words, "a very light picture, a very small picture. And, of course, we made it a phenomenon."

Just how is a little less clear. First, of course, there was the book, though that certainly didn't help with *Jonathan Livingston Seagull* (whose financial flight was presaged at Frank's grand-premiere press conference when Jonathan relieved himself in Frank's hand). Then there was the kind of sales hype Ted Zephro described. Further, Frank says, "We didn't let anybody see the picture; we built up a kind of mystique. And we had that copy line—'Love Means Never Having to Say You're Sorry'—which was an integral part of it, only because nobody knew what the hell it meant. . . . Then, of course, there was the whole romance of Bob and Ali." And there was also skillful attention to the right marketing and distribution details.

This does make a difference. On *Chinatown*, for example, Buffalo was out of line. "We moved the schedule ahead an hour," Frank says, "and the grosses immediately shot way up. In Memphis we opened up to sixty-eight hundred dollars the first week. We changed the ad, which was too sophisticated for Memphis, and we grossed eight thousand in the next *three days*." Or this: *Gatsby*, like *Godfather*, opened in five New York theaters. "In retrospect," says Frank, "perhaps we shouldn't have opened in five theaters, because had we only opened up in one or two, there was enough pressure on *Gatsby* to have built enormous lines, and those enormous lines would have buried the critical reviews. *Buried* them.

Because a person that reads Vince Canby and sees it's a terrible review, but goes out and sees he can't get into the theater, he's got to figure somebody's crazy—either the five thousand people in the line or Vincent Canby. And so part of the marketing strategy is, you want those lines. They feed on themselves." There is no question in Frank's mind, he says, that opening *Gatsby* in a single theater would have added millions to the eventual gross of the picture.

One knowledgeable man in the industry, who has worked extensively with Frank, says that even considering the tyrannical movie men of old, "Frank has alienated more people in the industry than anybody else ever did." Paul Newman, for one, has sworn he'll never make a picture for Frank—but then Robert Redford swore the same thing and has just signed to do *Three Days of the Condor.*

"Those [actors and directors] who are alienated," Frank says, "I would have to say are immature and don't realize that I have no personal animus towards them." He pauses a minute to reflect. "There *are* several I have a personal animus to, because I think they're unnice people. Really unnice people. I don't think I've made more enemies than Cecil B. De Mille or Jack Warner or L. B. Mayer or Harry Cohn. Nor have I made any more friends than they made. I do what I do the way I do it. I've never said that I'm the most popular man. But by the same token, I'm a lot more *decent* than some of the popular men. A *lot* more decent. Because I'm basically in a rejection business, and I will give a fast no and a fast yes. It's difficult not to alienate someone in a rejection."

CUT TO: Stanley Jaffe, Frank's predecessor. Stanley wants to make a movie from a screenplay called *Polo Lounge.* (In Los Angeles, everyone, including Frank, stays at the Beverly Hills Hotel. The bar is called "The Polo Lounge.") Evans and Yablans both hate the script. Stanley, hysterical (all right, well, I'm telling this story the way movie people tell it)— Stanley, hysterical, goes to Frank and says, "If I got George C. Scott for the lead, would you do it?" Frank gives a fast yes. Stanley asks how much he can offer Scott, who's been working for $1 million and up lately. Frank says, $100,000. Stanley, outraged but not licked, says he will make up the $900,000 difference himself, and, to everyone's surprise, signs Scott for $1 million. Stanley comes back to Frank, just a trifle triumphant, and announces that he's got George C. Scott. "Stanley you're f----ed," says Frank candidly. "We're not going to do the picture even with George C. Scott."

CUT BACK TO FRANK SAYING, "So I'm aware of some of the problems I have. I'm trying to refine them—I don't want to be an abrasive personality. But by the same token I'm not about to get off the lines of the mission that I see. . . . I'm a nice guy. I am not, I am *not* a killer. I am not a killer. And I would much rather help somebody than hurt somebody. But I'll also be very cold. And calculating."

Frank's intercom buzzes. *"What?!"* he demands. "I'll call him later."

"How do you handle *Gatsby*," Frank continues, "and do the outrageous things we do and make the outrageous statements we've made, and get eighteen million in advance, without getting a lot of other presidents' noses out of joint? And I can't help it if Redford feels that we turned *Gatsby* into a circus, and *yes*, I get upset when Redford says something about it, because Redford is going to make a million-six or a million-eight by the *fact* that we made a circus out of it. Because if we are to believe the critics are accurate—that they would have hated the picture anyway, without all the promotion—then the picture would have done three million instead of thirty-five million." ("I would like to have two critical failures a year like *Gatsby*," Frank is fond of saying.)

Frank says most of the Yablans stories that make the rounds are untrue. "I mean, to have Paul Newman say he doesn't like me because I'm a fascist—I mean, my God, you know, I'm a bleeding-heart liberal, not a fascist! Paul Newman and I met only once. So that's the kind of business we're in. We're in a vicious business."

Even so, says Frank, he has made "a concerted effort to find out what it was I was doing wrong." "Certain things," he admits, "I was doing wrong. Certain calls should have been made. . . . Maybe picking up the phone and calling somebody and saying, 'Gee, I understand that you heard such-and-such and I just want you to know that's not the way I feel.' And it's appreciated, you know. *That* kind of thing. But you can't spend all your time doing it. You really can't."

Some of the ego bruising he's done, he says, "was really due to my own peculiar sense of humor, which is quite acerbic at times, you know." For example, he says, he was asked to visit a columnist's home. "And the person was very proud of her new home," he recalls, "and she said to me, 'Well, how do you like it?' And I said, 'Well, you know, to me it looks like early Mediterranean Queens.' Which I thought was very witty. And everybody laughed, and she laughed—but she was angry as hell! So I had to call up, and I said, 'C'mon . . . how can you be upset at that?' "

One famous Paramount director describes Frank as "incredibly ambitious, a total egomaniac, publicity crazy—he wants to be very powerful and very wealthy, and in the course of it steps on people if he has to. I suppose he's okay if you know all that. But I don't respond to that kind of man."

But Peter Bogdanovich thinks Frank is "a terrific guy." "I have no complaints about Frank," he says. "I'll tell you something that somebody said about him, an actor friend of mine. He said, 'When you look into Frank's eyes, there's life there. And most of those business people tend to have rather stony, cold, dead eyes. Frank is full of impish fun and warmth.' "

Well, half full, anyway.

P.S. Dino got his three full pages in *The Times*, as Charles Bronson—BLAM, BLAM, BLAM, BLAM—murdered three more junkies.*

September 1974

---

* P.P.S. Frank was replaced as head of Paramount a few weeks later. FINAL CUT TO: a cat's head being stroked absent-mindedly by the fingers of a carefully manicured hand.

DID DAVID BEGELMAN NEED
THE MONEY?

PROLOGUE

On Thursday, September 2, 1976, a check in the amount of
$10,000 was drawn by Columbia Pictures Industries, Inc., to
the order of actor Cliff Robertson on instructions from David
Begelman, president of Columbia's film and television divisions. Robertson was not owed the money by Columbia—nor
would he receive it. Instead, David Begelman himself forged
Robertson's endorsement, took the check to his local Wells
Fargo branch, got the check initialed by a bank officer who
knew him by sight, and cashed it.

Some months later, Columbia's accounting department sent
a routine tax form to Cliff Robertson stating that he had been
paid $10,000 during the previous year. Robertson, puzzled,
remembered earning no such sum from Columbia. Eventually, after months of inquiry, Robertson's agent got a call
from David Begelman himself.

The mystery had been solved, Begelman reported. A young
man at Columbia had forged the check. The company was
dismissing him, of course (that's what you do when employees
forge checks), but inasmuch as it was his first offense and the
boy's father had come in pleading for mercy, Begelman said,
they had decided not to prosecute. Would Robertson be
equally generous? Robertson agreed not to press charges but
was advised by his accountant to obtain a copy of the check
for his records. When the copy came, the accountant called
the branch at which the check had been cashed and asked the
officer who had initialed it whether he remembered it. Yes, he

did. And who had cashed it? David Begelman, he said, president of Columbia Pictures.

When Columbia obtained an admission from Begelman that he had forged the check—but with his assurance that there were no other forgeries—the board of directors suspended him "pending a full investigation." The locks on his office doors were changed, and a vague statement was issued citing "certain unauthorized financial transactions." And here is what David Begelman, still drawing $4,500 a week while on leave, was telling *Newsweek*—which was as eager as everyone else to know exactly what the mogul had been suspended *for:*

"It involves things that I had relatively unlimited authority over," he said, "and I may have abused that authority." But, he went on, "I want to say that any judgment I made, I stand by. I like to think of myself as a doer, and if you are a doer, you are going to make some mistakes." Only later was it revealed—not by Columbia's board of directors, which apparently did not think it of material interest to the company's shareholders, but by the press—that the "mistakes" Begelman was referring to were in fact out-and-out forgeries.

Once out in the open, the affair quickly grabbed the headlines. Indeed, it was a case of Columbia grabbing headlines from itself, because up until David Begelman came along to dominate Hollywood/Wall Street consciousness, his employer, Columbia Pictures, and its movie *Close Encounters of the Third Kind,* and the company's stock, up from 7⅜ to 20⅞, were all anyone could talk about. Movie reviewers were reviewing the stock; at least one business writer has flown to a sneak preview in Dallas to review the movie (he predicted it would be a "colossal flop").

Autumn had been all speculation about *Close Encounters* —How high over $100 million would the worldwide gross go? And would that make the stock go up or down?—and now winter was nonstop speculation over David Begelman. What had he done to warrant suspension? And then, when the story finally leaked out—not through *Variety* or Rona Barrett (strangely mum on the subject of forgery) but in a *Wall Street*

Journal story by David McClintick, followed by a *Washington Post* exposé by Jack Egan and John Berry—how in the world could Columbia's board of directors ever have put him back at the helm? For that, after discovering an additional $74,208 in forgeries and expense-account theft, is what they did.

It is a story that speaks to the power structure of Hollywood, certainly, and to that community's ethical perceptions; but it goes further, inasmuch as the members of the company's board of directors, the final authority, come from a broader community. Matthew B. Rosenhaus, for example, the board member with the greatest number of Columbia shares (some 710,000 out of a total 8.4 million), is also vice chairman of the board of Nabisco, a $2 billion company. Herbert A. Allen, 37, the board member with the most power, is president of a Wall Street investment banking firm (Allen & Co., Inc.) and the principal second-generation member of an investment banking family whose fortune has been estimated at half a billion dollars. With his father, he made available $80,000 to Hugh Carey's New York gubernatorial campaign. He is a good friend of Vice President Mondale.

How could a man like David Begelman, born without money but Yale-educated, highly cultivated, handsomely compensated ($4,500 a week plus bonuses and elaborate perquisites), forge checks!

And then how could a man like Herbert A. Allen, born into "serious" money, Williams-educated, forthright, articulate, and well-intentioned, lead the board fight to reinstate him?

Let's start with David Begelman (the name is pronounced like the dog, not the doughnut), who, incidentally, is not Yale-educated, after all. He lists himself in *Who's Who* as having graduated with the Class of '47, but Yale has no record of his ever having attended.

HOLLYWOOD: LONG SHOT

In Hollywood you are what you drive, and anyone who is anyone is a Mercedes-Benz. David Begelman, even as Colum-

bia Pictures was fighting to stave off bankruptcy when he
signed on in 1973, was a Rolls-Royce. (Leased—but who
would know?)

In Hollywood you must live in Beverly Hills, Bel Air, or the
Hollywood Hills (unless you work for Universal, which keeps
a lower profile, or unless you live out at the beach); and you
must live in a house that, especially in light of your car payments, you cannot realistically afford. You think I'm joking,
but it's true. It's not that the houses are so grand, either, many
of them—just that, bid up and up by the status seekers, they
are so expensive. David Begelman's modest house with pool
in Beverly Hills might go for $150,000 anywhere else; in its
present location it is worth half a million or more.

This is an example of the kind of financial pressure everyone in the business who hasn't yet made millions lives under.
It is a poor example with respect to David Begelman, however, because in David Begelman's case the house is not
owned, it is leased; and the lease—at some $5,000 or more a
month—is mostly picked up by Columbia Pictures. It is a perk
the company agreed to when it lured Begelman from Creative
Management Associates, the talent agency he headed with
agent-producer Freddie Fields.*

(What Columbia did not know until the recent investigation
was who *owned* the house Begelman leased: Ray Stark's lawyer.)

This is Hollywood, and in Hollywood two kinds of people
drive expensive cars. First, there are the actors and producers,

* Begelman is the only Columbia Pictures executive whose resi-
dence has been subsidized. The house, moreover, is his only resi-
dence—so it cannot be argued that this is a "home away from home
necessitated by business." So far, the I.R.S. has allowed Columbia to
take its lease payments as legitimate business deductions; and, so far
as it is known, it has not required David Begelman to pay income tax
on the money. The company also pays for household help. The
Rolls-Royce he leases himself.

On the same subject: If David Begelman declared as income the
money he stole from Columbia Pictures on his 1975 and 1976 tax
returns, it would be news to us; and if he didn't, it would be tax
fraud.

and even a few agents and directors, who have hit big; and then there are their good friends who have power and status but no meaningful piece of the action—namely, the studio executives.

Ray Stark, for example, one of Columbia's prime producers (and owner of 90,000 shares), is a Rolls-Royce of the first kind. (Well, the Rolls is his wife's; he drives a Dodge station wagon —but you get the idea.) He is worth in excess of $10 million for having produced such movies as *Funny Girl, The Owl and the Pussycat,* and *The Way We Were.* David Begelman, who has long been a close friend of Ray Stark's—not least for his role in keeping client Barbra Streisand in line for Stark's movies while still her agent at CMA—is a Rolls-Royce of the second kind. (Nixon had the same problem. He was always socializing with men vastly more wealthy than he was, and it hurt.)

To the rest of the world, a quarter-million-dollar studio-head salary looks rich. But when the government takes half that salary in taxes and your friends are all millionaires, it pales. On at least one occasion, David Begelman found himself borrowing money from Ray Stark. At the same time, it was part of his job to deal with Stark on behalf of Columbia Pictures. A potential conflict of interest?

Leonard Goldberg of Spelling-Goldberg Productions, a highly successful television production company, is another good friend of Begelman's; and he, too, is a Rolls-Royce of the first kind. It is alleged that at one time, while Begelman was still an agent and during the period when he was gambling heavily, Len Goldberg arranged to send $300,000 in cash to Begelman in Las Vegas. Both men (through their lawyers) deny that any such loan ever took place—the source is a shady character who claims to have carried the money—but it is the kind of loan that a man like Goldberg could have afforded to make, and it is the kind of loan that a man like Begelman could never have made. (Begelman described his gambling as having stretched over a "four- or five-year period" in the early 1960s, when he wasn't so much a compulsive gambler as a "compulsive loser." And yet, in four or five years of compulsive losing, he estimates he lost only $50,000 or $60,000. Others estimate he lost a great deal more. It is said that Freddie Fields would get threatening calls in the middle of the night from shylocks and casinos trying to collect on his partner's debts, and that Fields, after negotiating the best deals he could, would pay off out of Begelman's share of the agency's proceeds. Fields denies this. In any case, no evidence whatever has been turned up—despite considerable digging—to suggest that Begelman has gambled at all since 1973, when he joined Columbia Pictures.)

Whether Len Goldberg ever loaned money to David Begelman or not—and I hasten to add that as far as I know there is nothing wrong with one friend's lending another a large sum of money—it *is* true that when David Begelman and his current wife, Gladyce, got married, they invited Len and Wendy Goldberg along with them on their honeymoon. It is also true that shortly after David Begelman was reinstated at Columbia this past December, he signed a multi-picture deal with—that's right—Leonard Goldberg.

I imply no sinister quid pro quo. The movie business, like any other (but more than most) is incestuous. Hollywood is a tight-knit community where everyone knows everyone and where the interlocking favors and feuds and friendships and fiefdoms raise the specter of countless conflicts of interest. But what are you going to do—put together movies with sealed bids?

Business is business, and whom you like and trust and owe one to has as much to do with your deals as does merit. And then he or she owes *you* one. Eventually, the hope is, we'll all get rich together. How would you write specifications for a movie? "Must run 102 to 106 minutes in length, be highly affecting and 'accessible,' funny in spots, with enormous box-office appeal. Lowest bid accepted." Can't be done. Neither can the choice of directors or producers or writers or studios be put out to bid. It is a business of people—mostly lawyers-turned-agents or agents-turned-producers or agents-turned-studio heads or studio heads-turned-producers (give me a good deal on this one, and when I'm a producer I'll give you a good deal on the next)—and these people are inevitably torn between two desires: first, the desire to make truly wonderful and important movies; second, the desire to make truly vast and sensational amounts of money. Since you can't make truly vast and sensational amounts of money without delighting at least some millions of people in the process, even if their number does not include Pauline Kael, Frank Rich, or Vincent Canby, this second desire is not necessarily such a bad thing. (And there is always Judith Crist.) In any case, the desire will never go away.

Which brings us to:

HOLLYWOOD: CLOSE-UP

Allan Carr, who made his first millions with a Mexican quickie about athletes eating other athletes called *Survive,* but who will shortly be giving us the rather more palatable *Grease,* is throwing a Christmas party in his Benedict Canyon home for Gladyce Begelman and the book she co-authored, *New York on $500 a Day (Before Lunch).* Whatever the party cost, complete with six elaborately costumed carolers, dozens of red and white poinsettias, perhaps 200 guests and a buffet table that would do any caterer's brochure proud, it must have been substantially more than Gladyce could ever hope to receive in royalties from the book. But Allan Carr is nothing if not generous, and book sales are not the point. He loves to give parties, and this one is wonderful.

Each invitation included a make-believe Master Charge card in the name of Gladyce Begelman. The cocktail napkins bear the printed greeting WELCOME GLADYCE, as do the plastic cups (tell me how they print on curved plastic and I will tell you how I fry eggs on my radiator). The guests include David and Gladyce, of course; producer Ray Stark (who was largely responsible for placing Begelman at the head of the studio in the first place); superagent Sue Mengers (who was given her start in the agency business by Begelman and now handles Barbra Streisand—and just about everyone else— herself); Columbia's head of production, Danny Melnick (number two at the studio to Begelman), with girl friend Tina Sinatra; producer Marty Ransohoff; Candice Bergen; David Geffen; Ed McMahon—as well as a fair number of the poor- but-chic-and-aspiring.

The book lies on a table off to the right of the enormous living room—more in the style of a "great hall." (If you like this house, friends say, you should see Allan's house in Mal- ibu, where the 80-foot beachfront lots—just the lots—go for $500,000 and more.) The book was obviously written with tongue in cheek. "How terribly taxing for you to have to plan whether you'd prefer your massage before your manicure or after," runs one passage. But it purports nonetheless to be based on personal experience—"We picked up a super sport- coat for just $1,300 last year"—and it was unquestionably so- cialites, not socialists, who wrote it. ("How anyone manages in New York without a chauffeur is beyond our comprehen- sion.")

The irony of this book, and of this party—which is taking place while Hollywood's inner circle is all abuzz over David's indiscretions—does not go unnoticed. Here you have Gladyce Begelman, who all agree is a lovely and right-spirited woman and who used to be married to Lew Rudin, one of the largest realtors in New York and a Genuinely Rich Man. She knew David Begelman in those days, because the Rudins and the Begelmans went everywhere together and were, as couples, the best of friends. And then, around 1969, you had Gladyce Rudin deciding to become Gladyce Begelman instead, and suddenly she is living with a man who had a Genuinely High Income, but No Real Money. (The prior Mrs. Begelman, Lee, who had to be divorced to effect this switch, is alive and well in New York and not as bitter as most of the reporters who have called her had hoped. About the only intimate detail she would reveal in her generally glowing description of her ex-husband is that he used to do the Sunday *New York Times* crossword puzzle in ink. The very *first* Mrs. Begelman, Esther —back in the days when David Begelman was just a life insurance salesman with a prospect named Freddie Fields— was lost to her husband in a long, tragic fight with cancer that must have been both emotionally and financially exhausting.)

Which is all a long way of saying, did David Begelman need the money he stole? Of course he needed it! As one well-known Hollywood millionaire put it to me, "If you can spend five hundred dollars a day before lunch, can you spend a thousand a day by the time you go to sleep? If you can do that, that's three hundred sixty-five thousand dollars a year *after taxes*. David didn't make anywhere near that kind of money!" (This young fellow, by contrast, makes five times as much just by sitting back with his investments.)

True, Begelman could have borrowed the money from friends—he has friends in abundance. To pay back Columbia the money he stole, he is said to have borrowed from his friend Sy Weintraub, a retired multimillionaire. But David Begelman is a proud man (that is the real punishment for his crimes—the public embarrassment of the past couple of months), and the proud are reluctant to ask for help. Moreover, loans do not solve the problem. There *were* loans; some say lots of them. But unless expenses are cut back, the debt just grows and grows. Perhaps one reason Begelman entered into a long-term seven-figure lease on Ray Stark's lawyer's house was, in a roundabout way, to pay off some debt, financial or otherwise. Everyone denies this, but who knows these things? (The lawyer has many clients besides Ray Stark, so there may be no connection whatever.)

It may be true, too, that Begelman's subconscious motivation in forging the checks was self-destruction. This is how he himself would eventually explain it. But what was he thinking *consciously* each time he ordered up another check, forged someone else's name, and then drove over to the bank to receive the cash?

My guess is he was thinking he needed the money.

People have made much of the analogy of the millionaire who shoplifts. They point out that a man in David Begelman's position could easily have stolen much larger sums, principally through deals with distributors overseas, and that he would not have been the first to do so. While there may be some truth to the shoplifter analogy, it should be pointed out that David Begelman's stealing $84,208 was *not* "like a millionaire with a compulsion to shoplift." It was more like a man with minimal assets, and perhaps heavy debts, stealing $84,208.

And bear in mind: in Begelman's tax bracket, $84,208 stolen is as good as $180,000 earned. Only in Hollywood does such an amount seem small.

MEANWHILE, IN NEW YORK

David Begelman, throughout all of this, was not the chief executive of Columbia Pictures Industries, Inc., merely president of its principal divisions. Alan J. Hirschfield, a Harvard M.B.A. (really—we checked) some fourteen years Begelman's junior, was chief executive of the parent corporation. While Begelman was running the studio out in Burbank, Hirschfield was dealing with corporate matters, largely financial, at headquarters in New York. (Coincidentally, last year Allen & Co., Inc., moved its offices into the same building.) As a team, with Begelman perhaps deservedly getting the larger share of the credit, these two men had engineered Columbia's remarkable recovery. They had transformed a company on the verge of failure into a company flush with cash and panting for acquisitions.

When Alan Hirschfield first got a call from the Beverly Hills bunco squad advising him that David Begelman had forged Cliff Robertson's name on a $10,000 check, he thought the caller was Ray Stark, who is partial to this kind of prank—and very good at it. "Come on, Ray," he said, "I'm busy." When he realized it was not a joke, and when David Begelman not long thereafter confirmed the report, he was shocked, but sympathetic. He asked Begelman whether there was "any more." "No, no more," Begelman assured Hirschfield. He told board member Allen the same thing.

The company suspended Begelman on September 30, 1977, and set its accountants, Price Waterhouse, and its lawyers, Weil, Gotshal & Manges, upon an investigation that would take several weeks and cost Columbia shareholders in excess of $250,000. In a matter of weeks it was discovered that Begelman had forged the names of director Martin Ritt and of restaurateur and man-about-town Pierre Groleau; had overbilled the company for a screening room it had authorized him to build in his home (rather, Ray Stark's lawyer's home); and had padded his expense reports.

(He had stolen nothing from Robertson, Ritt, or Groleau themselves, because they were not due the money. Indeed, Groleau was astonished when first told that he was the "third name," which had not yet surfaced in the press. Weeks later, after his name *had* appeared, he still knew nothing. "David, to this time, to this moment, has never said anything to me," he told me, "although we have met several times recently. It's just 'Hello, David,' 'Hello, Pierre,' as though nothing has happened. I don't know the reason and I don't want to know, because I do like him very much—he's always been terribly nice to me.")

Soon the stream of discoveries stopped. Columbia's investigation went on for some time, including close scrutiny of all company transactions over the preceding four years, as well as an examination of Begelman's personal checkbook—even his wife's—but nothing more was found. Herbert Allen would describe the search as "possibly the most intensive corporate investigation of its kind in history."

So there it was. On the one hand, the man had helped to make perhaps $100 million for the shareholders of Columbia Pictures; and on the other hand, he had misappropriated around $80,000—now paid back with interest. What should Alan Hirschfield and the board of directors do about it? Should they reinstate him as president? Or should they give him a lucrative independent producership to retain his talents but shunt him out of the line of fire? (No one on either side was advocating prosecution.)

Two points to help you decide:

• First, the minute Begelman's suspension was announced, telegrams began to pour in to the board of directors "from every good name in the business," as one would put it, affirming admiration for and support of David Begelman. Although doubtless genuine, these testimonials were not entirely spontaneous. Sue Mengers and Ray Stark, principally, had organized an intensive lobbying effort. Many of the telegrams were sent from Sue Mengers's office with clients' approval. Jack Nicholson found out about the telegram he sent only a week after Sue had sent it for him—he'd been out on location and unreachable at the time. "By the way, Jack," Mengers said, explaining what she had done. "You've got some balls, kid," Nicholson said, acquiescing.

In most cases the expressions of support were general. They did *not* say, "Having considered the extent of David's misdeeds, we nonetheless conclude that the proper action of the board of Columbia Pictures, a public company, should be to reinstate him." Most, in fact, were sent before the specifics of his misdeeds were known. But an effort was made to convince the board that without Begelman, the company would collapse. It was intimated that Barbra Streisand would not work for the studio. Ray Stark said he would not work with Alan Hirschfield.

• Second, concurrently with the investigation of his finances, David Begelman began visits to Judd Marmor, "psychiatrist to the stars." (Begelman also spent much of his time during this period with another prominent Beverly Hills psychiatrist, his good friend Aron Stern. Dr. Stern, who is also a producer, has a deal going at Columbia. He categorically refuses to discuss the advice he gave Begelman during this period but does say it was "anything but self-serving. Quite the contrary.") After a handful of sessions with David Begelman, Dr. Marmor flew to New York to meet with a group of Columbia board members. He told them that Begelman's actions had resulted from emotional, not pathological, problems; that they had been manifestations of self-destructiveness; and that, having gotten this all out into the open and understanding now the motives behind what he had done, Begelman would be very unlikely ever to do such things again. The experience had served as a sort of cleansing.

To hear board member Matty Rosenhaus tell it, it was nothing short of a miracle: "In six weeks' time, believe it or not, we got a report from [Marmor] saying that he believed this man was cured and would never do a thing like this again. Never, never, never again."

Are you saying that he's no longer self-destructive?

"*I'm* not saying that. I want you to know that *the psychiatrist* told us that. He said this man, in his estimation, was cured. He was very thrilled with that analysis. He would be willing to testify before anybody that this was a cured man."

Rosenhaus was equally thrilled with the analysis, as he interpreted it, because it provided a justification for reinstating a man he hoped might be able to make yet another $100 million for his company.

Rosenhaus, part of whose fortune was built on Geritol, whose tired-blood advertising claims the Federal Trade Commission fought for years as misleading, controlled two out of eight votes on the board. Chalk up two votes for reinstatement.

THE CASE FOR REINSTATEMENT

"Look, Andy," said one of the powers involved in all this, trying to help me understand. "If I have a secretary who's working for me, who has worked for me for five or six years and done a terrific job, and I find out that she has forged some checks, right? I have to make my own character judgment. I can't let the world make it for me. I have to decide, do *I* want to prosecute this secretary? Do *I* want to fire her? Do *I* feel she's worth a second chance? That's *my* decision. This is *Columbia's* decision; they know David Begelman better than the people who are writing about him, better than the public, better than the stockholders. It is their considered opinion that despite the wrong he did—and no one is saying he didn't do wrong—they want to give him another chance. You talk about freedom—that's freedom!

"Yes, David Begelman did something wrong. And he did something illegal. But within the tenets of the law, from what I've been told, it is up to the people that he harmed to decide, based on whatever—personal relationships, business achievement—whether or not they want to punish this man any more than he's already been punished. Because when you talk about justice for the rich versus justice for the poor, strangely enough—if you really analyzed it—a man like Begelman is suffering probably as much, with the public disgrace he is being subjected to, as the guy who has to serve six months for forgery. Okay?"

Okay, but at the time the board moved to reinstate him, no word of Begelman's actual wrongdoing had appeared. He had suffered no great public embarrassment.

In Herbie Allen's view, it was a mental problem, not a moral one. The man was not a criminal, he was emotionally disturbed. And the *really* humanistic thing to do, he felt, post-Watergate morality or no, would be to give this fundamentally good man a second chance. "Whatever happened to the idea of compassion?" he wonders.

To Herbie Allen, just as sad as seeing what Begelman had done was to see a friend, Hirschfield, not defend a friend, Begelman. In his view, those who opposed Begelman's reinstatement—Hirschfield chief among them—were "taking a moral stand when there was *no moral issue*." Allen points out that "when Clive Davis signed on to run the record company, you didn't see Alan Hirschfield objecting, and Clive came in under an even bigger cloud."* Hirschfield argues that Begelman's wrongdoing was more serious than Davis's, and that it

---

* CBS had dismissed Davis for charging his son's lavish bar mitzvah to the company—not such a preposterous thing to do within the context of the record business—and there were fears, which proved groundless, that he might have had some connections with the underworld that would have jeopardized CBS's broadcasting licenses.

occurred while Begelman was at Columbia, not before he arrived.

"What I'm saying," Herbie Allen says, "is that I think there's a particular lack of understanding in this case for this guy. The shareholders have a piece of paper in their hands that's worth a hundred twenty million dollars, and when they first got involved, it was worth twenty million. Now doesn't anybody think about that? He did it honestly, he did it decently—doesn't he get any credit for that?"

Although he was reinstated, Begelman was stripped of two titles and lost stock options. A deal that he had been negotiating with Hirschfield was canceled. Had it gone through, he would have, at the end of his contract, received $1 million. ("He always sort of focused on that figure," Allen says.) "Don't you think all that makes a difference?" asks Allen. "How much punishment does a guy deserve? Should he have more than that?"

THE CASE FOR "INDY PROD"

Alan Hirschfield never wanted to "punish" David Begelman, only to move him aside into an independent producership. In fact, when Hirschfield and Melnick committed Columbia to buying rights to *Annie*—for an unprecedented $9.5 million—it was with the expectation that Begelman would be given the project to produce.

Beyond whatever selfish and/or moral motives Hirschfield may have had for wanting to fire Begelman, there were practical considerations.

• How can you keep a guy who steals? What does this say to others in the company who might want to steal, too? (When, some time earlier, it had been discovered that a Columbia employee was using the transcontinental "pouch" to traffic in cocaine—albeit at no material expense to the shareholders—the man was immediately dimissed. How could a public company do otherwise?)

• What does it say to Wall Street? (Not all that much, apparently. The day the *Wall Street Journal* story broke, Columbia closed up three-eighths. The First National Bank of Boston, however, which had some $30 million in loans out to Columbia, threatened to pull the loans if Begelman did not go—then it relented.)

• Additionally, what kind of weapon does keeping such a man at the top give to unwilling managements of potential Columbia Pictures acquisitions? (The company was reportedly in the midst of trying to acquire Mattel, the toymaker, for one, and there was talk of other potential takeovers.)

Then there were the questions about how a self-destructive man might try to self-destruct next and, assuming he didn't, how uncharitable Internal Revenue agents or relentlessly uncharitable journalists might try to do it for him. And think of the stockholder suits the board would be opening itself up to!

Bad as anyone may or may not have felt for David Begelman —and most people, even in the press, really did feel bad for him—you just couldn't reinstate him.

Ah, but you could, was the thrust of a 47-page opinion letter prepared for the board of directors by Columbia's New York lawyers, Weil, Gotshal & Manges. Just take him off the board and strip him of his corporate vice presidency. That way he will not, technically, be an officer of this public company— even though he may for all intents and purposes be given the authority to run it—and stockholders, should any of them sue, won't have a leg to stand on. (It would be a very recalcitrant stockholder indeed, argues Herbie Allen, who would sue the board of directors for retaining one of the key men who had turned the company to gold.)

THE ENVELOPE, PLEASE

Of the board members, only two, ultimately, were opposed to reinstatement—Alan Hirschfield, president of the company, and Leo Jaffe, chairman of the board. The outside directors all favored reinstatement. Allen & Co.—which had been brought in and given effective control in a deal arranged by Ray Stark in 1973—and Matty Rosenhaus controlled those outside votes.

The boardroom fight became bitter, and soon Hirschfield realized that it was he more than Begelman who was in danger of losing his job. "*I* didn't forge any checks," he said to friends more than once in dazed disbelief.

Yet his detractors claim he was not as naïve and wholesome in all of this as he would have them think. They saw his stand as a callous grab for power. Moreover, as one of them explained, "What you don't understand is that Alan was never able to offer solutions. If Alan had been able to say, 'Hey, fellas, what are we worried about—I've got John Calley coming in' or 'I've got Alan Ladd coming in' or 'I've got Bob Evans coming in,' that's one thing. But he had no viable solutions."

On Sunday, December 4, even before word of the forgeries had hit the press, Alan Hirschfield reluctantly offered Begelman his job back.

Begelman refused.

He didn't want to come back if he felt Hirschfield didn't really want him. (If accounts from insiders are to be believed, the issue, and rancor, was never really between Hirschfield and Begelman—they remained on relatively good terms—but between Hirschfield and the board, especially between Hirschfield and Herbie Allen.)

Thus it was to nail down the provisions of his "indy prod" deal that Begelman showed up at Hirschfield's Scarsdale home the following week. At that meeting, Hirschfield surprised everyone, including the board, by again offering him his job back, and this time persuading him to accept it.

When looked at with hindsight, it was not a prudent job offer for Begelman to accept. For one thing, he stood to make more money as an independent producer. But friends say he was motivated in large part by a desire to clear his name and "do right" by the company by making it even more successful. It was also the kind of job, with fifty projects up in the air at any one time, that would be far more to his liking and suited to his temperament than that of a producer, who may spend two years or more on a single project. And, of course, there may have been a touch of the self-destructive drawing him into the climax of the drama.

"If you look at this thing with any kind of perspective," comments a ranking insider, "you have to conclude that David's willingness to go back into the management job, which brought with it the barrage of media, as anyone could have seen it would, was perhaps the final and most effective method of self-destruction."

Hirschfield's motives in offering reinstatement are equally hazy. Basically, it was his belief that the board would never allow him to run the show on his own. Perhaps he had just bowed to his notion of expediency.

Perhaps, too, he had the foresight to realize what would happen next:

The reinstatement was announced, all hell broke loose, and within less than two months, Begelman was once again vacating the office of the president, this time of his own volition. He would "go indy prod" after all, guaranteed to earn some half-million dollars a year. Columbia stock, which had fallen from around 20 to 13⅝ despite the continued success of *Close Encounters*, jumped smartly on the news.

SERMONETTE

The day before Begelman was first suspended—back on September 29, 1977—Herbie Allen happened to be sitting in the Roosevelt Room of the White House with a score of other film-industry executives, chatting with the President of the United States. He was the first to ask Carter a question, and his question—to the horror of his industry colleagues—was essentially: Isn't our crackdown on "dubious payments" abroad wrecking our balance of payments? Aren't we losing a ton of business because we can no longer bribe foreign officials like everyone else?

The question was unrelated to the movie business, but not entirely unrelated to this story. Allen is a practical man. A decent man, and a practical one. He thinks it's crazy for us to try to legislate the morality and the business customs of governments overseas—an effort he thinks is doomed to failure anyway—at the cost of billions of dollars in lost foreign trade. "Our enemies laugh at us," he later wrote the President in a letter of elaboration, "and our friends cry for us." He thinks most of the President's advisers are "hopelessly naïve."

And on the issue of foreign payments, a significant chunk of America's business elite agrees. One attorney I spoke with, who had had a position of responsibility throughout three administrations—Eisenhower's, Kennedy's, and Johnson's—feels very strongly that Allen is right. The S.E.C. should never have been allowed to bring all this dirty laundry out into the open, he says. In the reality of international politics and commerce, it could only prove harmful to all concerned.

The connection between the foreign-payoff question (which is not a simple one) and the Begelman forgeries (which I think is) is pragmatism. Not immorality, but perhaps a dose of amorality.

When the board of directors of Columbia decided—unanimously—not to press charges against David Begelman for his thefts, they were acting "humanistically," they say; and I find it hard not to agree. What they saw was a weakness or sickness on Begelman's part, not a calculated plan to do in the shareholders.

When the board of directors decided to continue Begelman's salary and perks much as they had been, retaining his talents as an independent producer, they were giving him a very generous "second chance." Here you could argue they were being too kind. Perhaps they should have required that he reimburse the company, over a period of time, for the costs of its investigation. Perhaps they should have severed ties altogether, although it might not have been in the shareholders' interest to do so.

But, before that, when the board of directors of this public company actually moved to reinstate him (having paid him all the while he was on leave), they truly made a practical and, I think, an ethical blunder.

The man forged checks. Not once, in a drunken stupor—but at least three times. You can argue that a bar mitzvah attended by all your industry colleagues is good for business—and hence deductible. You may not win the argument, but you can make it. You can argue that illegal wiretapping, if done in the belief that it would save the country, has some supralegal moral justification. You may not win the argument, but at least you can make it. You can argue about marijuana, you can argue about draft resistance, you can probably even argue about the millionaire with a compulsion to shoplift at the five-and-dime. You may have to make these arguments from behind bars, and you may lose them—but you can make them.

How can you possibly argue about forgery?

A board of directors in today's corporate America cannot describe a series of forgeries as "certain unauthorized financial transactions" and then reinstate the perpetrator, hoping that no one will notice or make a stink.

The best that can be said is that in doing so, out of compassion for a friend and in hopes that he could make their company yet another $100 million, the board of Columbia Pictures made an honest mistake. It is a mistake I think few other boards of public companies would have made.*

March 1978

* Early in 1980 Metro-Goldwyn-Mayer tapped Begelman to run its film division, at a salary "close to half a million dollars a year."

II
Money Clips

IF THEY'RE SO SMART,
HOW COME
THEY GAVE ME $10,000?

On the surface, it was a most intriguing proposition. Not only was I being offered a column in *Esquire,* a publication I had long admired; but as it was to be a column about money, I would be given some to play with.

"Some what?" I asked, blinking. It sounded as though "some" referred to "money," but we have all lived long enough to know that magazines do not give their writers money "to play with." Rich men give it to their wives, Parker Brothers prints it with their games, but . . .

Then I remembered (with money, as with most things, there's no substitute for having been around a little) that this same editor had, at a different magazine, once conned a different writer, Jon Bradshaw, into writing a delightful story about the New York State Lottery in return for a thousand $1 lottery tickets. Anything he won he could keep. The readers got their vicarious thrill, the magazine got its delightful story, and Bradshaw got $196.

"Ah," I sighed, "the old Bradshaw con."

No, said this editor. I was to be paid a normal columnist's fee for my writing. The $10,000—ten thousand dollars!—was extra. For me to play with in the stock market. And to report back to the reader on my gains and losses.

"And if there's anything left when I'm done playing? Who gets that?"

"*You* do. Don't you understand? It's *your* money. You can

do anything with it you want, and the more you make with it, the more you'll have." Here was Michael Anthony dispensing John Beresford Tipton's tax-free million to a disbelieving schnook—so that the audience could enjoy watching it wreck his life.

Now let me back up to say that having been offered quite a few deals and opportunities in my young life, I have come through harsh experience to know that the world is divided into two things: things that are too good to be true, which constitute the vast, overwhelming, wildly disappointing majority of things; and, once in a rare while, things that are simply a very good thing. I was beginning to take this offer for the latter. It was only after mentally furnishing my apartment with the $10,000—Oriental rugs, they say, are a wonderful investment; likewise art, antiques, and a good wine cellar—that I realized, finally, the catch. (There was a catch, after all.) The catch was that what I would *really* do with $10,000, were it to float in my tightly weather-stripped window, is invest it in two $5,000 municipal bonds due to mature in 2005—or some equally boring but eminently prudent thing. Only that would be the stuff of a column that appeared every 28 years, at purchase and redemption. Or at best every six months, each time I clipped two coupons.

You see, I believe that by and large you can't beat the system. It is very hard consistently to do appreciably better than average with investments. In fact, the harder you try, the more (odds are) you lose. The more risk you take, the more likely you are to lose; the more frequently you switch from one thing to another, the more money you give up to the house. Patience, not pizzazz, is rewarded when it comes to money. But patience is boring, and I knew *Esquire* was not hiring me to be boring.

"You're asking me to violate all my investment principles," I said, seeing the trick. "You're asking me to set a poor example, an example of exactly the kind of so-called investing I do *not* recommend.

"I'll take it," I said.

What's more, unbelievably, they sent it. Ten thousand dollars.

All right. I grant you that $10,000 is really not such an extraordinary amount of money. In New York, if you are single and earning, say, $26,000 after deductions, almost $5,500 of any $10,000 windfall goes straight to the government; the remainder is barely enough to buy a large-screen TV. (This gift was not only smaller than John Beresford Tipton's, it was fully taxable.) Nonetheless, as one who recurrently dreams of finding loose change in the street (well, in the gutter, if you must know, although I can't imagine there being any significance to that), with those dimes and nickels leading to more dimes and nickels, and *quarters* . . . which really couldn't add up to more than twenty or thirty bucks, tops (although that was a goodly sum in my childhood, when the dream presumably was scripted) . . . as one who has had that dream on and off for twenty-odd years, the idea of finding $10,000 *in the street,* $10,000 just *to play with* . . .

I gurgled happily all the way to the bank.

Now it is appropriate that I set forth, as modestly as is possible under the circumstances, my credentials for losing $10,000 in public (apart from the considerable practice I've had with smaller sums in private). In other words, If I'm So Smart, How Come I'm Not Rich?

Here's how smart I am:

Some time ago, I was sitting next to one of the ten—surely one of the fifty—most powerful men in the world, Walter Wriston. Wriston is chairman of Citicorp, by a country mile the world's leading global megabank. Citicorp is vastly more powerful than most nations; Wriston runs it; and from my limited dealings with him, I say that if anyone has to be that powerful, I'm glad the board of directors chose him. In me, at least, Wriston engenders great respect and trust—and not every banker does.

This was an off-the-record dinner Citicorp hosts at the River Club each year for the two or three dozen financial writers the bank has found least offensive. The food was good (lobster claws were served—as hors d'oeuvres); the small talk was on a reasonably high level (when somebody from the bank went down to Washington with Pat Patterson—Ellmore C. Patterson, chairman of J. P. Morgan & Co.—to go "eyeball to eyeball" with Jerry Ford at the height of the New York City crisis, Ford pointed to a scar above his eye and said to Pat, "This is the cleat mark you left." Turns out they had played opposite each other in college).

Placed neatly under each guest's butter dish was what looked for all the world like a two-page college quiz. With our names already typed for us across the top, no less. This, it was explained for the benefit of first-timers like me, was the annual "Fearless Forecast," in which we, the press, were to make our economic projections for the coming year.

Terror seized me by the lapel. Because if the truth be known, I am only vaguely aware of this year's G.N.P., let alone capable of knowledgeably projecting its level twelve months out. As for such things as the M family (M_1, M_2, and the rest), or the way the Fed *expands* the money supply by buying *in* government bonds, let's just say that I have been known to get these things confused. (At business school, our classrooms had no windows. The joke in accounting class used to be "Debits by the windows, credits by the doors." I still don't understand what they were talking about.)

To my great relief, for each question—G.N.P., unemployment, Dow Jones industrials, Consumer Price Index, etc.—Citicorp had charitably included the statistic from the year just past. So, while they were handing out a gold-plated perpetual-motion clock to the winner of the prior year's forecast (Clem Morgello, formerly of *Newsweek*, currently editor of *Dun's Review*), I was busily adding a rough 10 percent to the previous year's statistics, much as a cook might add seasoning to the stew. A little for inflation, a little for growth—and a lot for convenience, as it's a great deal easier to figure 10 percent and round off than to figure 8.3 percent on the dot.

When it came to the last questions—who would be the 1976

Democratic presidential nominee and who would ultimately be elected—I was going to put Hubert Humphrey as the nominee and Jerry Ford as the winner, but the man to my left, Wriston, had let slip over dinner that *his* money was on Jimmy Carter (so to speak). So, figuring his guess was better than mine, I put Carter as the nominee; but—figuring he was crazy —I stuck with Ford to win. (How did Wriston *know*, eleven months before the fact? The first primaries hadn't even been held! It's scary.)

A year later, Carter was in the White House and I was back at the annual dinner, no longer at Wriston's table (these things rotate, naturally), and he was up at the podium handing me the gold clock. I had won, he said, by a very wide margin. It wasn't even close.

All of which I submit to prove to you that I am indeed as smart as the next guy (never mind the fact that I couldn't figure out how to get the clock to work) and, in this instance at least, lucky as hell. If I were always this lucky, I *would* be rich.

Anyway, the $10,000 was mine, and having made every conceivable excuse for losing it, I set about investing it. My broker could only marvel at the zest with which I churned my own account. There were the dumb little stereo and electronics companies that nearly went bankrupt, the little oil-field service company stocks that quadrupled (shortly after I sold them), and more. By the time the exercise ended, nine months later, the $10,000 had become $13,992, which was split five ways. The largest share went to the federal government; smaller but significant shares went to New York State and New York City; $1,281 went in brokerage commissions; and I got the rest—more than enough to furnish the hallway outside my new apartment.

June 1977

HOUSEHOLD FINANCE

Probably the best, most sensible, most potentially lucrative and rewarding investment you can make today, regardless of where you live or what your financial situation, is to buy a cooperative apartment on Manhattan's increasingly fashionable upper West Side. I want to stress that my saying this has absolutely nothing to do with *my* just having purchased such an apartment, nor with my intense interest in seeing its market value rise. What I am telling you is totally selfless.

The case for New York is clear enough: The Carter Administration is pledged to the city's solvency; griping and emigration to the suburbs have given way to boosterism and migration back into town; business in Times Square's colorful theater district is booming (and theater attendance isn't bad, either); Westway, the billion-dollar West Side beautification project, is about to get rolling [Three years later it was still about to get rolling.]; the immense submerged sludge reef that is creeping mysteriously up the ocean floor toward Long Island beaches will soon be driving shoreline residents back into Manhattan; and California's superquake, when it comes, will do likewise. Except for a few nettlesome problems—gangs of marauding thirteen-year-olds, an eroding economic base, etc.—all the city's indicators are thumbs up.

Now, granting all that, you may still wonder why you should pay $40,000 or $50,000 or more for the privilege of paying $600 or $800 a month maintenance on a modest two-bedroom apartment. Especially if you don't live in New York.

Aha!

To begin with, by buying an apartment you get to know the difference between a condominium and a co-op.*

Further, you get to borrow a great deal of money from a bank. And in addition to the prevailing 10 percent interest rate on New York co-op loans, you get to pay a variety of imaginative one-time fees, including one to cover appraisal of the apartment and another to cover appraisal of you. However, you do not get to *see* either of these appraisals—you just pay for them. "The appraisal report and credit report are confidential and it is bank policy not to release copies to anyone other than bank personnel."

While your loan application is pending, you get to suffer not only your own traumas—My God, am I doing the right thing? Am I crazy? Am I paying too much? Can I afford it? Will the Tenants Committee approve my application? (They can turn you down without even being obliged to tell you or the seller why.) What if the depression comes and other tenants can't afford it and I have to pay their maintenance, too?—but also the traumas of the sellers, who in my case blew hot and cold like a trade wind. One day I was being adopted as their son, and the next, when a competing real estate agent told them he could get them an extra few thousand for the apartment if they got out of their deal with me, I was not someone they wanted to do business with.

Finally the deal goes through, and you get to meet New York's not inconsiderable legal community, which shows up en masse at the closing to collect $200 apiece. There are your lawyer and their lawyer; your bank's lawyer and their bank's

---

* With a co-op, you are buying shares of stock in a corporation owned jointly with the other tenants, and you lease your apartment from that corporation. Technically, you don't own the apartment and thus cannot mortgage it (although you may borrow against the value of your stock); nor can you depreciate whatever portion of it might be used for business. With a condominium, you own the apartment itself and have the right to finance it and rent it out to whomever you please, much as if it were a private home. Corporations may not purchase co-ops; they may purchase condos.

lawyer; the lawyer for the building and the lawyer for the managing agent of the building; the real estate agent's lawyer, if it's gotten sticky enough; and lawyers who, passing in the halls, stop to see why such a crowd has gathered.

The lawyers are seated in a special gallery that the host law firm sets up, with attendants, called paralegals, passing out programs and selling drinks. As each check, waiver, note, proprietary lease, or duplicate thereof is signed, initialed, notarized, photocopied, or affixed thereto, the lawyers demurely applaud. When all the papers have been dispatched, when it has been established that it is not *your* seller who has a $25 parking ticket outstanding against him in Staten Island but a man of the same or similar name (because *were* it the seller, your bank's lawyer fears the city might come after the seller for the $25 and, in the event they couldn't get it, seize his erstwhile apartment instead, leaving you out on the street and the bank without security for its loan)—when, in short, every conceivable contingency has been considered and protected against, the host law firm announces that it will not consummate the deal until each of the lawyers in the gallery is paid $200. A cheer goes up from the stands.

Besides getting to throw a closing, by buying your own apartment you get to paint it. When you rent an apartment, the landlord sends around a nice Greek man with a latex roller and a six-pack of beer. If you ask what the beer is for, he will smile and indicate, through hand signals, that, well, it's all Greek to him (never mind that he majored in English at Oberlin and only dropped out of law school when he discovered he could make even more money as a painter). One therefore assumes that the beer is used to wash down the walls before the paint is applied. A large apartment takes two days to wash down and roller over. Another half day is required to seal shut the windows, cabinetry and radiator controls. The job costs you nothing, and it's a bargain.

However, when you own a co-op, you are responsible for your own painting. (Also your own floors, your own toilet, your own sink, your own outside hall—everything but structural damage to the building, as in the case of a plane crashing into the side of it or the onslaught of Dutch brick disease.) You get to hire your own Greek, supply him with your own beer (it should be imported) and choose from hundreds of shades of white, at $11.95 a gallon plus tax. It takes weeks. You think one man with one roller can do a so-so job in two days, so two guys with two rollers can do madonna-with-child in four? It took *three* guys with *three* rollers *three* days just to do the room I've set aside as my office. Of course, you can get firm estimates from respectable union painters and be sure in advance just what the job will cost you. A man I know was painting his seven-room Park Avenue apartment around the time I was painting mine. He did get estimates. They ranged from $10,000 to $27,000. Honest to God.

I could tell you how, when I took possession of the apartment, only a few forty-watt light bulbs had been left behind —presumably too high to reach. I could describe the scene I envision having taken place between Mr. Seller, begging her to leave them, and Mrs. Seller, determined to take even the half-depleted rolls of paper from the johns (they compromised and left one). I could tell you air conditioner stories that would freeze your heart. But as it turned out—through dumb luck (and inflation)—the $11,000 cash I put into this deal, my own home, was by far the best investment I ever made. Me and 40 million other Americans.

July 1977

THE SACCHARIN-BAN SUGAR BOOM OF 1977

If you are at all "into money," and perhaps even if you're not, you are constantly being bombarded with, and forced to make determinations about, different investment alternatives. Some succeed; some fail; most of them you choose not to become involved with at all. Here is the anatomy of one such investment decision, made with all the clarity of thought and professional aplomb you would *expect* of a sophisticated business school graduate.

It began with a letter from Merrill Lynch, which is always on the lookout for ways to make me some money. I got this form letter letting me in on ML's latest thinking on sugar. ML's latest thinking on sugar was: Buy.

Admittedly, the letter admitted, commodities speculation isn't for everyone; but for those for whom it is appropriate, the play in sugar offered some really good leverage and lots of upside potential. (In the investment business there are "upside potential" and "downside risk." Why there are not simply "potential" and "risk" is a point I have never fully grasped.) By anteing up $2,000, I could control a "contract" for future delivery of 112,000 pounds of sugar—enough for anybody's cereal—and stood to make $1,120 for every penny sugar rose. If it rocketed back up to its 66-cent 1974 high, I stood to make $63,000 on $2,000 in a matter of months.

Ordinarily, I toss such letters away without a second look.

What do I know about sugar? What kind of schnook makes his investment decisions reading form letters? But having some extra cash on hand—to keep, lose, or multiply, as might be the case—I read the letter through and mailed in the coupon for ML's full report. I don't believe I included my phone number, but they got it anyway, as I knew they would. Instead of the report, I got a phone call from a very sophisticated version of the kind of person who calls to sell you a magazine subscription. We went through the obligatory preliminaries, in which I feigned surprise at getting a call instead of a research report and he feigned surprise at my not yet having received the report. He then moved on to qualifying me as a prospect— mainly, had I ever traded commodities with Merrill Lynch before—which, as a matter of fact, I once for a brief period had. From the dryness of my tone, he knew enough not to ask how I had made out.

Sugar. Ah, the sweet opportunities in sugar. What with the Russian and Chinese surprise purchases having moved off some of the producer overhang, he said, and the possibility of government price supports or import quotas, although, but, perhaps, in which event, our opinion, with stops at 8.50 on the July contract, upside potential, downside risk—how much of a position was I considering taking?

Well, I explained, I was considering taking no position at all, because I didn't know what he and I knew about sugar that everybody else didn't know. And if we knew no more than everybody else, what edge did we possibly have?

I should note that this is more of a problem for the client than for the broker. The broker makes the same commission whether sugar goes up or down—although the longer the client keeps from getting wiped out, the more times he can be traded in and out of various positions (soy beans look promising this month, too), dropping $60 or so each time into the brokerage firm's tin cup.

Each of my questions was met with a polite, if glazed, response, as if much of it were being read, with understandable boredom, from a printed research report on the broker's desk.

Doubtless I was not the first of the day to be read to from this report, nor would I be the last.

We agreed, after about half an hour back and forth, that I would wait to see the research material ML would now certainly send, and that I would follow sugar daily to see how it was moving. If I didn't invest this time around, maybe I would take a flier in some future commodity speculation. The broker (I assume) flipped my index card over onto the growing pile on his right, and began dialing the number on the next card.

Then I started thinking. Sugar *had* been as high as 66 cents in 1974, and now *was* down to a pitiful 9 cents. True, there was a time when they traded onion futures, and the price of the onions fell to less than the cost of the sacks they kept them in. But how much further could sugar possibly fall? It's all-time low in recent memory was slightly above 5 cents in 1972 —unless your memory stretches back to 1969, when it was 2 cents, or 1967, when it was little more than a penny.

Part of me argued that sugar actually was awfully cheap, and that Merrill Lynch might have a point. Certainly, brokerage firms never let on, if they realize deep down in their corporate consciences, that what they are providing, mainly, is adult entertainment rather than any genuine way to beat the financial odds. Presumably, Merrill Lynch really believes that if you follow its advice, you will do better than if you don't. It may even be true!

However, most of me argued that even successful professional commodity speculators lose money on most of their trades, so that unless I were very lucky placing this bet, or unless I decided to get into this game on a continuing basis in the hope of occasionally making a killing to offset all my little losses (and all my little brokerage commissions), I had best steer clear.

But how interesting would that be? How could I write a column about not speculating in sugar? I decided that, all things considered, the smartest, the *classiest* thing for me to do would be to go into sugar, as ML suggested, but to go *short*, instead of long. (Going short a commodity, or anything else, means selling it rather than buying it, in the hope that it will go down rather than up. Eventually you have to buy it back, to "cover" your short and close out your position, but if it's gone down in price, you get to keep the difference between what you sold it for and what you had to pay to buy it back. Never, during any of this, I hasten to add, do you ever actually see any sugar.) My idea, in other words, was to bet that Merrill Lynch, although well meaning, was wrong. To bet against the crowd. Contrary investing. However, to give myself a little room, I decided to wait until sugar had gone up a little, say to 9.5 cents or 10 cents, before I made my move. I figured that on the basis of ML's worldwide marketing effort alone, the price of the stuff should go up that much.

I would let Merrill Lynch take its position. Then I would take mine.

Two nights later, all having been quiet on the sugar front thus far, I was lying awake at three in the morning listening to all-news radio—and I hear out of the blue that the Food and Drug Administration has just moved to ban saccharin, the world's prime artificial sweetener. Just like that!

Just why the F.D.A. would suddenly announce this at three in the morning I did not stop to consider. I read a lot of newspapers and magazines, and listen to a lot of all-news radio, and I remembered having heard absolutely nothing that would suggest such an action was in the offing. Apparently, the F.D.A. had kept its secret well and had sprung it in the middle of the night. (Or so it seemed to me at the time.)

I got out of bed and went to check the research material Merrill Lynch had by now sent me. Nowhere was there any mention of the possibility of a saccharin ban. This was not one of the factors the market was considering. ML, those lucky bastards, had just been in the right place at the right time. It was as if they had accidentally recommended domestic oil stocks the day before the announcement of the Arab oil embargo. Sugar prices would doubtless go through the roof.

I tried to go back to sleep, but was kept awake by the specter of what would have happened had I indeed gotten around to shorting sugar as I had planned. Wham-o, there would have been the end of my much ballyhooed $10,000. COLUMNIST

GETS HIS SUGAR CUBES CRUSHED, some smart-aleck financial editor would headline somewhere, and I would feel like crawling into a safe deposit box and shutting the door behind me. Because with commodities, putting up $2,000 doesn't mean that all you can lose is $2,000. Hardly. When a commodity is really moving, one way or another, it can go up or down "limit" the minute it opens for trading—and not trade for the rest of the day. You can't get out of your position, sometimes for days. You have only put up a couple of thousand dollars' margin, but technically you have bought, or sold, 112,000 pounds of sugar (or 36,000 pounds of pork bellies or 22,500 dozen eggs or 100,000 board-feet of lumber) worth maybe ten or 20 times your down payment. All sugar would have to do would be to close up limit a few days running, with me short and losing $1,120 a day . . .

I fell asleep around five, mightily relieved that I had not tried to buck the wisdom of Merrill Lynch, after all. And I awoke as the bell (if they have a bell) rang on the New York Coffee and Sugar Exchange. I called my broker. Not the man from Merrill Lynch, but the man I have come to know and trust through thick and (mostly) thin. He, too, is forever speculating in commodities and egging me on to do likewise, and I thought that perhaps now, on the off chance sugar hadn't already closed up limit and I could still get in, I might just take a flier with him in sugar. On the long side, of course. All thoughts of being classy had now given way to a single burning conceptual ideal: making a killing on the inevitable Saccharin-Ban Sugar Boom of 1977.

Oddly, sugar was up all right, from 8.98 cents a pound to 9.25 cents, but by no means up limit (a full penny). Yet there was the news headlined in the morning paper, just as I had heard it on the radio. My broker plunked down $2,000 of his own to buy a sugar contract at 9.25 cents; I wavered and chickened out.

Wonder of wonders, by the end of the day sugar closed at 8.98 cents, and my broker was out $302.40 plus commissions.

How could this be? Had the market known about the possible saccharin ban, after all, and had it thus already been discounted? (Yes.) Did it not make much difference, after all, because saccharin users would in most cases not be switching to sugar? (Yes, again.) Did the saccharin ban really make all that much difference? (No, apparently not.)

Saccharin, it seems, does not compete with sugar, when you come right down to it, but with other artificial diet sweeteners. *Corn syrup*, if they ever banned it, is the thing that would turn sugar into gold.

It was one of those rare investment episodes: I was no poorer, but wiser.

September 1977

THE
GREAT
CHAIN ROBBERY

Over the past couple of years, apart from the general rigors of city living, I have had reason to fear for my life only twice.

In the first instance I picked up the phone to be greeted by an F.B.I. agent who suggested—so that I would be sure this was for real—that I hang up and call him back at the F.B.I. Soon I was back on the phone with the same agent. He was calling, he explained (even though now, technically, it was I who was calling), to notify me that the Bureau had reason to believe that I and four others were on a Palestinian terrorist assassination list. Just why this was, the F.B.I. man did not profess to know, but I was in exceptionally good company: columnists Joseph Kraft and Jack Anderson, Senator Henry Jackson and President Anwar Sadat. Thrilled to have been included, I asked what the F.B.I. was proposing to do to protect me. That was not his department, the agent said; the Bureau's job was simply to notify me. However, while he could not assess the seriousness of the danger I might be in, he said, he did want to point out that the Mideast is a hotbed of plots, few of which ever actually get . . . "executed."

(What I had done to get on the list, I figured out later, was write a story for *New York* magazine that looked into the use of military force as a means to break the O.P.E.C. cartel. At the time, this option was being discussed openly in such power centers as the locker rooms of the Yale and Harvard clubs of New York. My story, "War—The Ultimate Anti-Trust

Action," concluded emphatically that such action would be unthinkable on several grounds. But the *cover* of the magazine, which I had no hand in designing—honest—looked like an *Action Comic*, with Ford and Kissinger in Marine fatigues, storming the desert beaches, oil rigs dotting the background, and Ford saying, "Are we gonna let these wogs kick sand in our faces?" The whole thing was reprinted not long afterward in *Paris Match*, where the terrorist leader—himself a Princeton alumnus—presumably saw it.)

The second threat, a good deal less serious and entirely unrelated to the first, was received last week. It was contained in the second paragraph of a handwritten chain letter.

"Trust in the Lord with all your heart," the letter began, "and all will acknowledge Him and He will light your way." The letter purported to have been sent to me for good luck, same to manifest itself within four days—providing I did not break the chain. "Don Elliot received $60,000 but lost it because he broke the chain," the letter declared, which would have been reason enough, heaven knows, to make and send the twenty lousy photocopies. But in addition there was the chilling experience of General Walsh. "While in the Philippines," the letter warned, "General Walsh lost his life six days after he received the letter. He failed to circulate the prayer. However, before his death he received $775,000 he had won." (It was probably the taxes that killed him.)

The letter had been around the world nine times, originating in the Netherlands, it said, and I have no doubt that it has been, because I and many of my friends have gotten it, with slight variations, several times before. (I do wonder, though, who lets everyone know when it is time to replace "around the world eight times" with "nine times" and "ten times," etc. It must be the same man who changes the billions on McDonald's signs.)

I have always been fascinated by chain letters and by their cousins, the pyramid-sales schemes, Ponzi schemes, overnight for-profit religions, and the like. I have never originated or passed one on, although I've been tempted, but I have done some research on those who have, to find out how they've done. They have done very poorly.

Chain letters, of course, can't work, because very rapidly you run out of people to keep them going. Say I put my name at the end of a list of four, sending $1 as requested to the top name on the list and then crossing it off. (My chances for success are just as good if I *don't* send the dollar, which is one of the bugs in the system.) I send the letter to twenty people, who put their names beneath mine, moving me up to three; and those twenty in turn send the letter to twenty more each —400—which moves me up to second place; who send the letter to twenty more each—8,000—all of whom, if these letters are to be believed (and, of course, they are not), send me $1, as they enter their own names at the bottom and, in effect, start 8,000 new chain letters. By the time the folks who each supposedly sent me $1 get to the top spot, 64 million people have to have joined at the bottom, and for each of *them* to reap the promised $8,000 return on his dollar yet another 512 billion folks, give or take, must join in.

An otherwise savvy staffer with Arthur D. Little, the prestigious consulting firm, sent me a chain letter once with the following note (he was a very junior staffer): "I've *never* done this before, but my curiosity is aroused. The person my mother got it from says it *really* works—*if* you send it to the kind of person who would go along with this kind of freaky thing!" Then, apparently considering that I might not be such a person, he added: "*Please* mail it back if you're not interested."

The letter asked for $1 and promised close to $8,000 within 90 days. "We have had, at the present time, almost one-hundred-percent return to the people carrying out this promotion," the letter stated. "The majority received $7,800. If everyone had worked, they would have received the full $8,000."

I checked later with the people in the number two spot on the letter—the people, in other words, who were just one level away from cashing in. "I never got a cent. The place the

letter supposedly originates from in Knoxville *doesn't exist,"*
one wrote me, as if genuinely surprised.

There was a time when there was more enthusiasm for this
kind of thing (and most others), even if the results were no
better. Nowadays, few people consider participating in the
chain letters that still occasionally appear in their mailboxes.
They have to be disguised as franchise opportunities or mysteriously surefire tax-shelter schemes if they are to stand a
chance of enriching their authors.

Not so in 1935. In that Depression year, a send-a-dime letter
sprang up in Denver that sent mail volume zooming. At the
peak of the mailing, the Denver post office—"strained to the
breaking point," according to postal officials—was handling
about double its normal volume of mail, an extra 160,000
pieces *a day.* By the time it was over, Denver postal workers
had had to put in 28,000 man-hours of overtime (at 70 cents an
hour) to handle the crush.

Soon chains were sweeping Omaha, Kansas City, Los Angeles, Spokane, Seattle, and Topeka. In New York, no fewer
than 70 members of one ad agency were churning out letters.
At the White House, President Roosevelt received hundreds
of send-a-dime letters.

To skirt the postal regulations, some avaricious souls re-
sorted to $5 and $10 telegram chain letters. Others went face-
to-face. Others broke into mailboxes in search of funds. One
postal carrier, at least, was arrested for plundering his sack.

Of course, at a dime a crack, or even $10 or a pint of whis-
key,* these letters were only a very modest form of mail fraud
and one that was swelling postal coffers munificently. One
citizen calculated that "we do not have to go [very far in the
geometric progression] to solve all the ills of this country and
of the entire world, and possibly any financial worries that
may beset the next." Unbroken to the twenty-third level, he
calculated, there would be circulated something on the order

* The Liquid Assets Club, originated in Lincoln, Nebraska, held
out the prospect of 15,625 pints in return for the 1 sent.

of 10 quadrillion letters. "The post-office revenue for sending ten quadrillion letters, at two and a half cents each," he wrote, "will reach $250,000,000,000. If Mr. Farley cannot show a real honest-to-goodness surplus on *that* . . ." Indeed, envisioning a world without need of further taxes, the writer suggested sardonically that it be made illegal to *break* the chain.

Meanwhile, in Springfield, Missouri (according to the Associated Press), "Chain-letter 'factories,' with $18,000 changing hands at three of them within five hours, turned this southwestern Missouri city into a money-mad maelstrom today. Society women, waitresses, college students, taxi drivers and hundreds of others jammed downtown streets. Women shoved each other roughly in a bargain-counter rush on the numerous chain headquarters [that had been established] in drugstores and corridors, anywhere there was space." The chain had been started the night before as a joke. "By sunup, it was the city's biggest business." The letters, in $2, $3, and $5 denominations, were sold from person to person. That each of these people did indeed send the requisite sum to the name at the top of the list was attested to by a notary public; this was supposed to ensure the validity of the scheme. Once notarized, the new owner set about selling copies of the letter to two others to recoup his investment and keep the chain going. "Professionals" offered their services to folks who were too shy to do the selling themselves—in return for a 50 percent cut.

By the following evening, "sad-faced men and women walked around in a daze . . . seeking vainly for someone to buy their chain letters. . . . The craze which swept over this city yesterday subsided because almost everybody had a letter to sell, thus draining the buyer market dry."

Less than two months after it all began in Denver, *The New York Times* was able to report to a partially sobered up world: "The recent chain-letter mania seems to have run its spectacular course."

Except that, as the story went on to say, "in its wake . . . is a series of astonishing requests—petitions, not for dimes, but whiskey, hay, postage stamps [quilt patches, golf balls, postcards, earrings, recipes], dates with college girls, elephants . . ."

And having largely run their course in America, the chains —or "snowball schemes," as the British call them—surfaced for an equally brief but tumultuous run in Britain.

And then it was over.

In the present decade, the lemming prize would have to go to the managers of the big bank trust departments. The Ponzi prize* would be awarded jointly to ex-commodities magnate Harold Goldstein, who at 28 was selling $25,000,000 of nonexistent commodities options a month, to Stanley Goldblum, founder of Equity Funding Corporation, whose fictitious life insurance sales ran into the hundreds of millions, and to Robert S. Trippet, whose Home-Stake oil-drilling tax shelter looted the likes of Jack Benny, Bob Dylan, Walter Wriston, and "Adam Smith." And the chain-letter prize would go without dispute to Glenn W. Turner, mink-oil salesman extraordinaire.

But lest I leave chain letters with a totally bad name, I should point out that they have, on occasion, been put to unselfish, nonfraudulent use.

A chain letter to aid the family of slain civil rights worker Medgar W. Evers, in 1964, flooded former Mississippi segregationist governor Ross Barnett with 5,000 one-dollar checks made out to Evers, with Barnett to serve as trustee. Barnett termed the episode "harassment."

In the 1950s, when coffee prices rose to an astonishing $1 a pound, American housewives circulated a chain letter that urged a boycott. Brazilians began circulating their own chain letter: "If the United States does not wish to pay a fair price

---

* In a Ponzi scheme, investors are promised fat returns—and paid them—out of the investments of new investors. As long as the flow of money into the scheme keeps increasing, there is enough cash to pay back old investors, with plenty to spare for the organizers. This can go on for years—and frequently has—before it finally collapses of its own weight.

for our coffee," it read in part, "why should we pay absurd prices for the junk they are selling us?" Pass it on.

An environmental chain letter not long ago called for recipients to wrap and mail a pound of garbage to the corporate polluter of their choice.

My favorite, however, was sent to me by an associate at Morgan Stanley, the nation's leading investment banker. Apart from the instructions, it reads as follows:

1. The president of the largest steel company, Charles Schwab, died a pauper.

2. The president of the largest gas company, Howard Hobson, is now insane.

3. The president of the New York Stock Exchange, Richard Whitney, was released from Sing Sing prison.

4. The greatest wheat speculator, Arthur Cooten, died abroad, insolvent.

5. The greatest bear of Wall Street, Jesse Livermore, died a suicide.

6. The head of the world's greatest monopoly, Ivor Kruger, the match king, died a suicide.

7. The president of the Bank of International Settlement shot himself.

The same year, 1923, the winner of several of the most important golf championships, Gene Sarazen, won the U.S. Open and the P.G.A. Tournament. Today he is still going strong, still playing an excellent game of golf, and is solvent.

CONCLUSION: STOP WORRYING ABOUT BUSINESS AND GO PLAY GOLF.

August 1977

PUTS

The obvious thing to have done on Friday, June 3, 1977—an opportunity now long past—would have been to buy or sell a put, thus to participate in the historic First Day of Put Trading. One could have done this, via any stockbroker, on any of five exchanges—the American, Pacific, Philadelphia, and Midwest stock exchanges, or the Chicago Board Options Exchange. Rather than enter the put pit, however, I chose to sit pat.

What is a put?

In the first place, a put might more properly be called a stick. For the whole point of a put—its putpose, if you will—is that it gives its owner the right to force 100 shares of some Godforsaken stock onto someone else at a price at which he would very likely rather not take it. So what you are really doing is sticking it to him. Who wants to be forced to buy 100 shares of IBM at 280 when it is selling on the open market at 240? What kind of a bargain is that?

Puts (and calls) are options, a put being the opposite of a call, just as bearish is the opposite of bullish, short the opposite of long, selling the opposite of buying. Puts are the anti-matter of finance, long having existed in principle but just now coming into their own. (By the end of June, 1977, 180,608 put contracts—at 100 shares per contract—had traded hands.) Puts are also a backbreaking exercise in the double negative. You buy a stock when you think it is going to go up. You buy a put on that stock when you think it is going to go down (not up). You *sell* a put when you think it is not going to go down but, rather, up (not not up).

Example. Vaguely related to the fact that there is a sprawling industrial complex in Rochester, New York, called the Eastman Kodak Company, with $5 billion in sales and well over 100,000 employees, there is a stock called Kodak that you can buy or sell currently for around $60 a share. (Buy 150 million shares and you will own practically the whole thing.) If you think Kodak stock is headed up, you can buy some. If you buy planning to hold it awhile, that's called investing. If instead you think the stock is headed down, you can short some (sell it now, hoping that when you go to buy it back to return it to your broker's computer, it costs you less than you were paid for it). That's called speculating. Or—depending on which way you think the stock is going to go over the next few days, weeks, or months—you can buy a put or a call on it . . . or sell a put or a call. That's called betting. Indeed, if you haven't any idea which way the stock is headed but feel it is headed someplace, you can buy both a put *and* a call on it. That's called a straddle, and involves enough commissions to keep your broker smiling all week.

Let's say you decide Kodak stock is in trouble (never mind how the *company* is doing; over the short run the two are only marginally related), and you want to buy a put. Looking in the paper under E for Kodak ("Es Kod" or "Eas Kd"), you find puts that allow you to stick 100 shares of Kodak to the stickee at $60 a share, and others that allow you to stick it to him at $50 a share. Clearly, the former are more valuable, and so cost you more. You also get to choose among three expiration dates. Options do not run forever; the longer you want yours to run, the more you will have to pay for it.

You write the six possibilities on a piece of paper, disembowel a turkey, and choose the January 60—namely, the put that gives you the right to stick 100 shares of Kodak to him at 60 any time up until mid-January.* As Kodak stock was only 57⅞ on the day from which I am drawing this example, you

---

* Never mind who "him" is. Your broker's computer keeps track of all that.

were already "in the money" with this put. That is, the right
to sell at 60 stock you could simultaneously buy at 57⅞ was
already worth 2⅛ a share. The 4⅝ a share—$462.50 in all—
you were paying for the put represented in part this "intrinsic
value," and in part a premium to the seller for taking the risk
of getting stuck.

Now. If by January Kodak has fallen to $23 a share, which is
unlikely, the right to sell 100 shares for $6,000 while simulta-
neously buying it for just $2,300 will be worth approximately
the $3,700 difference. And that $3,700, less commissions and
the $462.50 you paid for the put, will be a short-term capital
gain. If, on the other hand, Kodak is 60 or higher by the option's expiration date, the right to sell at 60 will be worth
exactly nothing. You will have lost your $462.50 plus commis-
sions.

Meanwhile, in Rochester, Herb Benderbacker is dutifully
ratcheting lens divets, as he always has, oblivious to the drama
being played out over your morning coffee each day as you
check the stock pages of your newspaper to see how far you
are ahead or behind. (Assuming, that is, that you can restrain
the impulse to call your broker twice a day to check—which,
if Kodak begins to fall sharply and you are making $100 a
point, believe me, you can't.)

The problem with puts, as with calls, although they are
great fun and can serve a risk-limiting purpose, is that it is a
zero-sum game (for each winner there is an equal and opposite
loser), without dividends but with *lots* of commissions. What's
more, puts and calls are available only on those stocks that are
most widely followed—exactly those stocks whose move-
ments, study after study has shown, cannot be outguessed
with any more assurance than the flip of a coin.

Which is not to say I don't try.

November 1977

HOW
WALL STREET
MAKES AN EXTRA
$100 MILLION

I shorted 200 shares of a $40 stock the other day, and as I was returning the phone to its cradle, just before the line went dead, I heard this yowl of joy come ringing through the receiver. At first I assumed it had come from my broker . . . but that couldn't have been right. I had placed this trade through my *discount* broker. Discount brokers, I have found, are not nearly so emotional as the regular full-commission variety are. And as the entire commission for this $8,000 trade was a mere $30 (a regular broker would have charged $140), I could hardly see that there was much to get excited about.

I did a little research, however, and found that in these days of hard-won Wall Street profits—hard-won because of niggardly, chiseling customers like myself, who will only pay $30 to make an $8,000 trade—there is nothing quite so welcome as a short seller. (Commodities speculators and options addicts are warmly welcomed too.) It was not my broker himself but the financial community as a whole that was yowling its delight through the phone—to the tune of perhaps $100 million a year in hidden profits.

Most people know that "shorting" a stock means selling it —even though you don't own it—in the hope that it will go down. You then buy it back at a lower price, clear your account, and pocket the difference.

But few people understand just how such a transaction is handled—or how profitable it can be for the brokerage firms. On that 200-share trade of mine, if I were to wait a year before buying back the stock (to "cover" my short), the brokerage commissions would have come to $60 in all. (Or to $280 with a full-price broker.) But on top of that—and this is the part very few amateurs and not all the pros realize—there would have been another $900 or so in profit for the brokerage firm. Total gross profit for the full-price broker: $1,180 on an $8,000 trade.

Here is how it works—and how, in the aggregate, it amounts to tens of millions of dollars in added profits to brokerage firms, especially large ones.

When you sell shares short—shares you don't own—your broker must first borrow them. In practice, the lender is likely to be some other investor with an account at the same firm. He won't even know the stock has been lent. (If dividends fall due, they will be paid to his account—out of yours. It is all done by computer.) Now the broker has the shares you want to sell, and he *sells* them. He actually does. And when he sells them, his firm gets *money* for them. Real money. In the case of my trade—$8,000.

Now! Who do you suppose gets to earn the interest on that money? You, for whose account the broker borrowed the stock? You, in whose name the broker sold the stock? You, who are taking all the risk (should the stock go up instead of down)? The interest, thank you very much, is kept by the brokerage firm.

The way the brokerage firm earns interest on this money—your money—is by lending it out to clients who buy stocks on margin. These days, brokers are lending money to their margin accounts at around 13.5 percent, which is around 2 percent above what the banks charge *them* for the money. These loans are so safe, backed as they are by securities in a vault, that banks generally lend to brokers at a fraction *below* the prime rate. As is readily apparent, 13.5 percent interest on $8,000 for a year ain't hay. Even at 11.5 percent, which is what the brokerage firm currently saves by not having to borrow from the bank, it comes to $900.

Granted, interest rates are not ordinarily this high. [By the end of 1979 they had climbed substantially higher.] And, granted, a year is a long time to hold a short position (many shorts are placed one day and covered the next). But at any given time, the total "short interest" of all traders dealing with all firms runs to 50 million shares or more. So, to take just the roughest stab at it, figuring $25 as the average price of the shorted shares, something well in excess of $1 billion would be in "float" at any given time—cash from short sales that is earning interest for brokers instead of clients.

A billion dollars! At current rates, that comes to more than $100 million a year in additional gross profit for the large Wall Street firms, which is as much as (for example) Bache, and Paine Webber, and Shearson, and Dean Witter earned in 1978 —combined.

"The big firms don't like to talk about it," says the head of one smaller firm that borrows a lot of stock for its short-selling customers, "but you have uncovered one of the last little areas of real hidden profit in the business. Very few outsiders understand this." In other words, interest on the cash balances from short sales may be just a footnote, but it's not a small one. Or, as one of my finance professors was fond of saying, "A hundred million dollars may not be much to *you*, but . . ."

The crowning blow, by the way—and it happens very often —is in the case of the investor who owns a portfolio of stocks that he has bought on margin but who is short some stocks as well. Here is a man whose broker is in effect *lending him his own money*, at 12 or 15 percent interest.

As bad if not worse is the man who does *not* own any appreciable portfolio of stocks but who wants to short one. He will be required to put up cash as security. It is reasonable that such a cash deposit be required—but is it reasonable that it not earn the client interest? At many brokerage firms, it would not. In this case, you have a man shorting, say, $8,000 worth of stock—on which cash he earns no interest—and at the same time having to deposit $4,000 in cash to secure his account. *He* is, in effect, lending the brokerage firm *$12,000* interest free.

The point is not that brokerage firms should be prevented from earning as much as they can in profits, this way or any other legal way, nor that they have been somehow immoral with regard to this issue—although they have hardly gone out of their way to explain it.

The point is that brokerage statements are so confusing that many short sellers have never understood the bonanza they were providing their brokers. Given Wall Street's new competitive environment, if a demand arose for brokers who would share the interest earned on the proceeds of short sales, at least some brokers might begin offering to do so.

It's not as though the firms fail to appreciate what good business this is. Brokers actually compete to lend stock, offering borrowing brokers—but not borrowing clients—a portion of the interest that is earned on the cash left as collateral. Your cash. It is the large firms that make out best, having as they do substantial inventories of shares to lend.

One man I know, who shorts not 200 shares at a time but 2,000, 20,000 or even, on occasion, 200,000, does have an arrangement whereunder he splits with his broker the interest received on cash from his short sales. But very few investors are large enough or savvy enough to cut that sort of a deal. More should try it.

Brokers will argue that there are extra expenses involved in shorting stock—and there are. However, the considerable bookkeeping chores involved are done mostly by computer, at minimal expense. If a lending broker is willing to pay interest to a borrowing *broker* to get him to borrow, why not pay interest if the borrower happens to be a client?

April 1979

MAYHEM
AT CITIBANK
BRANCH 007

I sent a friend a check for $10 million some years ago. It was his birthday, and I had run out of conventional birthday cards. Ass that I have subsequently discovered him to be, he deposited it.

Just what the teller at the Cambridge Trust Company thought when this young Harvard Business School student presented his slip and my check, with its handwritten birthday messages on it, I can hardly imagine. I had purposely pegged it at *$10* million rather than one so there could not be the least possibility of its being taken seriously by anyone. Be that as it may, a loud electronic hiccup momentarily convulsed the Federal Reserve regional check-processing system; Bankers Trust in New York canceled my checking account of five years' standing and my line of credit; Cambridge Trust canceled his; and that is how, more or less, my checking account came to be domiciled at branch double-O-seven of First National City Bank—now Citibank.

If you "have a friend at Chase Manhattan" and if "the chemistry is just right at Chemical," if Bank of America is the free world's largest private bank and Morgan its most prestigious —then surely Citibank is banking's leading edge. Citibank was first to introduce the consumer loan, first with certificates of deposit, first to float "floating rate notes"—and the list goes on. Now Citibank is leading the way toward the stainless-steel-faced electronic banking of the future.

Just how aggressive and innovative a bank ought to be (given its special fiduciary role), how much risk it ought to take, has always been a matter of some debate with respect to Citicorp. Bankers *ought* to be somewhat stodgy, some would argue—and less adept ones have gotten burned trying to play Citicorp's fast game. Nevertheless, Citicorp profits—the true measure of a bank's health and strength, the bank would argue —have grown magnificently since 1961. Until this past year. In 1977, Citicorp profits actually declined 6 percent, sending the company's stock from a high for the year of 34 to just a shade below 20.

But while others were looking to Australia or Zaire for an explanation, I was looking to Broadway and 72nd Street— branch 007. Because in point of fact, most of the bank's growth, lo, these many years, I realized as I stood endlessly in line to cash a check, must have come from this one branch. But by 1977 it had become physically impossible for this branch to take on even a single new account. With the refusal of the adjacent Yum Yum Ice Cream store to move, all prospect of expansion in Citicorp profits melted like frozen-yogurt on a midsummer day.

This all became clear to me some months ago when, fighting my way to the only working ball-point in the branch, I found myself at the protective barrier from behind which bank officers field complaints, deny requests, and initial checks. Being in one of those moods, I asked one of the officers, "Is it always like this?" And as she was beginning to reply ("No, sir, this is an extraordinarily busy day"), customers to either side of me began answering for her: "Worse! It's actually worse!" "Worst damn bank in the world!" "A zoo! It's always like this!"

I finished filling out whatever it was I was filling out and went to stand on the kind of line I can remember having formed at the Bedford Playhouse the day *The Wizard of Oz* came to town.

Shortly thereafter, I received my bank statement. This statement not only lists all your checks but lists them, through the magic of computer technology, in the order you wrote them (assuming you wrote them in order). There were my 40 entries for the month, in order—but included with the statement were not *my* 40 canceled checks (light blue ones) but 40 belonging to a Chinese laundry in Queens (big yellow ones), drawn on an entirely different branch of the bank.

Down to the bank I went with these checks, where I was told that the laundryman was probably doing the same thing himself with mine, so why not relax and wait to get something in the mail? Sure enough, in less than a month I received a fat envelope from Citibank devoid of any covering communication but filled with my 40 canceled checks, *plus seven others* belonging to a Mr. Sid Silvers.

What Citibank seemed to be moving toward was a system of sending out canceled checks at random, relying on its customers to sort them out among themselves.

"*My* checks?" asked a surprised Sid Silvers when I called to let him know I had dropped them in the mail.

"Yes."

"You got a bunch of *my* checks?"

"Yes."

"Holy Christ, are they idiots."

Sid Silvers proceeded to recount a tale of woe about *his* branch that would have horrified anyone but a client of my branch. "I'm just so disgusted that I'm ready to pull out of the bank altogether," he concluded, although for the sake of convenience—an extra block or two has a lot to do with which bank a customer chooses—he was loath to do so.

And now for the happy ending.

Many tens of millions of dollars and more than 180 newly installed electronic banking centers later, there is hope for Citicorp shareholders yet. (If the stock goes much lower, I may become one myself.)

In December, heralded with blue bunting and a sweepstakes, branch 007's first-generation out-in-the-freezing-cold cash machine, which was always either out of cash or out of order, was replaced by a pair of second-generation indoor video-screen machines that do everything from dispensing cash—$20 to $200 up to five times per customer in any one day—to taking deposits and loan payments, giving account information and even giving receipts. Each of these new machines is out of cash or out of order only half the time. There being two of them, the chances are three out of four that at least one will be working when, desperate, you arrive. As the bugs are debugged, the odds will rise even higher.

With the advent of the new "tellers," lines have shrunk within the bank during banking hours; the level of cursing at the cash machine on a Saturday has subsided from a din to an intermittent buzz—all this even as nearly 1,000 new accounts have been signed up by the branch (bringing the total of checking and savings accounts to around 12,000).

In one week the two 24-hour tellers handled 7,200 transactions. That is, roughly speaking, a line of customers more than a mile long who no longer have to crowd the bank during the 32½ hours a week it is open. For these customers, the bank is open 168 hours a week.

The same system of CATs, as they're known within the bank (customer-activated terminals), has been installed in more than 180 other Citibank branches in New York. Even for an institution that does much of its business abroad, and much of the rest with large corporations, this is a major step. It also points to the day when most of the tellers in banks around the country—and, for that matter, the cashiers in department stores and supermarkets, where the terminals may be installed as well—will be made of stainless steel and "accessed" (rather than greeted) with the thrust of one's bank card. Contrary to popular conception, the movement toward electronic funds transfer and the "cashless society" is not dead—just gradual.

If the way branch 007 has been turned around is any indication, and if countries like Zaire can somehow be bailed out (little problems like that), things may be looking up for Citicorp. Yum Yum Ice Cream can stay where it is, and the bank may still be able to turn out record profits year after year.

Of course, to the layman, the kind of foul-ups of which the bank is now capable seem all the more awesome when multiplied ten thousandfold by the power of the computer. But the experts have thought of everything, I'm told, and everything should flow without a hitch.

So far, so good.

March 1978

III
Driven Men, Driven Woman

JAMES DINES:
IN GOLD
HE TRUSTS

"I know what happens in a Crisis," wrote "Adam Smith" in *The Money Game.* "The Bank Rate goes to 7 percent, business goes down the tube, and the stock market crumbles to powder."

Yes, but what happens when the prime rate pushes *12* percent?*

Everyone knows that interest rates have climbed to undreamed of levels, that the Arabs will soon have all the world's dollars, that the hoarders already have all the world's pennies, and that the only power in the Western world without a leadership crisis is Coca-Cola (and even that could change when Pepsi gets the bomb).

Everyone knows these things, but almost no one knows what to make of them. Things clearly can't stay this bad for long, but will they get better or worse? The Dow Jones industrials, blue chips which have held up far better than most stocks, are now, adjusted for inflation, selling for less than they were in 1955. Does that mean the market has crashed— or is it just about to?

James Dines, editor of *The Dines Letter* "for traders and investors," cuts through the fog of uncertainty and the endlessly qualified prognostications like a refreshing breeze. In this, the spring of 1974, he is certain he knows what is going

---

* Or, six years later, *20* percent?

to happen to our inflation-racked economy. Says this refreshing breeze: We are going to have a full-scale economic collapse within six months. A year or two at the outside. It has already begun. Inflation is accelerating and there is no stopping it short of collapse. Wall Street will collapse, the dollar will collapse, corporate and personal bankruptcies will abound. There may be violence in the streets.

And you can make a lot of money while it's happening. Dines plans to. Not out of malevolence or with any sort of glee —it would just be foolish not to. His investment advice, though he acknowledges that different people have different needs and temperaments, is very simple. He outlined it for me, along with the apocalypse, over a pleasant $49.50 pre-depression lunch at "21." (This was his suggestion, not mine, but since he normally charges $500 an hour for private consultations, I perhaps got off easy.)

• Sell all your stocks and bonds, he advises—yes, even at these seemingly depressed levels.

• Get some money out of the country and into a Swiss bank (either in Swiss francs or in gold coins) while it is still legal to do so—an amount covering not less than five years' overseas travel expenses, he recommends—in case you yourself decide to get out at some point.

• Put as much of the rest as possible, as quickly as possible, into gold and silver stocks—yes, even at these seemingly heady prices.

• And then, if you are not 100 percent committed to gold and silver (or, by buying on margin, even more than 100 percent committed), consider using what you have left to sell stocks short.

• P.S. Forget real estate. Real estate values will plummet in the depression. No buyers.

That's basically it. Not unlike the gist of Harry Browne's best-selling *How You Can Profit from a Monetary Crisis,* though Dines says he was there first. Of course, if worldwide depression doesn't materialize on schedule, this bold investment strategy could cause a localized depression to gather right over your own head. But don't worry, the collapse *is* coming. (And I shouldn't worry?) The "morons" at the Treasury Department, Dines says, by printing more paper than we had gold to back it up with, and by piling up a half-trillion-dollar national debt, have painted themselves into a 40-year corner, and there is really no way out. Blame Lord Keynes, if you like, or F.D.R., but buy gold. "Not only am I personally fully invested in gold and silver," says Dines, "but I am there on margin." He is that sure. He is a gold bug; to him, gold represents fundamental value and financial defense.

Now, if Dines's investment advice smacks of the buy-high/sell-low syndrome that is all too familiar to some of us—in the sense that the precious metals Dines would have us bet on are near their all-time highs while the stocks and bonds he'd have us sell are in the pits—don't blame him. He has been recommending gold in his *Letter* consistently, week in and week out, since 1961. If you had listened to him then, and bought stock in ASA Limited (which in turn invests in South African gold mines), you would have multiplied your stake about fifteenfold. But again, "Don't worry," because, Dines says, "it's never too late to buy ASA." He sees the price of gold, now around $155 an ounce, going to between $400 and $1,000, in which case the profits of gold mines should benefit, over the long run, more than proportionally. Or, as one Dines slogan puts it—and slogans are important when it comes to speculating in a commodity whose chief "use" is the faith people have in it—"All the way with ASA!"

"It is helpful to reflect," leads off *The Dines Letter* of May 17, "on how really dangerous the human beings around you are capable of being, particularly in these days when religion has been replaced by opium derivatives as the new 'opium of the people.' Never forget that Himmler was a chicken farmer before Hitler made him head of the dreaded Gestapo. Similarly, don't think for one minute that just because the world is sunny and nice now that it cannot quickly degenerate into an unpleasant period. While we cannot escape our destiny, perhaps *The Dines Letter* can anticipate it, and thereby help you survive a bit better.

"One businessman was quoted this week as saying, 'The

only problem our economy has today is inflation.' Our riposte
to that one is, 'All I have wrong with me is terminal cancer.' "

Dines told me at lunch that he figures the current inflation
rate in the United States at 25 percent a year—the 18.8 percent the wholesale price index went up over the last twelve
months, plus an allowance for "lies" from the government.
Lies? "The U.S. government is in charge of its own statistics,"
he says, "so it's a question of what you want to believe.

"The real secret is this: the politicians have discovered that
all they have to do is promise anything, run the presses to pay
for it, and get themselves re-elected! It's a beautiful game.
And it's *over*. It's the end of an era."

The result of such irresponsible policies, Dines explains, is
massive debt at every level. "We are going to have to liquidate
that excess of debt forcibly," he says. "There's no other way
to do it. You can't pay it off; it's too large."

Forcible liquidation, continues Dines, means mass bankruptcy, including devaluing the dollar from its official $42 per
ounce of gold to more like $500 an ounce. "You've got a
hundred and thirty billion [in Eurodollars] sloshing around
Europe—I got that number from a speech [Under Secretary of
the Treasury Paul] Volcker, that moron, gave; it's probably
higher by now, and that's before lies, all right? Now, that
hundred and thirty billion dollars is backed by eleven billion
dollars in gold [figuring our gold reserves at the official $42 an
ounce, and ignoring the fact that we no longer back our dollars
with gold]. . . . This is what de Gaulle was screaming about a
few years ago: we were running the printing presses and buying his goddamned country! He was furious, but how could he
stop us? Don't tell me we wouldn't do it—we did it! We did
it!

"Now, we've got eleven billion dollars of gold at the old
price, and a hundred and thirty billion dollars in claims
against it, which means the dollar is bankrupt at least ten
times over, which is why I'm looking for a price of gold at
least ten times higher than the official price. . . . It's a Chapter
Eleven [bankruptcy] on the U.S. dollar."

The blindness, not to mention the immorality, of men in government staggers Dines's rather fertile imagination. What would *he* do if he were Secretary of the Treasury? "Resign," he answers instantly. "I would resign immediately. The country isn't ready for what I'm saying. They're going to have to bleed first. And there's nobody who could put through the kind of policies that could save us at this point.

"In Washington, they remind me of the captain reshuffling the deck chairs on the *Titanic*. . . . The man on the street has no concept of the dimensions of this crisis. . . . Inflation never slows down, it always accelerates until there is a massive climax and then a collapse of the currency. . . . This is a really big story, and it's a serious, serious situation. And it has yet to break. When it breaks it's going to be like pricking a balloon full of water—it's all going to go *plahhh*. And then they're all going to say, 'What happened?' Or, 'Why didn't anybody see this?' "

Dines sees margin calls leading to forced selling, leading to more margin calls. (Though it should be noted that the institutions, which account for most market activity, do not buy on margin.) He sees corporate bankruptcies brought on by the murderous interest rates. And he sees a critical mass being reached one way or another that will spark financial panic. Then the jig will be up.

"This is not just some casual article about some kook, you know. I've got a track record that's way beyond the kook phase. I had to put up with the kook comments for a long time, but"—Dines pauses to think a moment—"you look at the Value Line average, for example. It's down sixty percent since 1968 [let alone in real dollars adjusted for inflation]. Now, that's beyond kookism, that's a real fact. And it's not a funny one either."

And that's true. Much of what Dines says cannot be dismissed out of hand, even though most people, with the same available information, do not arrive at the same dire conclusions. For example, in its more thoughtful, more sophisticated, and more highly regarded market analysis in the same week that Dines was predicting imminent disaster, the Smilen & Safian, Inc., *Dual Market Principle Report* led off: "Events, stock market behavior, and new economic, corporate, and technical data published since our last report have confirmed our judgment that the investment climate is comparably favorable to that of the early 1950's and that the firm foundation has been set for a new bull market whose longevity will be measured in years."

In other words, almost everyone agrees, including Dines, that since the late 1960s we have been going through a sort of slow-motion market crash, with all but a few stocks declining 40, 60, or 80 percent or more, particularly when allowance is made for inflation. And if the economy holds together, most people, including Dines, would agree that stocks are anything but overpriced. The question is whether the economy can hold together. Most people think that it will; Dines is sure that it won't. He says things like "Don't underestimate the human stampede," and he quotes people like Nathaniel Hawthorne saying, "The calmer thought is not always the right thought."

If we retain confidence in our system and institutions, then we weather the storm; if we panic, then *Titanic*. That's true of any system at any time.

Either way, Dines persists, gold is the thing to buy. He is convinced that the world monetary system, which essentially cut free of gold the day the United States stopped backing its paper with gold, must again return to gold as the basic measure of value. Otherwise you have a fiat currency, where money is printed at will and where you have more and more paper chasing the same amount of goods.

"You know," he says, "we Americans are not very bright when it comes to gold, and it's because of the Keynesian tradition of treating it as a barbarous relic. It's *not*. The function of gold is as a fuse. If you print too much paper, it forces you to stop. . . . You've got to have some relation between paper and reality. I don't care if it's diamonds or neon or whatever the hell you want to make it. But gold so far is accepted by at least three billion people." That is, they have faith in it. And faith, or confidence, is what we are talking about.

It's true that the Europeans have a much deeper appreciation of the meaning of gold than do Americans. But at least one European we know, a New York–based investment banker named Paul Le Percq, is convinced that "gold has had it." "It has hit its peak," he says, and his reading of the slow progress toward international currency reform is that gold definitely will *not* be the cornerstone of the new system, which will instead be based on something like the Special Drawing Rights of the International Monetary Fund.

Neither gold bugs nor chartists have ever been in very good repute in financial circles (except among gold bugs and chartists), and so James Dines, who is both dean of the gold bugs and deeply engrossed in his charts, has had a rough time of it, credibility-wise. Nor have people forgotten that in 1972, with the Dow Jones Average around 1000, Dines became boyishly bullish on the stock market for a time (though never breaking faith with gold).

Dines retorts with slightly twisted logic that "even a broken clock is right twice a day." That is, even he can be wrong. As for charts—they *really work,* he says. And, as a matter of fact, he says, he is *not* a gold bug. A gold bug perennially clings to gold as the only hedge against anarchy, which is perennially imminent. Dines plans to be the first one *out* of gold when the time is right, he says, just as he was the first one in.

The man is a classic. He wore a pitch black shirt to lunch at "21." He talks of "anti-gold nuts coming out of the woodwork." He writes things like "Only the most superficial observer can look at the D.J.I. [Dow Jones Industrial Average] and conclude that there are no problems. THIS IS A TRICK!! In *The Dines Letter's* opinion the D.J.I. will be the last one to go. Until then, the little *Dines Letter,* almost alone, fearlessly hurls the epithets 'liar' and 'cheat' at the D.J.I."

The first ideology Dines can think of that comes closest to

describing his own is—anarchism. He doesn't vote very often. He thinks the government should provide little more than protection to its citizens, and that progressive taxes should be abolished. He would abolish all present taxes and have the government automatically print 1 percent more paper at the first of every year; at the same time all prices would automatically be raised 1 percent. An inflation tax. When it was pointed out that 1 percent of the country's paper wouldn't come anywhere near covering even the $85 billion defense budget (which he favors), let alone anything else, he offered to raise his tax to 2 percent or 5 or 10 percent—whatever it takes. Don't bother him with details.

Is James Dines a fanatic? He told me that in thirteen years he has never missed a newsletter (he writes or edits them every Thursday), and he claims to have dictated one of them a couple of years ago from a hospital operating table after a head-on collision with a truck.

One would think that in thirteen years of stating much the same opinion week in and week out, not to mention having most of one's assets (plus margin) invested in a particular idea, one would become less than fully detached and objective about that idea. But is Dines "a person with an extreme and uncritical enthusiasm or zeal, as in religion, politics, etc.," as my dictionary defines fanatic? Well, he is extreme. And he spends very little time qualifying his opinions. Complex as the world is, it is all fairly clear to him. Everything fits. He sees Con Ed not as having been strangled by politicians and regulators, but as the first of the companies to fall before today's record interest rates. [It recovered.] Asked why Brazil and other countries which have long had inflation rates far worse than ours have not already collapsed, he says simply, "I don't know very much about Brazil. But their story isn't over yet." As proof that gold will be the basis of the currency of the future, he cites the fact that all the foreign governments "are hanging on to it." "They'll sell you anything else," he says, "but not their gold."

As for "enthusiasm or zeal, as in religion or politics"—his gold seminars are said to hold more than a faint resemblance to revival meetings—he definitely has a "message"; and belief in gold predates Christianity.

But if James Dines is a fanatic—and it would only be by the weakest definition of the term—he is certainly a fanatic of the high-class variety. (And a pleasant one to have lunch with.) Number one, he's rich. Number two, he's supersmart, the tone and content of some of his writing notwithstanding.

He's quick. (I started to ask him whether the schedule of the *Letter* would prevent him from, say, going off to Australia to hunt up aborigines; and as I got to the word aborigines, having in mind an anthropological field trip of sorts, he was already saying, "No, I don't believe in killing for sport.") He's impatient. ("Two twenty-two and sixteen seconds," he shot back, checking his Pulsar, when I asked him for the time.) He's not modest. (He's filmed a segment of CBS's *60 Minutes*, to be shown this summer. "It's the most dynamic and explicit explanation of inflation I've ever seen in my life. . . . I've never seen a more clear explanation of the gold crisis, money, and inflation. It's *incredible*," he says, with real wonder in his voice.)

Self-assured, self-centered, articulate, intellectually arrogant (but without the grace of a Galbraith or a Buckley), not terribly warm. His manner suggests he knows he's not particularly easy to get along with and that he doesn't care. He calls a great many men "morons."

He won't talk about his "personal life," by which he means to include where he was born (not relevant), where he went to high school (not relevant), or how old he is ("Twenty-nine bid," he laughs). In fact, the first thing he says to an interviewer is that he won't talk about his life-style, and, at least in my conversations with him, his passion for privacy became a recurrent theme. Yet he wound up allowing us to take pictures in his apartment—a first, he said—and he even asked our photographer if he knew any of the various models he had at one time or another dated or lived with. (Dines is a bachelor.)

So who *is* James Dines?
He was born in Ohio on November 14, 1931, but looks about

five years younger. He is trim—a poster of a Sumo wrestler hangs on his refrigerator door; he declined dessert at "21." Fit —he does push-ups and sit-ups in the morning and likes to ski.

He majored in French literature and the natural sciences at Oberlin; won a full room-board-and-tuition one-a-year National Honor Scholarship to the University of Chicago Law School; got his law degree from Columbia; went to work for military intelligence; was "seduced" by the stock market, giving up law to take a $75-a-week clerical job with a small Wall Street firm (his predictions had been so good as a customer, they asked him to join); started writing his letter in 1960; and struck out on his own in 1962. He now has over 30 people working for him at *The Dines Letter.*

He speaks fluent French, Spanish, some German, and taught himself Swedish with a bunch of LP's. He has a lot of friends and some relatives in Sweden, a country he visits often.

His books run from *The Joy of Sex* to *The Bread and Soup Cook Book* to seven copies of *The Money Game*—in which Adam Smith likens him to a prophet of doom "somewhere to the right of Nahum the Elkohite." The best financial book he has ever read, he says, and reread, and reread, is Charles Mackay's famous *Extraordinary Popular Delusions and the Madness of Crowds,* written in 1841.

He lives in a top-floor ultraluxury apartment on the upper East Side, the first tenant to sign a lease in the building, he says. He walks to his office on 41st Street. From his terrace— a *fabulous* view—you can see an apartment building on 46th Street which had its side blown off. This is, more or less, what he sees happening to our economy.

Dines says he is "semiretired," working only three days a week, and that he's "a very happy man." "I've understood life, at least for myself . . . I'm into a philosophical thing, and I'm not interested in that whole ego trip of scrambling for power or glory and all that stuff. This is the Thoreau side of me, if you will. [Well, I'll think about it.] I'd much rather go ski in Switzerland or spend a quiet evening at home with a few *very* carefully selected friends. It's just my life-style. I will permit nothing to interfere with that."

Dines is rich, handsome, confident, content, intelligent, and, I think, all wrong in his one-track dire predictions. Everyone in government is *not* a moron; he is not the only man in the world to whom it has occurred that we have a national debt. It's true, curbing inflation is absolutely critical (runaway food and fuel prices may already have slowed to a jog), and unfortunately that means higher unemployment, not tax cuts. Yes, some marginal businesses will be shaken out in the face of murderous interest rates, but that can leave the system all the more healthy. The chief danger that occurs to me—and of course it has more to do with psychology than economics—is that if Nixon and Patty Hearst ever give themselves up, the hottest story will be the economic news. If that happens, and if the press competes for the scariest stories without providing proper perspective, the confidence that holds things together could come unglued. It's one thing to sensationalize the pending divorce of a movie star or to speculate on possible impeachment scenarios, quite another to turn everyone's thoughts to possible disaster and to treat, say, Con Edison's problems as the beginning of the end.

June 1974

SOMEDAY
WE MAY ALL
LIVE
IN LEFRAK CITY

It's not hard to make fun of a builder who can't pronounce "condominium." But Samuel Jonathan Lefrak, who pronounces his name *Lef*rak (except on social occasions, when it's Le *Frak*) and condominium "condomini*un*," has housed more New Yorkers in larger apartments at lower rents than any other man in town. He is landlord to a quarter of a million people, mostly middle-income residents of Brooklyn and Queens. A quarter-million more, mostly in Bedford-Stuyvesant, Brownsville, Williamsburg, and East New York, live in buildings his father built and sold between the First and Second World Wars. With roughly $10 million in rent rolling in each month, a few million dollars of Texas oil, a few million dollars of big-name art, a few homes with a few in help, a stable of race horses and a "100-foot yacht" that conscience sometimes compels him to admit is only 85 feet long, Sam Lefrak is one of the richest men in the world.

Says he: "A lot of people call me a philanthropist, a civic leader, a community planner, a master builder—I'm an engineer, a 'colonel,' a 'doctor,' I was knighted by Pope John, I wear all kinds of hats—but just call me just plain Sam. I'm a very informal kind of a guy. I guess you get that way when you have a love of people, and that's the way I feel."

Says one real estate man: "Sam is vulgar, ruthless, egotistical, lacking in any real human warmth, and utterly without taste. But when you get all through detracting from him, the fact remains that in his field he is phenomenal. He knows his business like nobody else." Though many characterize Sam's personal traits less harshly, virtually all agree that he knows his business like nobody else.

The largest individual builder-landlord in New York, if not the country, Sam Lefrak is worth an estimated half-billion dollars. Litton Industries and the Great Atlantic & Pacific Tea Company, based on their current market values, are worth nearly as much. Of course, when you are that wealthy, just how wealthy you are is a subjective calculation, and Sam prefers to keep his own estimate to himself.

His latest and most ambitious project, the planned $1.1 billion Battery Park City, is 91 acres in the shadow of the World Trade Center, where Sam envisions "a complete urban microcosm, a city within a city, encircled by a monorail, where a person could be born, live, and die without ever leaving."

Sam says that Battery Park City will comprise 14,100 apartments, 14 percent of them renting at about $40 a room to low-income tenants (of the senior-citizen rather than the welfare variety, Sam points out), 56 percent renting at about $80 a room to middle-income tenants, and 30 percent renting as luxury apartments at about $120 a room. There will be nearly a million square feet of enclosed-mall shopping space, a 1,000-room hotel, underground parking, a marina for large boats, three schools, rooftop ice-skating rinks, a library, a hospital, a fire station, a police station, an esplanade along the river, movie theaters, banks, swimming pools, and Venetian blinds.

Right now the site is virtually barren. Yet Lefrak says construction will begin later this year and that his first tenants will move in an unbelievable fifteen months later. Instead of using bricks, he says, he may prefabricate his building blocks off-site and float them down the Hudson to avoid tying up city traffic, then lift them into place with helicopter sky cranes. He says he may not paint his apartment walls if he can find the right kind of plastic-coated material. He says he hopes to find a way to use the water of the river in his cooling system, and another way to recycle all the effluent from the project to make it pollution free. He wants to run just one water pipe into each apartment, which will have a self-contained heating unit, thereby eliminating half the piping in the buildings.

Will any of this dreaming come to fruition—let alone as budgeted and on schedule? It seems highly unlikely. But then Sam knows his business like nobody else.

Sam learned his business from his father, Harry, a French national brought up in Palestine who arrived in New York on January 5, 1900, 20 years old and penniless. Harry Le Frak immediately found gold lying in the streets in the form of snow to be shoveled at $4 a day. Soon he had set himself up as a glazier, mending broken windows with panes he would take from abandoned buildings. (The Lefrak Organization is still known for obtaining materials at the best possible prices.) In 1916, a gas explosion knocked out thousands of windows in Manhattan, and Harry was there with a crew of men to clean up. He used his profits to build rows of walk-up housing in Brooklyn for immigrants like himself who preferred large rooms and low rent to painstaking craftsmanship or novel design. By the end of the building boom of the 1920s, Harry had become by most standards a rich man, although not by comparison with his son's wealth today. Harry worked his tail off until he passed away in 1963.

Sam refers to his family as a dynasty and stresses the importance of father-son teams in the building trade. Great-grandfather Maurice built in Paris and taught his son Aaron, who built in Palestine and taught his son Harry, who built in Brooklyn and taught his only son, Sam. Sam learned to read blueprints as he ate around the ones that were always spread out on the dining-room table. He went to work for Harry part-time when he was eight. Sam's only son, Richard, began his apprenticeship when he was fourteen. Richard, Amherst '67 and Columbia Law '70, has thus far begotten only Harrison, who is one, and unemployed.

Sam went to P.S. 167, where he was periodically cracked over the knuckles for writing left-handed, and to Erasmus Hall High School in Brooklyn. At the University of Maryland he was a varsity two-miler, an enthusiastic student, and a dynamo of extracurricular activity. He roomed with a boy named Marvin Mandel. "Whoever thought he'd become governor?" Sam fondly recalls. "Buddy Mandel, governor of Maryland! The point is, he came on my boat one day and he said to me, 'Isn't it wonderful? You've got the money and I've got the power. Who's better off?' And I said, 'I am. With my money I can buy your power.' And this is the truth." *

Sam entered a pre-dental program at Maryland but switched to engineering, the story goes, when he found that left-handed dentists required specially made equipment. Upon graduation in 1940, he went to work for his father, investing in the business the $2,500 he had earned as a part-time retail shoe salesman. By 1948, at the age of 30, he became president. Two years later, recently returned from a Young Presidents' Organization one-week course held at Harvard Business School, he risked the family fortune to outbid 400 real estate buyers for a package of properties that was up for auction. Having put down a $50,000 cash deposit on his winning bid, which was about all the cash he and his father had, Sam had only to find the remaining $4,950,000. If no one had lent him the money, as for a while seemed likely, the Lefrak reputation would have been destroyed—in an industry where credibility is vital.

The phenomenal growth of the Lefrak Organization since then has resulted largely from Sam Lefrak's inexhaustible energy—he runs on only five hours of "quality sleep" a night, he says—and from his remarkable acumen: "Sam often comes on dumb in business dealings," explains a longtime observer, "but he never makes mistakes. He is forever coming up with some new wrinkle to make a good deal even better. And he fights like hell."

Sam says his strategy is simply to "give people what they want at a price they can afford." What sets him off from all the

---

* Perhaps so. Later in the decade, Mandel would be convicted with five co-defendants of "mail fraud" and "racketeering" in a case that centered on legislation Mandel backed to benefit a racetrack his co-defendants owned.

other people trying to do the same thing, though, is that he is able to build more cheaply than anyone else—for a variety of reasons:

• He has kept his land costs low by buying in huge lot sizes and, often, by buying marginal properties. The site of Lefrak City in Queens was so swampy and so vast that he was able to acquire it for $4 a square foot. Its value is now estimated at around $100 a foot. Few builders can, like Sam, achieve the critical mass required of a project to transform marginal land into prime land. A small development on the same site as Lefrak City might well have failed for being too isolated. Sam doesn't build one structure and hope the neighborhood will improve—he builds the whole neighborhood.

• As no Lefrak project over the past half-century has ever failed, financial institutions fall all over themselves to lend to him, usually at the prime rate. Over the life of a 30-year $30 million mortgage, a point of interest makes a $4.5 million difference.

• Though they win no architectural awards, Sam's buildings are designed to be easily and rapidly built. He has a genius for editing the plans that Jack Brown, his primary architect of the last seventeen years, draws up. He visualizes the actual work they call for and makes changes to better match them to the skills and customs of his construction crews. He aims for the most efficient possible rhythm of work as floor rises upon floor. At the same time, he knows what concessions to comfort and aesthetics must be made to attract the kind of tenants he is after for any given development. And he knows which extra expenses in design will pay off over the decades in lowered maintenance costs. For example, his buildings tend to have more elevators than necessary, partly because he thinks his tenants appreciate it, partly because he has found that maintenance costs decrease significantly when elevators aren't overworked.

• Tremendous volume allows him to squeeze suppliers and subcontractors to the bone. "I'm the people's surrogate," he says. "I pass the savings on to them." When he was unhappy with the rate Con Edison was proposing for his all-electric Lefrak City, he threatened to supply his own electricity with a nuclear reactor (no less). Con Ed preferred lowering Sam's rate to calling his bluff, or so the story goes.

He snaps up batches of materials at distress prices and warehouses them, knowing he will be able to use them on one project or another fairly soon. He makes his own bricks. He has a core of 4,000 full-time employees, from architects and engineers to carpenters and painters to a sanitation squad and a 350-man security force. At peak construction periods, his payroll swells to 20,000, he says. Thus the profits of subcontractors are largely eliminated. Those subs he does use, he says, are willing to work for very slim margins because they know he can keep them working for a long time. Every Friday the subs line up like customers at a bakery for their progress payments. "Sam has progress payments down to a fine art," says a colleague. "He pays them just enough to be sure they can keep afloat, but not enough for them to recoup their costs and walk out."

• Lefrak wastes no money, works his people hard, and is known to raise his voice every so often.

As his son, Richard, pilots the Fleetwood through toll booths on the way from one construction site to the next—no need for the chauffeur today—Sam collects receipts for the Internal Revenue Service, which audits him every year. At lunchtimes the Fleetwood may pull in to a Burger King. (Sam prefers the Whopper to anything McDonald's has to offer.)

The Lefrak Organization headquarters on Queens Boulevard is more shirtsleeves than show. The reception area has linoleum on the floor and a huge wooden coat of arms hanging on the wall with the Lefrak motto. It is *Labor Omnia Vincit,* which, loosely translated, means that Lefrak employees had damned well better work their asses off the way Maurice, Aaron, Harry, Sam, and Richard did and do.

As for Sam's raising his voice on occasion, one who has seen him in action says, "He acts on every job as though if it fails, he'll go to the poorhouse. He's abrasive, superaggressive, and certainly no diplomat." But then one must consider that getting anything built in New York, let alone as much as Sam gets built, is a very tough business. "You can engrave the entire ethics of the real estate industry in New York on a flea's behind and still have room for the Lord's Prayer," explains a Lefrak spokesman.

• Perhaps most important, Sam builds extremely fast. With construction costs rising like a Master Charge loan at 12 percent to 15 percent a year, the faster a project is completed the less it costs—and the less interim financing is needed to carry it until the first rent-paying tenants move in. Also, the sooner a project is finished the less chance it will be caught in a strike and delayed still further.

On a routine surprise visit to Harrison Towers (named after Sam's unemployed grandson) in Franklin, New Jersey, Sam and Richard ascertained that there were two stories down (up), and eighteen to go. The site foreman said the men had settled into a rhythm of one floor a week, despite the difficulties inherent in pouring concrete in 10-degree weather. Richard thought for a minute (Sam was on the phone taking directions to some nearby real estate a broker wanted him to look at) and explained to the foreman that one floor a week was too slow; it would have to be two floors a week. He said he would see about sending more men down to help.

Though Sam has a corps of lieutenants to oversee construction, and an NCR 315 computer (owned, not leased) full of critical-path programs that are supposed to neatly coordinate all facets of a construction job, Sam explains that there is no substitute for getting out into the field and pushing, which he and Richard often do, unannounced.

What all this adds up to—"the bottom line," as Sam would say—is that Lefrak buildings are notable for how little they cost to live in. When he built the four-building Kings Bay cooperative apartment complex in Brooklyn years ago, the price was so right that 3,600 people waited in line, some of them all night, to apply. (Sam had coffee, doughnuts, and even some blankets rushed in.) His most recent offering was fully rented in two weeks.

Still, there is more to Lefrak marketing strategy than price. "Live a Little Better with Lefrak," read the signs on his buildings and the wrappers on the cigars he gives out to visitors. In addition to large rooms, he offers prospective tenants his reputation as a landlord, which is quite good, and, in many of his complexes, such "amenities" as carpeted hallways, attractive lobbies, terraces, swimming pools, recreation areas, day care facilities, parking, convenient transportation, and Venetian blinds. (Venetian blinds, for some reason, are always featured in Lefrak brochures.)

Sam's own apartment, though not Lefrak-built, offers some amenities, too. He has one floor of a Fifth Avenue co-op; Richard has the floor below. They often ride to work and back together. Some of Sam's art collection is here, the rest at his homes in Woodmere and Palm Beach. One who has been his guest at dinner—"Sam calls Asti Spumante 'champagne' and proposes an absolutely stomach-turning toast"—thinks Sam buys his Gauguins, Chagalls, and Picassos "by the square foot." Not so, says a friendlier observer: "Sam can't say, 'I love this Renoir'—he's embarrassed to talk in such terms. So he says he bought it for $50,000 and just turned down $300,000 for it. But that doesn't mean he lacks taste, just that he's reluctant to express his feelings. You'll notice that his dress is not ostentatious—and, really, he lives quite simply for a man so rich." This month Sam was named to the board of the Metropolitan Museum of Art.

Sam lives with his wife, Ethel, and with the youngest of his three daughters, Jacqueline, who is eight. He is proud of his older daughters: Denise, who turned down a Hollywood career, he says, to teach retarded children; and Francine, who, at 24, is already head of the customer service department at the Parke Bernet gallery. Yet one suspects he may be just a bit envious of the likes of Meyer Rothschild, whom he is fond of quoting (along with Napoleon, Diogenes, Oscar Wilde, and many others), and who was blessed with five sons. Had Harry or Sam been blessed with five sons, we or our children might *all* be living in Lefrak City.

Like Rothschild in the Jewish ghetto of Frankfurt, Sam is quite conscious of being Jewish. He grew up at a time when many of the same sections of town that now are trying to keep out blacks were keeping out Jews. "The University of Maryland used to have a quota on Jews," he says almost defiantly, "and now they're naming the school of architecture after me." Through three foundations he has established, Sam helps support a host of philanthropic organizations, many of them Jewish. Rather than give out his exact address, for security reasons, he says he lives "near Temple Emanu-El."

Lefrak took some flack for a series of $90 donations made to Nixon's campaign by more than a score of his companies (the Lefrak Organization comprises about 350 in all, he says). However, Sam himself gave some money to McGovern and says he is "above politics," although he lives for the day, he says, when the present Mayor, "that -------," leaves office. "To me," he says, "I want to be loved by all, I don't want to be classified. Basically, I'm very independent. I would say that I'm to the liberal side."

Indeed, he is a curious mixture of guilty-Jewish-millionaire liberalism and self-made hard-hat patriotism-conservatism. He says things polished New York liberals don't say. "I recruited three Watusis for the basketball team," he tells a fellow Maryland alumnus. Or, "I'm not saying that you can come up with architectural gems, but how many architectural gems do you have to have?" he asks a *New York Times* reporter. Yet Lefrak has hired, trained, and secured union membership for substantial numbers of blacks and Puerto Ricans. His buildings are integrated (though his blanket policy against renting to welfare clients leads Jack Goldberg, former Commissioner of Social Services, to call him "one of the subtlest racists in New York"); and he is currently completing turnkey housing projects in Bedford-Stuyvesant and the South Bronx, where other builders were either afraid to build (each unit requires a 24-hour guard dog) or saw no profit in building (there isn't much, Lefrak says). As for architectural gems—well, how many *do* you have to have? His new 33-story Squibb Building at 40 West 57th Street, which will soon become Lefrak's head-quarters as well, is not as innovative or impressive as Sheldon Solow's new building across the street. But it is attractive, and it rents for about 20 percent less.

Sam's hard-hat patriotism is not uncharacteristic of a largely self-made multi-(to put it mildly) millionaire. "Frankly," he says, "all I can say to you is this is a great country, this is a great city, the dynamics around us are fantastic, there are dia-monds lying in the street. It's only the intelligent, wise man who's willing to work for it can make it good. And all I can tell you is God bless America."

Although his birth certificate reads "Le Frak," Sam says he now goes by Lefrak so as not to sound too "Euro*peen*." "I don't want to be accused," he says lightheartedly, "of being anything other than an American, as American as apple poy." And it suddenly hits the listener how very like Archie Bunker he looks and sounds. (His secretary's name, as it happens, is Edith.) Meanwhile, from over his left shoulder he looks re-markably like his good friend Nelson Rockefeller.

Rockefeller's picture is one of the 58 that hang on Sam's office wall ("Here I am with my good friend Bernard Baruch"), along with numerous trophies and awards, portraits of the family tree, and signs Sam has had made up with the tenets he says he lives by, among them: "1 + 1 = 3"; "Think" ("Old man Watson gave me that one"); "There is nothing im-possible, it just hasn't been done before"; "Self-preservation is the first law of man"; "Be genuine, be simple, be brief"; "Some people see things as they are and ask why; I dream things that never were and ask why not."

His office wall is matched only by his six-page closely typed biography, which ranges from his chairmanship of the Senior Prom Committee (1940) to his chairmanship of the 1961 Boy Scouts Lunch-O-Ree; from his honorary membership on the New York State Harness Racing Commission (1965) to his membership in two dozen clubs; from his having been "ac-claimed as one of America's Outstanding Builders" by Gen-eral Electric (who supplied 5,000 kitchens to Lefrak City—

you bet they acclaimed him) to his more substantial awards and achievements.

Whatever there is about Sam that makes him such a collector of approval and recognition must also be the force that drives him to build so much and so effectively. "One guy says to me, 'What makes Sammy run?' And my answer is 'because everybody's chasing him.' They all want to put gloves on with the champ." And who is chasing him the fastest? It just may be the man with the heavy foreign accent who would tell his only son when he got back from school, number two in the whole class, "You still have one to beat."

March 1973

THE
SIGHTLESS WONDER
OF WALL STREET

Laura Sloate arrived on Wall Street in late 1968, a 23-year-old Columbia Law School dropout. She turned bearish on the market in November 1969, then selectively, and successfully, bullish in September 1970. Such fortuitous market timing and a knack for securities analysis attracted a small following, six-figure commissions, and rave reviews from money managers. "Laura is a super analyst with terrific timing, right on top of the right ideas," says one. "She's great at eliminating the garbage and the fiction—and zeroing in on exactly what counts," says another.

None of which would be particularly remarkable were it not for the fact that Laura Sloate is blind.

Granted, some money managers would have improved their performance over the past few years if they had simply shut their eyes every morning as they read the *Wall Street Journal* and recommended whatever their index fingers happened to fall upon. But Sloate's approach has been far more conscientious and painstaking.

She gets up at 6:45 most mornings and squeezes orange juice for her father, who for the past twenty years has been managing the profits he accumulated in "the junky ladies' underwear business," as his daughter puts it. While she squeezes, he reads her the financial section of *The Times*. Then, around 7:30, he leaves for the Fifth Avenue Synagogue. Laura, an agnostic, rides her Exercycle, dresses, and walks to the Wall Street express bus or to the Lexington IRT, "depending on how rich I feel," she says. When she was younger and less concerned with her appearance, she dressed so sloppily that people sometimes mistook her for a beggar child and offered her change for the bus to school (which she angrily refused).

Laura arrives at Drexel Burnham & Co. before nine A.M. Her rather drab office looks smaller than it is because banks of file cabinets jut out from two walls; her fifteen cabinets have overflowed out into the hall. "I'm a terrible paper collector," she says. The office is distinctive only for the pictureless picture hooks hanging on the walls (she has been meaning to replace the decorations of the former occupant) and for the small but powerful German shepherd who sits quietly eating a cheeseburger in the corner (bun and all).

Ora, Laura's seeing-eye dog and constant companion of the last eight and a half years, does not usually eat cheeseburgers in the office. Usually she just lies lazily in the corner or demands attention from a visitor (with surprising force—this dog knows how to handle people), content to wait for supper at home. Supper at home consists of three-quarters of a pound of steak each night and ice cream. Both dog and mistress, Laura concedes, are spoiled.

Laura's morning mail is staggering. Six hundred letters, press releases, proxies, prospectuses, annual reports, newsletters, and journals were waiting for her when she returned from a recent week's business trip to California. ("The weather out there was terrific. We had one of the ten days all year when you can see the mountains from downtown . . . or so I was told," she says without self-consciousness.) Sloate opens the mail herself, she explains, to keep her hands from reaching for one of the 30-odd Marlboros she smokes each day. "My only vice. I don't drink, because I have a hard enough time keeping track of things as it is," she says in a way that suggests the idea is really a little frightening. But then she grins: "And I was the only virgin in my graduating class at Barnard."

Even if corporate treasurers issued their financial statements in Braille, Laura would have her mail read to her anyway. Though she does know Braille, she believes in a totally aural approach, which permits no laziness: no turning back a page, no referring to notes. Whatever is worth remembering must be learned on the spot. Whether this approach forces the mind to use more of its capacity, or whether her mind simply has more capacity than most to begin with—probably both—the result is nothing short of incredible. Laura has the aural equivalent of a photographic memory. She has never seen a balance sheet, and when she closes her eyes—a reflex left over from the time when she had some light perception—and puts her fingertips to her temple in an effort to remember, she does not visualize anything, she says; the numbers she wants just pop into her head. She has never *tried* to remember anything, she says, except vocabulary words in school. She just remembers.

When asked whether she had heard of Leisure Dynamics, a quiet over-the-counter issue the writer wished *he* had never heard of, she said she didn't know anything about the company—just that it was a small toy and game company out of Minneapolis, started by a bunch of ex–General Mills executives, whose performance had fallen short of projection recently in an industry where . . . When asked if she had ever heard of Wagner Electronics, another of life's little disappointments, which trades maybe 600 shares on a really big day, she said she didn't know anything about Wagner except that it was two-thirds owned by Studebaker and, as a captive company, investors shied away from it because its affairs could too easily be manipulated by the parent, and that the auto parts industry . . .

Obviously Sloate spends a long, long day absorbing this kind of information, analyzing it, and passing it on to her clients. Her pace is grueling because it is slow, limited by the speed of her readers. To keep her mind occupied, she often does something else while being read to. She may listen to a ball game, calculate profit margins in her head, or even talk on the phone while listening to the latest issue of *Chain Store*

Age, Electronic News, or *The Journal of Accountancy.* Up to a point, she claims, she can concentrate on two things at the same time, presumably filling the pauses in each activity with the substance of the other. She has not yet managed to have two readers going simultaneously, but makes up for her limited speed with long hours. She often leaves the office by six, but has one Columbia doctoral student read to her three evenings a week until 11:30; and another reads to her from nine to six on Saturday and Sunday. Around midnight on weekdays, her mother reads her the *Wall Street Journal* for an hour or two.

Ironically, Laura has less trouble keeping awake through her long dusklike days than she has falling asleep after them. Though she appears calm and even lethargic when she rests her head on the desk and listens to a balance sheet, she actually is tense—a hard-driving, fiercely motivated woman who hasn't taken a vacation in twelve years. And even after a nineteen-hour day, it is difficult for her to fall asleep, lacking as she does any contrast between light and darkness to help. (Long meetings in which she plays no active role have been known to do the trick, so she avoids those.) To turn off the lights in her mind, she takes long hot baths before going to bed, often dozing off for an hour or two in the tub; and she always leaves music on while she is sleeping. She does not see anything when she dreams; she dreams in dialogues.

Laura was born in Brooklyn in 1945 and began to lose her sight to glaucoma, extremely rare among children, when she was three. She retained some sight until she was seven, largely obscured by the bandages of a long series of unsuccessful operations, and some light and color perception until 1972, but she says she doesn't know what a tree looks like. She knows what it feels like. For that matter, she doesn't know what she herself looks like.

Fortunately, Laura had a family that could afford to give her anything she needed, and an IQ that when she was twelve measured 165. She had private tutors until she was fourteen.

"I used to make them put the names of the subjects on scraps of paper and I'd pick out the one we'd do next. I would fold 'Recreation' a certain way so I would always pick that." She admits, and her mother confirms, that she was a difficult, spoiled, bratty child.

"My mother gave up twenty years of her life for me," says Laura, "and I owe her everything." Mrs. Sloate beams with pride as she discusses her daughter's accomplishments. "I made her use her mind," she explains. "And I put her into everything. Did she tell you how she won a cha-cha contest when she was thirteen? Did she tell you how she used to play basketball?" Laura used to play basketball very badly, as you might imagine, but she remains an enthusiastic sports fan. "And she really knows her stuff," one of her clients told me, incredulously. "Things like—how's Willis Reed's knee?" She is a Knicks, Mets, and Jets fan. When the Dodgers were in Brooklyn, she was a Dodger fan. She recalls with amusement the thrill it was, aged ten, to be hit in the head by a right-field foul Alvin Dark blasted out to the bleachers during Carl Erskine's no-hitter, and how she got to keep the ball.

It took her three and a half years to get her B.A. in medieval history from Barnard. After a year at Columbia Law, and a brief run at becoming a Ph.D. in American history, she plunged into the hypertensive heart of American capitalism.

"I read in the Sunday *Times* about the great Freddie Mates, so I pestered him," she says. "He's a charitable guy, and he gave me a job with his fund. I deserved a job in the fall of 1968 like John D. Rockefeller deserves welfare." Later, she became the assistant to Meyer Berman, a well-known Wall Street broker.

Laura was not an easy woman to deal with in those days and their parting was not entirely affable. "Meyer would have thrown Laura out the window twenty-five times over if she hadn't been blind," says one former associate. Another characterizes Laura as "a barracuda. A very self-serving person who uses her blindness to get people's sympathy and likes to climb on top of people. She's a sick girl."

"I was much too aggressive and brash in those days," Sloate agrees. "I had never really had to deal with people before. I think I am gentler now and more political."

One of her institutional clients who *is* very fond of her is awed by her independence and self-confidence. "I took her out to dinner once to a relatively popular restaurant," he says, "and the headwaiter, who was a bit of a stiff, simply said, 'I'm sorry, but we don't allow animals here.' Well, Ora was clearly a seeing-eye dog, and Laura was, uh, clearly blind. I'm not a very aggressive person, but *Laura*, just like a machine gun, spouted at him how such-and-such-and-such of the city code required seeing-eye dogs to be allowed into restaurants—and if you're going to argue this point, just say so and I'll contact the local precinct. Well, this guy—It was as if someone had hit him with a sledge hammer. 'How about this table here?' he asked us. And *Laura*, who I guess had been there once or twice before, simply realized that the table was not in that good a location and said no, she wanted one around the corner there. The headwaiter just rolled over. So she is not a shrinking violet. And yet she's a very human person. Very human, and yet very tough. She has to be."

Her sense of direction has confounded more than one disbelieving stranger. She once gave directions to a rookie cab driver, corner by corner, all the way from her office at 60 Broad Street over to the East River Drive and up to her apartment. Another time, a woman approached her on Madison Avenue and, amid considerable embarrassment, explained that she had just been given eye drops to dilate her pupils, so she couldn't see anything clearly. Would Laura mind walking her home? Laura sometimes even has to lead Ora. "She's trained not to go through tight spaces where we can't both fit side by side, so in crowds I sometimes have to pull her through behind me or we'd never get anywhere."

It is Laura's aggressive, if somewhat unrealistic, view that blind people are *not* handicapped but, rather, disabled—by which she means, essentially, that they can learn to do almost anything they want to do if they put their minds to it.

Of course, few minds are as gifted as hers; but at least this philosophy works for her. She says that if some miraculous operation could restore her sight, she is not sure she would have it performed. Being sighted, she explains, would require a great deal of readjustment. Indeed, such an operation would render superfluous many of the special techniques and abilities Laura Sloate has worked so hard to achieve, and which afford her obvious and deserved satisfaction.*

January 1974

*Sight or no sight, Sloate went on to found a brokerage firm which by the end of 1979 had more than $90 million under management, a string of blue-chip clients, 23 employees, a magnificent record of stock picks, and solid profits. She took up—and dropped—the guitar; began bicycling around Central Park (on a bicycle built for two); and, characteristic of her iron will, one day simply quit smoking.

HERB COHEN:
A Brief Course
in Power and
the Art of
Negotiation

So many people call in to Larry King's radio talk show between midnight and 5:30 each morning that—together with the late-night data transmissions of the C.I.A. in neighboring Langley, Virginia—the long-distance circuits are often jammed to capacity. While all the other area codes in the Bell System are computer-snoozing, with here and there a stray call, like a lone truck on a deserted highway, the 703 area code at three in the morning is lit up and blinking and buzzing with busy circuits as if it were high noon. *Particularly* on those nights when Larry is in touch with the planet Fringus.

Like tonight.

"Thank you, thank you, thank you, and good evening, everybody. This is the *Larry King Show*," Larry King announces with gusto. "It is network radio, the only coast-to-coast talk presentation." Some three million people are listening. "This is the night all America has been waiting for. In one hour from now we will go into direct contact with Fringus, our own personal planet. . . . We'll be talking to Gork, the public relations director of the planet Fringus.

"In our first hour I have a return visit from our friend Herb Cohen, who is president of the Power Negotiations Institute." (Also founder, owner, and principal asset.) "Mr. Cohen is a consultant to, among others, the F.B.I., the State Department, and corporations like IBM, Citibank of New York, and Chase Manhattan. Herbie was in Washington today on a State Department thing."

Herbert Cohen, 47, and Larry King (formerly Larry Ziegler), grew up in Brooklyn together, so Larry calls Cohen "Herbie." Today Herbie conducted his "negotiations" seminar at the State Department ($1,650), made much the same speech to the Food Marketing Institute ($2,000), and will spend the next five and a half hours, from midnight to 5:30, on network radio. The day before, he was in Sault Sainte Marie; the day before that, in Toronto. In the next two weeks, he will be in Chicago (home base), Washington, Hyannis, Chicago again, Sands Point, Ottawa, Rochester, Manhattan, White Plains, and Peoria. Typical weeks. Figuring an average of $2,500 in fees per day (expenses are billed separately), and working 250 days a year (his schedule is sold out for months), one estimates that Herb Cohen—former wise-ass kid from the streets of Brooklyn, former claims adjuster for Allstate Insurance (while he attended law school at night)—must now gross in excess of $500,000 a year. And, says his wife, fees are going up. He charges the Justice Department "only" $6,000 for a two-and-a-half-day seminar, because he likes the work; the National Dairy people, on the other hand, were milked for $4,000 for a single day's program. Subtract two secretaries and some office expenses, and Herbie must still be earning pretty close to half a million a year. And yet he keeps going. Whatever drives him, he is like an author on an eternal book tour or a politician whose campaign never ends. "It's not the money," he is fond of saying (meaning money as a way to buy things); "it's the *money*" (meaning money as a way to keep score).

The reason he will be on the *Larry King Show* until 5:30 in the morning, of course, is that after discussing the Mideast peace talks for an hour as Herb Cohen, he will be Gork. His voice electronically disguised, he will play the role of director of public relations of the planet Fringus. His wife Ellen told me later that neither she nor the children saw through the ruse. This is hard to believe, but charming.

Here is a man who looks and talks exactly like Walter Matthau (except when he does a sort of Buddy Hackett); who greets every audience with the news that we are *all* negotiators, from the time we first cry for our mother's attention (or deal with employers, employees, colleagues, customers, suppliers, or even the coatcheck person when we've lost our stub); and who will leave us, his voice resonating with solemnity, recalling "two men who lived two thousand years ago, two of the greatest negotiators in the history of the world. Of course, I am talking to you about Jesus Christ and Socrates." In between, whether it be a dessert-and-coffee luncheon engagement or a two-day management seminar, he is a Catskills comedian whom we half expect after every sketch to bow, thank the crowd, and disappear behind a curtain. Instead, his voice and diction turn suddenly oratorical—"And so I say to you . . ."—as he reiterates the point of his story. You must be an entertainer first, Cohen says, and a teacher only second if you want people to learn.

It is an open question whether attendees actually do learn to negotiate more effectively, or, if so, whether they will ever have a chance to try out what they've learned. But they never fall asleep in class. Writes one senior vice president of Chase Manhattan Bank: "Without a doubt, your sessions on 'negotiation' were the absolute high spot of the two week [Chase Advanced Management Course]. . . . In fact, I've already put to use one of your tactics in our N.Y.C. negotiations. I felt we were being 'diddled' by a key N.Y.C. official in our negotiation. We broke off any further talks. This triggered certain responses which brought matters back into better focus and cleared the air for further negotiations." I.e., they creamed New York.

Another fellow claims to have saved $3,500 on the purchase of his home, thanks to Herbie's lecture.

The mayor of Tulsa wrote, "Your presentation [to a conference of mayors in 1978] had a greater impact on me than anything I have had since becoming Mayor." The F.B.I. loves him. The mayor of New Orleans calls whenever he gets into a jam. Mexicans listen to him eagerly through translation. Private individuals pay $225 to attend the one-day seminars he sometimes gives for the public at large.

Having watched the *Herb Cohen Show* three or four times now, twice live, once on tape, and piecemeal in hotel suites, I give it to you here—not complete, to be sure, but not for $4,000, or even $225, either:

THE PRISONER AND THE CIGARETTE

"Power is nothing more than the capacity to get things done. It's not moral, not immoral—it's neutral. What people tend to do is they confuse the power 'over' with the power 'to.' Power itself is neutral.

"Power is based on perception. If you think you got it—you got it. And if you don't think you got it—you *don't* got it. Let me illustrate that point.

"A prisoner in solitary confinement. You know? All right, this prisoner is walking around holding up his pants; he's lost a little weight. He craves a cigarette. Notices the guard is smoking his brand. He walks over to the steel door and he knocks and the guard ambles up, opens the door. 'Whaddya want?' 'I'd like a cigarette.' *Bam*, the guard slams the door. He perceives the prisoner is powerless. But the prisoner thinks he has power. 'Hi, there,' he says through the bars. 'Let me tell you what's going on. If I don't get a cigarette in the next thirty seconds—see this head? [Cohen points with feeling to his head]—I'm gonna bang it up against that concrete wall, and I'll be all bloodied, and when they find me I intend to swear you did it. Now, they're never gonna believe me; but think of all the hearings you'll be attending, think of all the reports in triplicate you'll be filling out, think of . . .[and now Cohen's voice is plaintive indeed] as opposed to giving me one crummy cigarette and I promise not to bother you again.' Can the guy get the cigarette? Yeah.

"Every one of you in this room [a gathering of small businessmen hosted as a customer relations exercise by Citibank] always has more power than you think you have. You gotta start off believing it," says Herb Cohen.

Cohen's advice is similar when it comes to fighting Very Big Guys. Ask your adversary to step outside (so he will not lose face when he lets you go); then tell him, with maniacal conviction, that if he so much as lays a hand on you, he'll have to kill you. Anything less than that, tell him, and no matter what it takes, you will kill *him*. Maybe not then and there, but sometime. As Cohen explains it, no one really wants to *kill* a guy, so your disputant may well just tell you to get lost, even though he could easily beat your brains out. Why should he kill you? Or *not* kill you and worry for the rest of his life that you might just be crazy enough to stick him with a knife some night or dynamite his house?

Impeccable logic which Cohen admits to never having had to put to the test. Is it possible, for example, that the man you are advising to kill you will be in less than a rational frame of mind himself—or not speak English—and break you into small pieces? It is vital when negotiating, Cohen says, to take risks.

DELAWARE IS CLOSED

"People in this society are enormously affected by signs. If I were to tell you to do something, you would evaluate my request based on your needs, and if the two of them meshed you might comply. But if a *sign* directed you to do it, the chances of your complying would be much higher. Do you buy that?

"Holiday Inn. The checkout time is one P.M. What percentage of the people do you think check out by the Holiday Inn checkout time? What do you think? *Ninety-five to ninety-nine percent,* depending on where it is in North America. Don't you think that's a remarkably high figure? Fifty-five percent of the people vote, but ninety-five percent check out by the checkout time."

Or, asks Cohen, do you remember the time Allen Funt put a sign up on a major highway leading into Delaware: DELA-WARE CLOSED? "You'd see guys drive up in their car and they'd pull over and they'd get out and here's this Funt and they'd go, 'Hey, what's going on in Delaware?' And he'd say, 'You read the sign.' The guy says, 'Yeah, yeah, but I've got a family. When do you think it will be open again?' And so I say to you, Legitimacy is very potent."

Legitimacy. Cohen has some suggestions on using it to your advantage. E.g., don't just have the price you want to charge in mind, have it typed up formally on an authoritative-looking price list. Better still, keep that price list *under glass* on your desk. How can you change it if it's under glass?

You, on the other hand, should not be cowed by such things. Herbie isn't.

HIS TAX AUDIT

"Three years ago the I.R.S. called me in to audit my tax return. There was one area of questioning about a building which I had elected to depreciate over a number of years. Now, the I.R.S. claimed that number should have been thirty. I took the position during the audit that it should have been twenty. We're discussing this, the auditor and myself, we're having nice discussions. Suddenly the auditor reaches in the right-hand corner of his desk drawer, whips out a fat book, and as I am speaking he is turning pages. He comes to one page, looks up: 'The book says thirty years.' I get up, walk around the table, look at the book. I say, 'Does the book mention my name?' He says, 'Of course not.' I say, 'I don't think it's my book.' I say, 'Otherwise it would have my name and my building.' I start taking down other books. The guy says, 'What are you doing?' I say, 'I'm looking for my book.' He says, 'You can't look at the books.' I say, 'Why not?' He says, 'I dunno, no one ever did that before.'

"Now what was that book he had? That book was not written in stone. That book was thought up by two bureaucrats somewhere to the best of their ability to implement some regulations. The book itself was the product of negotiation—and anything that's the product of a negotiation is negotiable." Or, if you make people crazy enough and are willing to take enough time—if, that is, you have no sense of decency, dignity, or decorum—there's no telling what concessions you might get. Witness:

THE NIBBLE

"Why was it so hard for the United States to extract itself from the war in Vietnam? Because we had invested forty thousand lives in it. It's known as the nibble. Let me describe the nibble to you.

"You go into an exclusive clothier in the downtown area where you reside. You want to get a fine suit. You start trying on suits. Each suit you ask the salesman. He says, 'Terrific.' You spend three and a half hours trying on thirty-nine suits. Each one you ask the salesman. He says, 'Terrific.' The salesman is fed up with you. He's about to blow his cool when suddenly you say, 'I'll take the one right there for two seventy.' 'You will?' The salesman breathes a sigh of relief and starts writing up the order. He takes you to a little room in the rear where they do the alterations—you've been in that room, you know that room—the one with the three-way mirror and they stand you on this little box and there you are looking at yourself. The salesman is writing up the sales slip, calculating his commission. Beside you as you stand on the box is this little guy with pins in his mouth, a tape measure around his neck. He's taking these pins and shoving them in your cuff, he's poking you up the rear, and he's always saying to you, 'This is a beautiful suit. It hangs very well on you.' Wherever you go, the guy's got the same accent. Maybe it's not an accent. Could be the pins. Anyway, you get the picture. You're standing there on the box, the salesman's writing up the slip counting his commissions, man on the floor shoving in the pins, making the chalk marks—when suddenly you turn to the salesman and say, 'What kind of tie will you throw in?'

"The salesman stops writing. He looks at the guy on the floor; the guy on the floor looks up. He doesn't know whether to shove another pin, make another chalk mark. He lets go of your crotch. Ladies and gentlemen, that's what we call the nibble.

"Now, I ask you, What is going through the mind of the salesman after the first wave of heat has disappeared? He's thinking, Three and a half hours of my time, thirty-nine suits I put on the guy's back, thirty dollars on a two-hundred-seventy dollar sale—as opposed to taking four bucks out of my pocket. I'm going to give this guy a tie and hope that I never see him again as long as I live.

"Will you get that tie? Yes."

Was it worth the effort and demeaning yourself? No. But Herb uses examples like these only to illustrate larger points.

POOR HERTZ

"Have I ever shown you my legitimacy card?" Cohen asks over $5 cups of lobster bisque in his suite at the Hotel Carlyle.

Most people know that Hertz and Avis give a variety of corporate discounts—usually 20 percent—when you rent one of their cars, or if you use their credit cards. Hertz, according to Herb, gives IBM 37 *percent*.

"I find this out, and I think it's inappropriate for me not to get the same discount."

At most airports, Herb says, you need only say you're with IBM and the attendants don't even check. Off goes the 37 percent. But at LaGuardia, they're really sticky. "They say, 'Who are you with?' I say, 'IBM.' They say, 'Yeah? Let me see your card.' "

Whereupon Herb pulls out of his wallet one of those pre-printed cards that says IBM in the upper left-hand corner and has Herb's name typed in in the middle. He was a speaker at one of their conferences, where everybody gets a card to wear under plastic on his lapel, and Herb kept the card.

Not only does he get 37 percent off, he says, they throw in free collision coverage. Works with Avis, too.

The only problem—evaluate it as you will—is that you have to lie to get the discount.

BOREDOM AT CAMP DAVID

"Persistence is to power what carbon is to steel. If a rat gnaws long enough at a dike, it could sink an entire nation. This is how the Camp David peace accords were put together. Jimmy Carter, in my opinion, is a highly moral individual. High moral convictions. However, he is also one of the most boring people in the history of this country. So he got Begin and Sadat to go to Camp David. Camp David is a very boring place itself. It's not what you'd call a swinging modern-day Sodom and Gomorrah. He got thirteen people up there with two bicycles and three films, so by the fifth day they had seen all those films and had to helicopter in a fourth. He'd come around every day and say, 'Hi, I'm Jimmy Carter. Let's talk for another five boring hours.' And if you were Sadat and Begin, obviously you would have signed anything to get out of there and that's what they did.

"I think to some extent the same thing was true when he went to the Middle East. He would leave, he was supposed to leave—No, he's gonna stay a little while longer. In fact, I think he'd still be there, but to his credit the persistence paid off. I think he achieved a great deal."

And when did "concession behavior," as Cohen calls it, occur? When it *always* occurs—at the deadline. On the way to the airport. Cohen learned this lesson, and the importance of "time" and "deadlines," many years ago.

HERBIE'S FIRST NEGOTIATION

"Twenty-five years ago I worked for an outfit that was operating internationally. I was not, but the organization was. I had one of those top management jobs where they would say, 'Hey, Cohen, two with cream, two with sugar.' You know— one of those key spots. And people would come back from overseas . . . you'd meet them for breakfast. 'Where you been?' And they'd say, 'Aw, just got back from Singapore; pieced together this nine-million-dollar deal.' Somebody else. 'Where you been?' 'Abu Dhabi. Where you been?' I didn't even know where Abu Dhabi *was*. What could I say? 'Well, I went to the zoo . . . the aquarium . . .' I used to go in to my boss every Friday and ask for a shot at the big time. Send me out there. Let me be a negotiator. I bothered this person so much that eventually he sent me to Tokyo to deal with the Japanese. This was my moment.

"I'm on the plane on my way to Tokyo. It's a fourteen-day negotiation. I've taken along all these books on the Japanese mentality, their psychology. I'm really gonna do well. Plane lands in Tokyo, I'm the first guy down the ramp. I'm raring to go. Three little Japanese guys [at one time Cohen weighed in excess of 200 pounds; now 155] are waiting for me at the foot of the ramp and they're bowing. I liked that quite a bit. Then they helped me through customs, they put me in this large limousine, sitting there in the rear all by myself and they're sitting on those fold-up seats. I say, 'Why don't you guys join me?' They say, 'Oh, no, you're an important person. You need your rest.' We're driving along and one of them turns around and says, 'By the way, do you know the language?' I say, 'You mean Japanese?' They say, 'Right. That's what we speak. This is Japan.' I said no. They said, 'Are you concerned about getting back to your plane on time?' Up to that moment I had not been concerned. They said, 'Would you like this limousine to pick you up?' I say, 'Oh, yeah,' and I hand them my ticket.

"Now, I didn't realize it then, but what's happened? *They know my deadline, but I don't know their deadline.*

"So we start negotiating, or I think we do. The first seven days they send me to Kyoto to visit the shrine, they enroll me in an English language course in Zen, they . . . I'm begging these guys to negotiate. They say, 'Plenty of time.'

"We finally start the twelfth day. We end early, play golf. The thirteenth day we resume. End early for the farewell dinner. The morning of the fourteenth day we resume in earnest; and just as we are about to get to the crux of things, the limousine pulls up to take me to the airport. We all pile in and just as we arrive at the airport we consummate the deal.

"By the way, how well do you think I did?"

Cohen advises people to conceal their own deadlines as far as possible. Act as if you've got all the time in the world, even though you don't. (And if you can, take more time than you might have planned, because that extra time will pay off. Try to keep your deadline flexible.) At the same time, believe that your counterpart, cool though he is playing it, unconcerned though he or she seems, is also sweating a deadline. It may not seem that way, but it's almost always true.

THE NEW HOUSE

Nowadays it's not enough to issue orders and expect the job to get done. You've got to negotiate for the commitment of your organization—get them behind you. Otherwise they can kill you just by doing exactly what you say. It's called "malicious obedience."

What does it mean to have your organization behind you?

"Five and a half years ago I lived in a community in Illinois called Libertyville. A rustic community, acres of land; thought I was very happy there until my wife explained to me that we weren't that happy. She said this area is not quite right for us, we ought to move.

"Since I'm away from home a great deal, it fell upon her shoulders to move us. And, you know, when you've been out of the real estate market for seven years and then come back, you're in for a shock.

"She's looking two weeks, four weeks—and to be honest with you, it does not bother me that she's looking—but I call home every night. Wherever I am, I call home every night. I am not a creative telephone conversationalist, by the way. I have a standard opening every night: 'Hi, how's everything?' And I even have a preferred answer, which is 'Fine.' I always move on to my second question, which is 'What's new?' My preferred answer is 'Nothing.'

"Monday night, Tuesday night, Wednesday night, I got good answers. Thursday night: 'Hi, how's everything?' 'Fine.' 'What's new?' (What could be new? I just talked to her last night.) 'I bought a house.' I said, 'No, you phrased that incorrectly. Semantically you're wrong. You mean to say you saw a house that you liked. She said, 'Oh, no. No.' I said, 'Oh. You mean you saw a house you liked and you offered money on it.' 'Yes, except they accepted the money and we got it.' *A whole house? How could you buy a whole house?*' She said it was really easy."

It turned out, shortening the story a little bit, that Ellen had made the deal subject to her husband's approval. That cheered him up somewhat.

"Okay, I get home late Friday night, I'm up early Saturday morning. The wife and I are going to this home, and I, alleged technical titular leader, am ready to reject the whole deal. We are driving along, and I say to my associate, 'By the way. Does anybody know about this home you almost bought?' She says, 'Oh, yeah.' I said, 'Who could know? It just happened.' 'A lot of people know.' 'Who? Who? Who?' 'Well, all our neighbors, all our friends know. In fact they're throwing us a gala farewell party.' I said, 'Who else knows?' 'Well, our families know— your family, my family. In fact, my mother has already ordered us custom-made drapes for the living room. I called in the measurements.' I said, 'Who else could know?' She said, 'Well, our children know. They told their friends, they told their teachers, they selected bedrooms they like . . .'

"In other words, what is happening is that the organization

is moving away from the leader. It is the zigzag theory of organizational behavior. In this case, the alleged technical titular leader was in the zig, while his organization was in the zag.

"What do you think the alleged technical titular lonely leader did in order to keep the title of alleged technical titular leader? He ratified the decision his organization had already made. It seems my wife knows more about negotiations than I do. When the body moves, the head is inclined to follow.

"And so I say to you, See people in context, get the commitment of others in the organization. Find out who's important to you and influence the people who are important to that person and you'll influence him."

MEETING SEARS' NEEDS

"If you want to deal effectively with people, if you want to convince them, if you want to negotiate, if you want to persuade, then you've got to approach people based on their needs. And that's all negotiation is. It is meeting the needs of people.

"You want to negotiate with Sears about the cost of a refrigerator. So you go into Sears and say, 'Hey, I'll tell you what. I'll take twenty bucks off your price, but I'll pay cash.' Does that work at Sears? No. Sears is not any retail establishment. They want you to think they are, but in reality they are a financial institution. They want to grab off eighteen percent of your money on their revolving charge account. Does it work with somebody else, though—the guy on the corner with a cash flow problem? Sure it does. And so I say to you, Every approach should meet the needs of people."

(In fact, Cohen maintains, you *can* negotiate with Sears and similar "one-price" stores. Most people don't think so, so they don't try. But the salesmen are authorized to come down on prices, to arrange trade-ins, to deal on "floor models," and more.)

Cohen speaks of refrigerators, but actually has in mind larger things, like labor negotiations or SALT II. He was called upon several times by the State Department during the Iran crisis, and even received a thank-you handshake from the President.

"What you've got to do is somehow find out what the other side's needs are. How do you do this? You don't start out when the negotiation begins; people won't tell you anything then. You've got to see all your encounters with people not as an event but rather as a process. You see, we think literally in terms of When does it start? It starts April sixth at two P.M. But negotiations, like mental illness, are a process. When somebody has been declared mentally ill at two P.M. on April sixth, when do they actually become mentally ill? Does anyone think they were fine at one fifty-nine, and at two P.M. they went bananas? You've got to use your lead time to gather information. Also to give information. When you give information to people, it influences the expectation level of the other side. It takes people a while to get used to a new idea. Throw something out to somebody over here, well in advance, and they will say, 'I don't buy that. No sir.' You mention the same thing over here, a little closer to the event, but when you bring it up you change the name of it. Do this a few times and what happens? 'Oh. That's been around for a while.'

"It takes a while for people to get used to any new idea. Allow for acceptance time to occur."

THE CLOCK

"A husband and wife are looking through an architectural magazine and they see a magnificent clock. They agree that if they can get it for five hundred dollars they'll be happy. They spend months looking for this clock—flea markets, antique shops, weekend trips—and finally they see the clock of their dreams. As they near the clock, they see one potential problem, a sign that says seven hundred and fifty dollars. One of

them is appointed negotiator in an attempt to secure the clock.
That individual walks up to the person selling the clock and
says, 'Sir, I notice you have a little clock for sale. I notice a
little dust around that sign on the top. Now, I am going to
make you one offer and one offer only and I know it's gonna
thrill you very big. Are you ready for it? Here it is: two
hundred and fifty dollars.'

"And the seller says, 'You got it. Sold.'

"Now, how do you feel when that happens to you? Why do
some of you smile when you hear that? You smile because
you've *been* there, that's why; and I've been there, too. What's
your first reaction? Is it that you got a great price? No. Your
reaction is 'I could have done better. I was stupid. I should
have started lower.' What's your second reaction? 'What's
wrong with the clock?'

"If the seller had been a decent, compassionate human
being, he would have allowed you to fight for every dollar and
finally settled with you for four ninety-seven dollars. You
would have been happier.

"I'm saying to you that human beings have needs [beyond
money]. And they are different."

Creative negotiators, Cohen believes, can often turn the
process into a "win-win" situation, where *both* sides' needs
can be met. In essence, he says, successful negotiation lies in
finding out what the other side *really* wants and showing them
a way to get it while you get what you want. He recalls a
corporate acquisition he was once involved in where the
seller asked $26 million and refused to budge. The buyer of-
fered $15 million, $18 million, $20 million, $21 million, $21.5
million; the seller refused to budge. Only after some days, by
chance over dinner, did it develop that the seller's brother
had sold *his* company for $26 million. Suddenly Cohen's
group realized that their man had needs other than money.
They wound up working out terms that fell within their budget, but allowed the seller to feel he had done better than his
brother.

The incident of the clock also illustrates another of Cohen's basic tenets: Start low. Or, if you're selling, start high. Any three-year-old knows to do this, of course, but Cohen says, No, even lower (or higher) than that. This gives you more room to maneuver, tests the waters, and lowers the opposition's expectations. Of course, if you had already been planning to offer so little (or ask so much) as to be downright insulting, this advice could serve to destroy any chance of making a deal. Well, don't start *that* low, says Cohen.

THE SERAPE

"Ever see people who come back from southern climates, who take winter vacations and wind up at northern airports— ever see what they're wearing? A week away from New York and they're wearing muumuus. I myself own two Mexican serapes. To tell you the truth, I never thought of myself as being with a serape. I don't like them.

"Five years ago my wife and I go to Mexico City and we're walking through the streets and suddenly she says, 'Ah, yonder I see lights.' She speaks that way, you know. I say, 'Hey, I'm not going over there, that's the commercial area. I did not come here to wallow in commercialism. You go; I'll meet you back at the hotel.' I go off on my own, and as I'm moving with the ebb and flow I notice this person approaching me wearing serapes. He's calling out, 'Twelve hundred pesos.' I'm trying to figure out who he can be talking to. It couldn't be me. How did he know I was a tourist? I look straight ahead and keep walking. The guy walks right up to me—I'm not even looking at him—and says, 'A thousand pesos.' I'm still moving. 'Eight hundred pesos.' I stop. I say, 'My friend, I certainly respect your initiative and your diligence; however, I do not need a serape, I do not like a serape, I do not desire a serape. Would you kindly sell elsewhere?' I walk away; the guy's still following me. He's yelling, 'Eight hundred pesos.' I'm jogging; the guy's pursuing me. 'Six hundred pesos.' I'm running down the damn street, I'm hot, I'm sweating, and he's chasing me. He says, 'Four hundred pesos.' I'm irritated. 'Damn it, I just told you I don't want a serape. Now beat it.' 'Two hundred pesos.' I say, 'What did you say?' 'Two hundred pesos.' I say, 'Let me see the serape.' Why am I asking to see the serape? Do I need a serape? Do I want a serape? Do I like a serape? No. See how a man changes his mind? I didn't think I wanted a serape, but maybe I do.

"You see, the guy started at twelve hundred pesos; he's now down to two hundred. I don't know what the hell I'm doin', but—I mean, I haven't even started negotiating and already I got the guy down a thousand pesos. Now, I find out from this guy that the cheapest anyone ever bought a serape in the history of Mexico City was a fellow from Winnipeg, Canada, whose mother and father were born in Guadalajara. He paid a hundred seventy-five pesos. I get mine for a hundred and seventy, thereby giving me the serape record for Mexico City. I am now walking down the street wearing my serape. It is a hot day. I am perspiring, but wearing my serape."

He rushes back to his hotel to show Ellen. "How much did you pay," she asks him. "The guy wanted twelve hundred pesos, but the internationally renowned negotiator over here picked it up for a hundred seventy." Ellen opens the closet to show him the identical serape, for which she paid 150 pesos.

"Why did I buy that serape? Did I need a serape? Did I like a serape? I didn't think so, but on the streets of Mexico City I encountered not a peddler but an international psychological negotiating marketeer. By some sort of process he met needs I didn't even know I had."

It is Herb's contention that we all have a serape or two in the closet.

TIDBITS

• You have to remember always that people are different. They have different needs and they understand things differently. "In the Midwest you tell people a nine o'clock meeting. What time would you have to arrive at such a meeting before you would be considered late? You know what people tell me? Eight forty-five. It's Vince Lombardi time or something. Other people tell me eight fifty-five. In California they say nine-fifteen. In New York guys say, 'According to Jimmy Walker, as long as you get there before it's all over you're not late.' "

• Make things personal. "Commitments are never kept with institutions. They're too big, too impersonal. What's the difference if Chase loses $100,000? What you want to do, see, you're with Chase, but you negotiate on behalf of yourself. A guy waffles on his commitment and you say, 'Look, you told me you were going to do this, and I told my boss. You're not going to let me down, are you?' The guy says, 'Hey, you're not taking this personally, are you?' [Plaintive, not hostile]: 'Yeah.' "

• If you box people in to taking a stand publicly, they will tend to resist change. Do your negotiating before the public meeting if you can.

• It's much easier to say no over the phone. So if you want something, you'll do better getting it face to face.

• The caller is always at an advantage. He's prepared, knows just what he wants to say. If you are the callee, bury the caller with gratitude for calling, but ask if you can call him back. That gives you time to prepare. Or if that's awkward, hang up on yourself. Let him talk a little, start to answer—and in the middle of your own sentence hit the button. Must have been the lousy switchboard. Gather your thoughts while you wait for him to call back.

• If one of you is going to write up a memo confirming your understanding, you be the one to do it. That way you get the initiative, you set the priorities, you're controlling the situation. The guy gets the memo and has five problems with it. "You mean you want me to do this all over again?" You are incredulous, hurt, perhaps a trifle annoyed. The guy has to fight for each one of his five points and feels lucky to get three. (If he'd written it, the five problems would have been in his favor, not yours, and you would have been stuck with two of them—down two rather than up two.)

• Likewise note taking. Asks Cohen: Who's in a better position to interpret the chicken scratchings than the chicken?

• Don't be afraid to ask for help, to say you don't understand. People respond to that; it helps make the negotiations more "collaborative" and less "competitive" (making it more likely that you will both emerge more satisfied). Could he explain it one more time? Sometimes, in reiterating and explaining his list of outrageous demands, your counterpart—perhaps embarrassed by their outrageousness, or taking pity on you—will let one or two drop without your even having to argue.

• Consider timing. When is the best time for a hooker to negotiate—before or after performing her services? Anticipation is always (or almost always) greater than reality.

• Consider options. A man went out to Cohen's new house (you know, the one his wife bought) to install a couple of locks. The bill comes: $142. He was there 45 minutes, Herb says—$142. "So I call up the guy and he says. 'Look, pal, that's the price.' 'Maybe we can talk about it?' 'No, that's it.' I said, 'Well, do I have any options in this situation?' He says, 'What do you mean, options? If you don't like it, I'll take out the locks.' I said, 'Good. That's a very good idea.' He says, 'What do you mean? You'll have holes in the door.' I say, 'No problem; take them out.' He says, 'How about ninety-five dollars—would that sound better?' I said, 'Yeah.' "

GORK SUMS UP

It is 5:25 in the morning now, and Larry King and Herb Cohen—Gork—have been at it for nearly five and a half hours. Everyone but me thinks this is a scream—that Gork is a riot. The only concept I really like is that what we call UFO's are actually garbage from Fringus. They pack their garbage into Frisbee-like disks and send them flying off into space. I like that, although I have the nagging suspicion I have heard something like it once before.

Cohen has several more dates scheduled for the *Larry King Show*. He's been turned down by Tom Snyder and Phil Donahue. Tom Snyder he doesn't mind, because the people were polite. But he has decided to appear on *Donahue* if it is the last thing he does in life. How will he manage that? He starts reeling off for me the names of every staff member of the show. More than that, he has found out where they're from, what they're like, how long they've been there. He has all this in his head. He is determined to get on that show.

Why is he so eager to do it? And why is he giving me all his material to give you free? Yes, it's great for business, but can business really get much better? Is it ego? Of course. But I also give some credence to his own explanation:

"I want people to have power, and to feel they have power. To have options, and know that they have options. When people are powerless, it's bad for everybody. Either they become hostile and try to tear down the system, or they become apathetic and throw in the towel. We don't want that."

June 1980

IV
Placing
Your Bets

THE
CASE
FOR STOCKS

If you are not a person "of means"—if, to you, clipping coupons simply means 30 cents off the next can of coffee—please stop reading. Bad enough to have no appreciable nest egg without your having to know, in addition, that if only you *did* have one, a good basket has come along for you to put it in. (Well, not *all* of it, of course, but you don't need me to tell you that.)

The basket I have in mind is the U.S. stock market. The very same U.S. stock market that, as measured by the Dow Jones Industrial Average, is actually lower today, December, 1978, than it was fourteen years ago and that, *adjusted for inflation,* is back to the level that prevailed at the time of the Great Plague.

I am not suggesting that we have in today's stock market "the chance of a lifetime." We had that chance, or so hindsight might eventually confirm, in December 1974. Then the Dow Jones Average was at 580 compared with around 800 today. More to the point, a good many lesser companies that trade at $10 and $20 today were then selling at $1 and $2 a share.

Nor am I predicting that stock prices next month won't be lower than they are today. They well could be.

What I *am* telling you is that stocks are a bargain. There is a strong case to be made for placing a significant share of your assets in stocks. What's more, there is even a government-subsidized strategy, of sorts, by which to do so.

Eight reasons to buy stocks:

1. Everything else has zoomed with inflation. It stands to reason that corporations should eventually rise in price, too. The higher everything else rises while stocks stand still, the more attractive stocks look by comparison. When you go shopping, you buy the items that are on sale.

2. Moreover, you shop in the country where your money goes the furthest. With the dollar still severely depressed, the U.S. stock market offers shoppers—be they American, German, Japanese, or Kuwaiti—the best buys.

3. The alternatives look less and less appealing. "Fixed-income securities"—bonds, savings accounts, Treasury bills, and the like—offer safety and, currently, terrific yields. But after taxes and inflation, these yields turn out to be negative. To have one's entire fortune tied up in fixed-income securities is *not* the most prudent financial course. (Unless that fortune is too small to accept any risk, as—for older people especially —is often the case.) Life insurance should be bought, cheaply, for protection only. As an investment, it pales. Art, diamonds, Oriental rugs, and the like require that you buy at retail and sell at wholesale—a tough game to beat. Commodities speculation is stacked hopelessly in favor of the broker. Gold has had its big run and pays no dividends. The real estate boom shows increasing signs of peaking, or at least decelerating (although a home remains the first investment most people should make.)

4. *If inflation continues*, the value of corporate assets (land, buildings, machinery, coal deposits, et cetera) will continue to rise and profits and dividends very likely will too. AT&T stock is actually lower today than it was in 1962—which tells you that it was not a great buy in 1962. Since then, however, its dividend has risen steadily from $1.80 to $5, and may be expected to continue to rise—which suggests that it *might* be a great buy in 1979. (Why buy an AT&T *bond* that yields $95 in interest on each $1,000 you invest but can never grow, when you can buy AT&T *stock* that pays nearly as much—$93 in dividends on each $1,000 invested—and could be paying

twice that much ten years from now?) Much the same could be said of a great many other corporate giants—and midgets. With stock prices having been stagnant for so long, while assets and profits and dividends have been growing, you now get much more for your money than you once did. Dividends may continue to rise with inflation; the interest on a bond never does.

5. If inflation does *not* continue—stocks will soar.

6. Much lower inflation is the key to a bright American future. What's new, or relatively so, is that most citizens finally agree. That's bullish.

7. Higher productivity is crucial to lower inflation. To achieve higher productivity, you must have increased investment in more efficient means of production—which means increased incentive to invest and less government interference. We seem to have turned *this* corner as well: The recent easing of capital gains taxes means a better deal for the investor—and may signal more favorable conditions for business and investment generally.

8. Although we are not in a panic situation, alas, and the news has at times been gloomier (panic and gloom being particularly good signs of opportunity in the stock market), pessimism is nonetheless widespread, and there is a crew of credible experts predicting disaster.

Which leads to the one reason *not* to invest in the stock market right now:

1. They could be right.

But even that's not quite as persuasive a reason as at first it appears, because under at least some of the disaster scenarios, few investments would fare much better than stocks. (It is also worth noting that when the market was poised for crash in 1929, the Dow had run up some 600 percent in the previous eight years and was selling at several times its "book value." Today the Dow, which has run nowhere at all, sells *beneath* book value, which may itself be drastically understated because of inflation.)

You might imagine that a second commonsense argument

exists for passing the market by right now; namely, that low as it may be now, it could be a good deal lower in six months. Which is true—it could be. But one thing is sure: Neither you nor I stand much chance of predicting short-term fluctuations in the stock market. We may be able to make some appraisal of relative value; we may be able to guess the market's direction *half* the time (so can a nickel); we may be able to say with certainty that, other things being equal, it is better to hold a stock in which you have a profit for 366 days than for 364 (to qualify for the 60 percent long-term capital gain exclusion); but we really are kidding ourselves if we think we can call the short-term turns in the market.

Which brings me to my suggested strategy. It is a strategy that assumes you have $10,000 or $25,000 or $50,000 you can comfortably commit to the market and that you are in a fairly high marginal tax bracket.

The strategy is simply this: Buy stocks now (or any other time the Dow threatens to dip beneath 800). Choose a diversified lot, most of which, at least, sell at very low multiples of earnings, a fraction of their book values, and pay secure 6 to 9 percent dividends. Throw in a Texas Instruments or two (high-technology, low-dividend, great growth prospects)—but avoid with great care stocks that are in vogue. Now, make a note in your calendar to look at them in ten months. (Try not to look at them too much in the meantime or you will be tempted to neglect your legitimate business and become a stock trader—or, at the very least, neurotic.) Deposit your dividend checks. When ten months are up, your stocks will be either higher or lower than when you purchased them. If they are higher, congratulations—you've made money. But consider waiting at least two more months before selling so that you qualify for a long-term capital gain.

If some or all of your stocks are lower—if the excellent bargains you bought have become even more outstanding bargains—*buy more.* Double up on the stocks in which you have substantial losses, even if it means borrowing heavily from your broker to do so, and wait 31 days. Then sell the original shares in which you had losses* (thereby repaying your broker).

Doing so will provide you with a short-term capital loss. Up to $3,000 of any such loss can be deducted from your taxable income, with the remainder carried over to future years. If you are in the 50 percent bracket (including state and local income taxes), the government will thus absorb 50 percent of your loss.

Now take a look yet another ten months hence. Either the excellent bargains that became outstanding bargains are now *incredible* bargains (in which case, double up for 31 days *again,* pin down yet another short-term capital loss for tax purposes, and accept my profound apologies) . . . or else these stocks have recovered in price and perhaps climbed handily to boot.

If *that's* the case, consider holding them: (a) for a long time, collecting dividends and waiting for further price appreciation—unless you are convinced there are better opportunities available that would justify the brokerage expenses and taxes of selling, or (b) for another two months and a day, until you've held them long enough to qualify for long-term capital gains treatment.

You can see how by taking losses short-term and gains long-term (*in different tax years, or else the I.R.S. nets the two out*) you come out well ahead even if you just break even! You would suffer an after-tax loss of only $1,500 on before-tax losses of $3,000—and then reap a $2,400 gain, after tax, if you

---

* The I.R.S. requires this 31-day interval between buying and selling. If you jump the gun, they call your transaction a "wash sale" and disallow the short-term capital loss you are trying to establish. The other thing you can do is sell the stock first, wait 31 days, and then buy it back. This eliminates the need to double up and the cost of tying up that extra money for 31 days. However, if your luck is at all like mine, you know what will happen. The day you sell the original shares, the stocks will rally smartly. By the time 31 days have elapsed, they will have doubled or tripled, leaving you distraught at best.

merely recouped your $3,000 before tax. And all the while you would be collecting dividends.

The odds are actually with you three ways in this game. First, you get dividends (they pay *you* to play). Second, as shown, you can work the taxes to your advantage. Third, I am convinced there is a better than even chance that stock prices, over the long run, will be a lot higher than they are today.

January 1979

THROWING
DARTS

Even if this is a good time to buy stocks—even if they *are* cheap relative to other assets (and they are)—most people feel incompetent to choose the ones to buy. Either they pay through the nose to have someone else choose or they turn their attention to other, more palatable projects. But how highly trained must one really be to take the plunge? Not so highly as one might think.

A monkey throwing darts, it has frequently been said, can do about as well picking stocks as the average Wall Street professional. Or better. Invariably, when I make this claim—most recently on a spate of local talk shows—I get one of two reactions. From the Wall Street professionals: "---- you." From everyone else: "Where's the monkey?"

"The real problem," I say, warming to my shtick, "is finding a monkey that can throw darts."

"Where's the monkey?" the audience asks again.

"It is computer simulated," I admit. (Children are particularly disappointed by this.) "But it's true. A monkey is as good as a pro."

But *is* it true?

I recently had an opportunity to put my monkey where my mouth was, so to speak, using neither marmoset nor macaque (nor computer) but, rather, five obliging ladies from the studio audience of *The Bob Braun Show,* in Cincinnati.

Such experiments are not original with me. The editors of *Forbes,* in a now much celebrated bout of dart throwing, selected a portfolio twelve years ago that has consistently outperformed the bank trust departments, mutual funds, and popular stock averages. At last report, it was over 60 percent ahead of the Dow Jones average.

But it is one thing to read it in *Forbes* and another to confirm it in fact. I will admit to having felt some trepidation as the darts began to fly.

My first thought had been to pin up the stock pages from an old *Wall Street Journal.* But the *Journal,* it seems, keeps its back issues on microfilm. The gals would have had to be sharpshooters indeed. Instead, we pinned up that morning's *Cincinnati Enquirer,* March 9, 1979. And from a distance of five feet, in front of an estimated 306,000 witnesses (the show is carried on six other television stations as well as 97 cable systems), they threw. Each dart carried a hypothetical $1,000. One dart sailed over the backstop; several hit the government-bond and options tables and had to be rethrown. Eventually, we had holes in thirteen New York and American stock exchange common stocks. (One I eliminated because it had not been listed five years earlier.)

Herewith *The Bob Braun Show* portfolio (dart holes available for inspection on request): Bendix, Brockway Glass, Integon, Peoples Drug, Puritan Fashions, Talley Industries, and Wrigley (all on the New York Stock Exchange); Hampton Industries, Louisiana General Services, Michigan Sugar, Richton, and Sysco (on the American).

Of the dozen, I had never heard of eight.

I went home and pulled out the stock pages from March 1, 1974. On that day, the Dow Jones Industrial Average stood at 860.53. Five inflation-ravaged years later, as we threw darts, it stood at 844.85—slightly lower. Had you invested $12,000 in March of 1974 in the stocks that make up the Dow, your investment would have shrunk slightly to $11,784 by the time we threw our darts. The same investment in the stocks that make up the Standard & Poor's average would have grown to $12,420. But if you had invested in the twelve stocks that our ladies of *The Bob Braun Show* picked, your money would have grown to $22,803.

And you'd have earned some $3,000 in dividends on your investment to boot.

How could the monkey do so well? Is it possible he will continue to outstrip the pros? (The average money manager underperforms the popular averages because—unlike those averages—his results are diminished by commissions and fees.)

To begin with, it should be said that if you had bought this same dart-selected portfolio (or just about any stocks) in the late 1960s, you would have gotten killed. By any reasonable measures, the market was very high in the late '60s, much less so in March 1974 or March 1979. It always helps to throw your darts when the market is low.

Low as it was, however, as 1974 progressed, the market went straight down. Had you sold out in despair—as so many did—you would have lost money. But monkeys do not sell out in despair. Nor do they change their minds. They do not generate brokerage commissions and incur taxes by selling one stock to buy another.

But the real advantage the monkey had in 1974 was in bucking what was known as the two-tier market. Back then, the top few hundred companies were accorded particularly wide premiums over the smaller, unknown, or uninteresting companies. Big companies tended to be overpriced; *most* companies were unfashionable—but cheap. While money managers concentrated on a few hundred overpriced stocks, darts landed at random among thousands of bargains.

Today, the relative valuations of big and little companies, glamorous and unglamorous ones, seem substantially more rational. So it is unlikely that dart throwers will do better over the next five years than professionals. But neither are they likely to do worse. Indeed, recognizing the difficulty of outperforming the averages, some billion-dollar money managers have turned (in desperation?) to "indexing," which is the practice of trying simply to match the averages by buying all the stocks *in* the averages (or at least a representative sample). To the extent that managers index their portfolios, they are making monkeys of themselves. They have given up trying to assess relative values—even though some stocks *are* better values than others—and just buy a little of everything. But even at that, they will do poorly, because they will mindlessly stick to the large stocks that make up the averages, even at times when smaller stocks are better buys.

Of course, certain pros *will* consistently beat the averages. I don't believe this is impossible—just very difficult. But how do you find them? If you can spot the winning mutual fund, perhaps you can also spot winning stocks and save the fee.

I do not suggest that anyone seriously consider choosing stocks at random. However, it does seem wise to diversify (one dart won't do) and to ignore, as the darts ignore, whatever is the current fashion (this year: gambling stocks). One excellent and inexpensive source of good investment ideas—out-of-favor companies whose stocks are undervalued—is *Forbes*.

If the market is indeed low today (what else costs no more than it did fourteen years ago?), and if the world as we know it does not end (as after all it might not), then by choosing your own stocks, buying them through a discount broker, and sticking with them patiently, collecting dividends, you may not do spectacularly, but you are likely to do creditably well. Boring but true.

May 1979

THE CASE
AGAINST
GOLD

[I wrote when gold reached $227 an ounce in late 1978 that to buy it was foolish. Although it could certainly climb higher, I argued, the risks were great—and in any case the *big* run was obviously over.

With gold ushering in the new decade at $600-plus, it is apparent that buying it at $227 in late 1978 would not have been so foolish, after all. A slight error in timing. To buy it *now* would be foolish. Although it could certainly climb higher, the risks are great—and in any case the *big* run is obviously over.]

The basic disaster scenario—and the rationale for buying gold—is that despite all American efforts, the economy will move from the severe inflation we have now to double-digit inflation and from double-digit inflation to hyperinflation, and from hyperinflation to complete collapse. Banks will be collapsing too—along with most businesses—so you'd better keep your gold at home. Paper assets will be worthless. But you will have gold.

The French peasants understand this, we are frequently reminded. They have the savvy, born of centuries' experience with governments that come and go, to hoard gold. (And yet they remain peasants. For me, this is where the argument breaks down.)

Disasters of all sorts do lurk, and it does make sense to hedge against them—but not necessarily with gold.

Water is an inexpensive hedge against disruption or pollution of the water supply, which in turn might be caused by earthquake, sabotage, or, in the case of my own building, antique plumbing. Yet how many people do you know—even gold bugs—who keep a few gallons on hand?

Solar collectors, which are beginning to make sense for many homes on economic grounds alone, become irresistible in the context of economic collapse, riots in the streets, and (one assumes) uncertain power supplies.

Food is also a terrific disaster hedge (and, as noted elsewhere, bulk purchases of food and other staples—at sale prices and/or quantity discounts—can be thought of not only as an inflation hedge, but even as an excellent tax-free "investment"). If there is a panic that wipes the supermarket shelves clean—much as the gasoline panic not long ago made the purchase of gasoline inconvenient—you might be happier with a cellarful of food than a pocketful of gold coins.

This sort of hedge is socially useful too. For the citizenry to increase its inventory of staples—its collective fat—means the social fabric will be less easily torn, our neighbors less subject to panic.

Buying gold is a different matter. It is a socially repugnant investment—and this is one argument against buying it that's infrequently made. It is, for one thing, a bet against our being able to muddle through—a bet that the social order *will* collapse. People should be free to make that bet (just as, if you will forgive a slightly hysterical analogy, people should perhaps have been free during World War II to buy marks or yen, just in case): but it is a bet that I hope will not really become "respectable," as some say it has, because it is such a waste of potentially productive capital.

Unlike investments in housing, more productive machinery, new factories, mass transit, solar collectors, or research and development—all of which we make, indirectly, when we put money into savings banks, pension plans, life insurance, stocks, or bonds—an investment in gold is sterile. At best it means that a few more miners, mostly South Africans, will dig a little deeper. But to what end? We have vastly more gold than we could possibly ever "need." Indeed, current annual production outstrips industrial demand (including the manufacture of jewelry)—and at today's lofty price, production is bound to increase, while consumption shrinks. The only "use" for the world's huge gold surplus is psychological, as a store of value. In this respect, its usefulness derives from its scarcity—so mining more does nothing to enrich mankind. Wasted effort.

The Gold Information Center has been running a particularly striking ad for some time now—you may have seen it— in which a cube of gold, just eighteen yards high, is pictured next to the Washington Monument. That's how little gold, the ad says—that one little cube—man has been able to find throughout millennia of scraping around looking for it. Implication: The stuff's so rare, so precious, it's a bargain at *any* price.

Well, I offer an equally meaningless—but equally accurate —ad of my own. Here it is: If you took all that gold (two hundred million pounds' worth, actually), and if, rather than cubing it, you strung it out as thread (one of gold's properties is that it can be drawn exceedingly fine), *you would have enough 24-karat gold thread to circle the earth six million times.*

I don't say this would be practical, but according to simple calculations based on the Gold Information Center's own figures, it could be done. (You could also gild the entire state of Massachusetts—twice.)

So perhaps there's already quite enough gold sitting uselessly in vaults around the world, after all, and perhaps we don't need to break our backs, or other people's backs, to mine more. What we really need to produce are things like oil, copper, silver and food. Of course, as long as there's a dollar to be made mining more gold, more gold will be mined. But as this represents enormous wasted effort, perhaps what the gold ad should really picture is one army of people digging a hole next to the Washington Monument, while another army works just as hard to fill it up.

Americans do not save, which is to say invest, nearly as high a proportion of their income as the Germans or Japanese, which is an important reason why our productivity, competitiveness, and growth in real personal income have lagged so badly behind theirs. To cut our productive investments back even further, by siphoning off that many more investment dollars into gold, leaves us at even more of a disadvantage and in the long run poorer.

The high price of gold, which is another expression of the low value of the dollar, does serve one purpose: that of an alarm. It signals clearly that we've been flirting with disaster.

But once that's recognized—once Proposition 13 passes, once fully 70 percent in a CBS poll would favor a constitutional amendment requiring a balanced federal budget, once people are actually more eager for a cutback in the size of government spending than for a cut in taxes, which the same poll also suggested—then you have the feeling that help is on the way.

If so, gold may do what it did the last time the world didn't end. Plunge.

November 1978

HELTER
SHELTER

Killing as it is to pay half of every dollar in income tax, there is a consolation: At least you get to keep the other half.

In trying to hang on to the *first* 50 cents as well—a natural instinct, like ducking to avoid a punch or yawning at the sight of a textbook—it is not inconceivable that you will lose the whole dollar.

BROADWAY ANGEL

The first tax shelter I ever participated in involved $1,500 and a play called *P.S. Your Cat Is Dead.** It was through this investment I learned Broadway angels had to *pay* for their opening-night seats. Never mind. I bought them anyway. And who should I find myself sitting behind—rather, behind whom should I find myself sitting—but the venerable John Simon.

"John," I said, drawing shamelessly on our passing acquaintance, "I have a stake in this show—and I will thank you not to drive it through my heart." Just kidding, of course, but John is Transylvanian, or nearly so, so I thought the imagery might in some vague way appeal. Simon headlined his review: "P.S. So Is Your Play." Return after four years on my $1,500 investment: $168.

*Based on the very funny book by James Kirkwood. Kirkwood was opening another play the same month *(A Chorus Line)*, but that one was not open to public investors.

The idea of a theatrical tax shelter—if you can even call it that ("contribution to the arts" might be a better term)—is to deduct your investment *this* year and then recoup it—and more—in future years. If it works, all you really accomplish is to transfer income from this year's tax bite into that of future years. *As with most tax shelters, you are merely delaying, not eliminating, your liability.*

I have since learned that there are far better, bigger, more complex and sophisticated ways to shelter money from taxes —and, in the process, to lose it.

CATTLE BREEDING

You have doubtless heard, for example, of cattle-breeding tax shelters, wherein you buy a bull and three cows now, which, upon consumption of much feed and by means of much fornication, will someday multiply your tax-deductible investment into boxcars of hamburger at $1.89 a pound. That sort of thing. I ran into one such deal at *The Money Show* at the New York Coliseum in late 1978. From the brochure:

Registered Black Angus Cattle can be an investor's dream. They offer you, the investor, an opportunity to breed for top pure-bred animals like the "Seattle Slew" of thoroughbred horse racing. It [sic] also offers the romance of owning your own cattle and visiting the ranches where they are maintained and bred.

It's getting back to one's roots, the Old West, simply the good old days. [You know—before they invented the investment tax credit, which applies to cattle, the 20 percent additional first year depreciation, which also applies, and the $17,000 in management fees, all described elsewhere in the brochure.] Although registered cattle are *Expensive and Risky* they offer *Prestige*, the *Speculative Chance for a Big Profit*, and *Significant Tax Benefits*.

Not only that, but each potential investor is given a card to which is affixed his or her own personal vile—and I do mean vile—of genuine 100 percent pure Black Angus bull semen.

Financially alluring as the Old West surely is (this company is located in Miami), no one I know invested in this particular deal, so I cannot report results.

BEEFALO

I do have a friend, however, who's into beefalo. Beefalo are —well, I guess it's fairly obvious what beefalo are. My friend bought fifteen of them a couple of years ago, had them shipped to a farm he bought for the purpose in upstate New York (that part of the investment has worked out nicely, anyway), and hired a couple of fellows to look after them. From the back of the beefalo, this man is persuaded, will come the tenderloins of tomorrow, and he is out to breed all the thoroughbred beefalo bulls he can.

Yes, he is losing money, raising beefalo without looking to sell any yet, and in that way he is lowering his taxable income. But when the world turns to beefalo, it will, of necessity, turn to those few farsighted individuals like my friend, whose bulls will stand ready—and eager—to impregnate the thundering herd.

Imagine my friend's dismay, therefore, when he learned recently that his beefalo were about to give birth (the good news) but that they were, without any question, a full two months early (the bad news). Either the beefalo gestation period had been miraculously shortened—or one of the common longhorns from the neighboring pasture had jumped the fence, screwed my friend's beefalo and, with them, his tax shelter.

OIL AND GAS

Cattle shmattle, you say. Bring on the oil and the gas. And it's true: For the average individual, real estate and oil and gas deals are about the only remotely plausible ways to shelter income effectively.

The first oil deal I went into was with some classmates from business school, one of whom has since fled the country. I am not implying it was a bad deal, but I have yet to see a dime.

The second deal, I did *not* go into. It, too, was the creation of a classmate. (You are thinking, Ha! The one he didn't go into was the Big Winner. Not quite.) The deal offered a *guaranteed* oil well, all my very own—or your very own—for just $28,500. Admittedly, the well was not guaranteed to produce at any specific rate of flow. But even a few barrels a day, at $14 a barrel, adds up in the course of a 365-day year. These wells were to be drilled in places where you could hardly avoid hitting hydrocarbons. (Just as digging into the sand at the seashore will almost certainly draw seawater after a few feet.) On the off chance the driller *did* miss—well, then he would drill you a second hole at his own, relatively minimal, expense.

My own well. A dribbler, perhaps, but one that would allow me to deduct most of that $28,500 from my 1978 taxable income and that would provide a pleasing stream of (mostly taxable) royalty checks for years and years to come. I must say the idea was appealing when it was first presented.

I toyed with splitting the investment with a friend or two; I read the lengthy prospectus two or three times—all right, I skimmed it—and tried to puzzle out the pitfalls; I checked out my classmate's qualifications. Impeccable.

My classmate, for his part, had checked out the driller's qualifications—also impeccable. And although I finally decided the stakes were too high for me, "guarantee" or no, he actually managed to attract about a million dollars to the deal, in $28,500 chunks.

As it turned out, the driller, whose reputation is now peccable indeed, took the million dollars and relocated. Somewhere. My friend—at least as devastated as the investors who had sought a million dollars' worth of tax shelter in this deal—is in the process of trying to make good the money out of his own pocket. It could be a long process.

THE GOOD DEALS

I am not trying to give the impression that all tax-shelter deals are lousy. At least 5 percent are not. I know of one investment banker, for example, who managed to parlay a zero-cash outlay (he borrowed the front money) into enough of a write-off to wipe out his entire 1977 tax bill while actually producing enough oil revenue to put him in even greater need of tax shelter for 1978 and, it would appear, the next decade or two. After all, there *is* oil in the ground, it is in much demand, and *someone* has to find it. It just never seems to be us. (That particular deal was not open to the general public—not a doctor or a dentist in the crowd.)

Unfortunately, just because 5 percent of the tax-shelter deals are good (if that's the number), you are not assured a one-in-twenty chance of finding a good one. Unless you are very favorably situated—as a partner in a large investment or accounting or law firm, for example—you may *never* get to see the really good deals. Why? Simply because the lawyers and investment guys who design the deals in the first place are in serious need of tax shelter themselves; likewise, the tax accountants and others who peddle them. So if the deal is really good, it is likely to sell out to the pros long before there might be a half unit or two left for your Uncle Harry, the periodontist, or your sister Leslie, the newscaster, or even your brother-in-law Sven, the marketing vice president. The chances are good that by the time the limited partnership papers hit your desk—with a half-pound thud—several more savvy investors, who saw it first, will have already passed it by.

One solution to this—of sorts, anyway—is to set up your own tax shelter. Go in with a bunch of guys and develop your *own* shopping center, build your *own* porn-theater complex, breed your *own* Black Angus—and structure the deal yourselves. Obviously this is much more work, but nothing good comes easy.

MINOR LEAGUE HOCKEY

One fellow who had a chance to observe the do-it-yourself route is Robert Fierro, a business writer himself. Some of Fierro's friends decided to shelter their income a few years ago by setting up a minor league hockey team in —well, there already *were* hockey teams in New York and Chicago— Macon, Georgia. (Surely a better choice than, say, Key West or Port-au-Prince.) Fierro contributed, along with his dollars, the idea for the name of the team: the Macon Whoopees.

As he subsequently explained it, "The tax shelter in the Whoopees was the accelerated depreciation of the players' contracts. If a player had a $500,000 multiyear contract, you might be paying him $80,000 the first year but taking an *additional* $80,000 in depreciation on his contract."

Whoopee.

"As it turned out," Fierro continued, "you couldn't take the depreciation this way for minor league teams. Only in the majors." (A pothole in the loophole.) "The big lesson there is to do your homework . . . But more important," cautions Fierro, "the key to the Whoopees' failure"—for of course the team skated off the ice and into obscurity in about the time it takes to pry off a goalie's headgear and pound his face into crushed ice—"is that it was sold as a tax shelter when it should have been sold as an investment. And this is the biggest failing of the entire tax-shelter industry."

Time and again, that is the message: *Never invest in a deal for its tax benefits alone*—the primary attraction must be its business appeal. With the new tax law, this has become even more essential. You can no longer make money after tax by losing it before tax.

THE TAX PRO

"The new word in tax-shelter investing is *economics*," says Stuart Becker, who runs a high-powered tax accounting firm in New York. "A deal has to make sense as an economic proposition."

The biggest change is that from 1979 on—except in real estate—you may no longer deduct more on some deal than you actually have "at risk." Which means that the only way you can get a $25,000 deduction—which might *save* you $12,500 in taxes—is to risk *losing* $25,000 in cash. It used to be that you could risk, say, $5,000 to get that $25,000 deduction. So if the deal went bust, as it invariably did, who cared? The deduction saved much more in taxes than it cost.* But no longer.

The sense of this change is important. It is not unreasonable to encourage people to risk money in projects they think will make a profit. Investment is a good thing. And if profits do materialize, even more tax will eventually be collected. That is quite different from encouraging people to invest in *un*economic projects or allowing them to delay taxes by shuffling some papers without ever making any real investment at all.

Another change is that the I.R.S. is gradually becoming better at probing tax-shelter deals and throwing out the large number that stink. For example, if an agent happens across a deal he suspects while auditing one of the limited partners, he is now more likely to pull the tax return of the partnership as a whole and, eventually, if the deal's no good, the returns of all the other limited partners. Which is why more and more deals are now being structured not as limited partnerships but as "Schedule C" deals—individual proprietorships—wherein each participant is in business for himself. This way, two or three of the participants in the deal can have their deductions thrown out without flagging the returns of all the other participants.

In fact, the big gamble many tax shelterers take—in some cases knowingly, in some cases not—is simply that they will

---

* Although in theory, and sometimes in fact, the I.R.S. would eventually catch up with you and "recapture" much or all of the taxes you saved.

escape audit. Or that, if audited, their shelters will squeeze past an inexperienced or befuddled agent.

Take, for example, the Treasury-bill straddles that many sophisticated investors have been doing recently to shift income from one year to the next. The legal questions are exceedingly fine, but the essence of the matter is that T-bill straddlers take limited risk, buying and selling comparable T-bill futures contracts of different maturities purely for the purpose of trying to beat taxes. Inasmuch as two key tests of a valid tax shelter are that real risk be involved and that the transaction have a business purpose other than simply to avoid taxes, you would think that such straddles would not stand up under close I.R.S. scrutiny. "That's right," says Becker, who advises his clients against doing them, "but how many of the straddles will in fact be subjected to close I.R.S. scrutiny?"

The I.R.S. is outnumbered. A tax pro who earns well over $100,000 a year says it is very rare to find agents who really understand shelters. And when he does find such sharp agents, he hires them. Inevitably, the balance of brainpower remains heavily weighted against the I.R.S.

MASTER RECORDINGS

And yet even a three-year-old would be able to see through some of the deals taxpayers have been signing their names to.

"It's a combination of panic and greed," says ex-Whoopee fan Fierro, recounting the story of a young stockbroker we will call Ralph. It seems Ralph sent $10,000 in cash to some outfit in the Cayman Islands—people he had never met personally —to acquire the rights to a record album by a group of musicians he had never heard. In addition to the $10,000 in cash, he signed a "non-recourse note" for another $65,000 and wrote off the full $75,000 against his 1977 income, thus eliminating all tax. "Non-recourse" meant that the loan would only be repaid from proceeds, if any, from the album—Ralph would not be liable for the money otherwise.

Ralph told Fierro that he "couldn't stand an audit" but that, panicking again in November of 1978, he had just signed up for a second master recording deal with roughly the same particulars.

The man is perhaps suicidal, for he almost certainly *will* be audited. And when he is, there is a strong likelihood that his record deals will be thrown out. How, the I.R.S. is likely to ask for starters, did he arrive at $75,000 as the value of the first album? Why not $750,000? Why not—more to the point— $750? On this basis alone, Ralph's deductions are likely to be cut back to next to nothing, which will lead to a whopping tax assessment. He will have to pay everything he thought he saved in taxes, and very likely more. *Where will he get the money to pay?*

WALKING BANKRUPTS

Even tax shelters that *do* pass I.R.S. scrutiny, as many do, merely manage to defer taxes, not erase them. In theory, what one does with one's *temporary* tax savings is to invest them prudently so that when the day does come to pay, the money is there to do so. The problem is, a great many people *spend* their temporary tax savings instead. Feeling rich, they may actually be walking bankrupts, with huge tax liabilities hanging over their heads.

Nor can one assume that one's accountant will steer one clear of such pitfalls because he is an expert. (Never mind that he is an expert who may be receiving a hefty finder's fee for selling you a tax shelter.) It is astonishing how much poor tax advice is to be had—at a price, no less. Herewith at least a few of the caveats that sober-minded tax advisers have to offer:

• Never go into a tax shelter deal in a panic at the last minute. This is the surest way to get burned.

• Never go into a deal that, were it not for its supposed tax benefits, would be unattractive.

• Never go into a deal that seems too good to be true.

• Avoid deals that seem particularly "cute" or bizarre. (The more offbeat, the more likely to attract I.R.S. attention.)

• Never shelter income that would have been taxed at less than 50 percent (federally), only to have it come back as "unearned" income, taxed at an even higher rate.

• Always ask yourself why, if the deal is so good (or good at all), they are offering it to you.

• Avoid deals that are based outside the United States.

• Be aware that, other than in real estate, there is no longer any purpose to a non-recourse loan. So if you *do* sign a note as part of the purchase price of participation in a shelter, you might someday have to make good on that note, no matter how badly the deal has gone.

• Beware of deals that seem to have no economic function besides avoiding taxes. If that's how it looks to you, that's probably how it will look to the I.R.S. too.

March 1979

V
Sensational New Products

THE
LITTLE ENGINE
THAT DIDN'T

The last time Foote, Cone & Belding handled an automobile account was in 1957. They introduced the Edsel. Now, fifteen years later, Foote, Cone has another revolutionary auto to introduce—the Mazda—and things may work out better. The Mazda, as you may have heard, is the economy ecology backfiring racer with the little engine that could, can, and does . . . not to mention the world's fastest up-and-down electric radio antenna and a turn signal that goes click-et-a-tick-tick-tack, wipes and washes your windshield and dims and brightens your lights. Whatever you may have heard about it up to now is nothing compared with what you will be hearing next week, when Foote, Cone starts to spend half a million of the client's dollars in a six-week splurge for Mazda's New York debut.

Directing Mazda's marketing blitz is bound to be more fun than selling Edsels, but it is not likely to be a graceful way to grow old. The Mazda is one of those small Japanese cars— only it's not cheap ($2,900 to $3,200, plus). If the yen is revalued next spring, as is widely predicted, it will be still less cheap. Its styling is chubby and cluttered. It gets as little as 14, and no more than 22, miles to the gallon. It backfires. And if something goes wrong with the singular little engine, the now celebrated "Wankel" engine that is causing so much interest, there isn't one mechanic in a hundred who will know how to fix it.

At least when the Edsel was introduced there was Ford's

reputation and established dealer network to support it. The Mazda manufacturer, Toyo Kogyo, of Hiroshima, has no reputation to speak of in New York, and until a few months ago it had no dealers here, either. For all this, Mazda plans to be selling more cars in the U.S. by 1975—350,000 of them—than American Motors sells, even though American Motors has a twenty-year 2,000-dealer head start.

If it sounds like a marketing *Mission: Impossible,* it is. Every *Mission: Impossible* plot hangs on a technological wonder-gimmick that gives the good guys such a competitive edge that, really, they can hardly fail. In this particular episode, the edge is provided by Mazda's rotary engine. Consider:

The typical 120-horsepower engine has 166 moving parts— like pistons, rods, cams, valves and lifters—most of them either moving up and down, or engaged in translating that up-and-down power into round-and-round power. Each is a source of friction and vibration, and each is a potential source of trouble. Mazda's 120-horsepower engine has just . . . three moving parts. And they move round and round to begin with. So, it's quiet. At 70 miles per hour, the interior noise level of the Mazda is half that of the Vega GT.

Because it's so simple, Mazda's rotary engine is little more than half the size and weight of a comparable piston engine. It delivers nearly twice the power per pound. So, it's fast. From a standing start at 50th and Madison, a Mazda with a four-speed gear box will accelerate to 83 miles an hour by 55th Street, traffic permitting—and still be in third gear. (It should be noted that as the Mazda decelerates rapidly in anticipation of a red light farther down the track, the engine may very well let out one of its cherry-bomb hiccups from under the driver's seat. Harmless, but annoying.) Had they started alongside the Mazda, the $4,000 Porsche 914, the $4,500 Alfa Romeo 2000 Berlina, the $9,900 Lincoln Continental Mark IV, and the $10,900 Cadillac Eldorado would all have been left breathing in Mazda's exhaust.

But not much exhaust. This engine already meets proposed

1974 Federal emission standards; and no insurmountable difficulty is expected in meeting the 1975 standards that have Detroit climbing the walls of the Environmental Protection Agency. In effect, tiny Toyo Kogyo, with $800 million in sales to GM's $28 billion and Ford's $16 billion, has perfected what looks very much like the gasoline engine of the future.

In most places around the world, however, the Mazda hasn't been selling very well. In England and Japan, sluggish sales might be ascribed to the Mazda's uninspired gas mileage—no small matter where fuel is expensive—or to the absence of stretches of road long enough to get the Mazda into fourth gear. But what of poor sales in Florida, Texas, and the Northwest, where the car was introduced in 1970? The answer is that even a strong, perhaps revolutionary, product needs the right marketing stretegy to succeed, and until Toyo Kogyo hired C. R. (Dick) Brown to set up Mazda Motors of America in January 1971, it lacked such a strategy.

Brown, 39, with fourteen years' experience at Chrysler and American Motors, faced an unorthodox marketing challenge. Normally, an auto maker conducts extensive market research to find out what car buyers are looking for, or might fall in love with, and then orders up something from engineering that might fill the bill. In the case of Mazda, the engineering came first.

By the standards of any self-respecting marketing man, the car is conceptually quite sloppy. It's sort of an economy compact—but what about the gas mileage? It's sort of a hot performance car—with a station wagon in the line and styling like that? It's sort of a luxury car, but shouldn't it look more dignified and cost more? Shouldn't automatic transmission be standard equipment? And how come it runs on sub-regular gas? It's sort of an ecology car, only why all the zoom-zoom power at the expense of fuel consumption?

Few descriptions of the Mazda fail to highlight what *Car & Driver* magazine called the "irresistible urge to ease up beside more pretentious cars on the freeway, and then gas the Mazda and go sizzling away from them." "The Mazdas," wrote *The National Observer,* "are ideal for the Walter Mittys of the world."

"Is the car overpowered?" I asked Matt Lawson, Mazda's director of public affairs. "Definitely not," he said. An "overpowered" car, by Lawson, is one whose brakes or chassis can't handle the engine, which is not the case with the Mazda.

"All the same," I asked, "doesn't the car encourage speeding?"

Lawson, who has gotten only three speeding tickets in all the months he's owned a Mazda, didn't think so. (He would have gotten a fourth ticket, he says, if one of the troopers who stopped him hadn't become engrossed in a half-hour inspection of the engine.)

Dick Brown, president of Mazda Motors of America, confirmed that the Mazda does not have excessive power. It just seems that way, he explained, because "all the other small cars are underpowered." Brown, for one, tries to keep from greatly exceeding the speed limit, at least when he's in California, because one more ticket there and he loses his license.

Lou Scott, 48-year-old chairman of Foote, Cone's executive committee, has probably given this question more thought than either Lawson or Brown, because when a California judge heard that he had been going 100 in a 25-mile-per-hour zone overlooking Newport Beach, he sentenced Scott to four weeks of driving school, three hours a night. "The ticket was written up for a hundred," Scott confides, "but they never really caught up to me to clock it accurately." "No," he says, "the Mazda is not overpowered."

It's up to Dick Brown to find out what market segments the engineer-designed Mazda appeals to. So far, he has been able to narrow it down to, basically, "Everybody."

That's a pretty broad market segment. On the other hand, the Mazda has, temporarily, a monopoly. It's the only car sold here with the engine most auto makers are likely to be using by the end of the decade. When he took over in 1971, Brown lost no sleep over things like market segmentation. Instead, he blithely assumed that the Mazda line was good enough to become a major force in the U.S. auto market, and he based the rest of his decisions to expand that market—first the West Coast, now the Midwest and East Coast—on that premise.

After the product itself, which Brown had to take as a given, the dealer network is the most important element in an auto maker's marketing mix. In Florida, Texas, and the Northwest, almost anyone willing to handle Mazda had been signed up. Dealers in other makes took Mazda on as a second line, gas stations took it on, and even one lawnmower dealer was signed up.

Brown set stringent standards: dealers would have to have had long experience in the auto industry and substantial working capital. They would have to drop their present lines, or else build totally separate sales and service facilities for Mazda at a different location. In return, he offered large exclusive territories and an average $500 to $600 margin on each car sold, which is on the high side for cars in Mazda's price range. Ultimately, Brown plans 655 dealers nationwide, selling among them more cars than American Motors' 2,000 dealers, and accordingly, he hopes, with each individual dealer selling far more cars, at higher margins, than each individual American Motors dealer.

Though Mazda's dealers won't be on nearly as many street corners as their competitors, Brown reasoned that an automobile purchase is important enough to most buyers for them to drive across town—particularly while Mazda's engine is still unique. Also, in order to persuade people to gamble on a new, relatively untested car, he wanted big dealers whose own faith in the Mazda would be clear to prospective buyers from the size of the dealership and from the absence of any other make of car to help support the overhead.

One strategy would have been to scatter dealers all over the country as quickly as possible, so the man with rotary engine problems in Ohio wouldn't have a 2,000-mile tow to the nearest qualified mechanic. Instead Brown decided initially to hit one region hard—California, the nation's most competitive auto market. No import had ever been launched in California with such a big push before, but the gamble paid off. Mazda was introduced in May 1971 by 27 dealers. In the first three days, supported by the kind of massive advertising hitting New York next week, 86,000 people trooped through the showrooms, and in California, Mazda is already the fourth fastest selling import. The quick success in California brought 2,300 applications for East Coast and Midwestern dealerships.

As he set his dealer strategy, Brown simultaneously had to choose an ad agency from among the 50 that were bidding for the Mazda account. One agency presentation played down the rotary engine on the premise that it would be a liability. Who, after all, would want to take a chance on a relatively untested engine almost no one knows how to repair? Another agency got carried away by the engine itself, forgetting, meanwhile, to sell the car.

The West Coast arm of Foote, Cone & Belding, headed by Lou Scott, made an elaborate presentation stressing the rotary engine's high performance and promise of low maintenance costs—and got the account.

The advertising for Mazda's New York introduction will be much the same as it was for the California introduction. Virtually every newspaper in the area will carry an eight-page full-color advertising supplement in their Sunday editions headlined: INTRODUCING THE ONLY ROTARY ENGINE CAR IN AMERICA.

Four different television ads will go on the air to the tune of 500 rating points a week. A working definition of "500 rating points a week" is: enough rating points to make viewers see the ads in their sleep. Sports fans, considered a prime target, would be especially hard hit.

One Mazda executive admits that Foote, Cone's creative work for the Mazda campaign is nothing to shout about. But he points out that the Mazda is that rare thing—a product with a real product difference—and therefore doesn't need spectacular or highly creative advertising to differentiate and sell it. What's called for here, he insists, is informational advertising. "Foote, Cone," he says, "does very good journeyman ad-

vertising. They follow all the rules and are pretty straitlaced
—not trend-setting, but solid."

Lou Scott says, "The Mazda is an advertising man's dream,
but there's a temptation to get too hyperbolic. Other auto makers have bankrupted the language." Well, to take an analogy:
How would you advertise a margarine that really *does* taste
like butter?

To avoid sounding like everyone else, Scott's approach has
been "newsy and low-key, underpromising so as not to sound
unbelievable." The narrator of the TV commercials was asked
to convey "restrained enthusiasm." A sort of heartbeat sound
reminiscent of *A Man and a Woman* accompanies the Mazda
as it cruises around lush scenery. Scott calls this "a musical
accentuation to give a feeling of active dynamics to the commercial, and that feeling of restrained excitement." And in all
the ads, TV and print, extensive use is made of third-party
endorsements, which are unbelievably laudatory. (So much so
that one magazine editor said, "Did we really say that?" even
though they had, indeed, said it.)

Before developing their campaign, Foote, Cone tested the
following six headlines to see which produced the greatest
recall and created the most interest in buying:

A • THE ROTARY-ENGINE CAR IS HERE.

B • STARTING TODAY, YOU CAN DRIVE THE SUCCESSOR TO
THE PISTON-ENGINE CAR.

C • DETROIT IS SPENDING $50 MILLION FOR A CLOSE LOOK
AT THE ROTARY ENGINE IN OUR CAR. WE'LL SELL YOU
THE WHOLE CAR FOR $2,495.

D • G.M., FORD, AND CHRYSLER ARE ALL STUDYING OUR RO-
TARY ENGINE. THEY OUGHT TO STUDY THE WORKMAN-
SHIP IN OUR CAR, TOO.

E • IF EVERY CAR IN LOS ANGELES HAD A MAZDA ROTARY
ENGINE, YOU COULD SEE THE MOUNTAINS TODAY.

F • THE ENGINE OF THE FUTURE WILL GO 100,000 MILES
BEFORE MAJOR REPAIRS. OURS WILL DO IT TODAY.

The test proved what Foote, Cone calls "a basic rule of good advertising." If one believes this rule, one can tell from the headlines themselves how they will rank in the test results, or at least which two will be highest. The rule is that good advertising has to be more than newsy, even if the news is momentous—it has to emphasize consumer benefits. That, they say, is why F pulled best and E next best. It's not clear from the rule why A pulled better than B, C, and D. Perhaps there is another rule operating here about people preferring short sentences.

In the creative strategy Foote, Cone prepared for Mazda they said, "In order to position the Mazda, the prices . . . should also be mentioned [in every ad]." Brown did not agree. He felt the price itself was not a selling point and that it might discourage some prospective buyers from going for the all-important test drive. Others might automatically assume the overall quality and performance level to be about the same as other cars in the same price range. So you won't see any price in Mazda's ads.

If Dick Brown has been making the right marketing decisions, there may be quite a few Mazdas speeding past Cadillacs and Continentals along the nation's highways, cherrybomb hiccupping as they ease back into the slow lane. But the giant auto makers too plan rotary-powered cars, perhaps as early as the 1975 model year. "Our real job," says Lou Scott, "is to exploit the exclusive lead time we have to establish an image as the leader in rotary technology." Dick Brown thinks introduction of rotary-powered cars by other auto makers will simply help establish the rotary as the predominant automobile engine of the future.

November 1972

GOOD NEWS
IS
BAD NEWS

The Gillette Company—with production credits that include Flair disposable pens and Cricket disposable lighters—has put a new razor into national release. You could call it a sequel to Trac II, which itself sounds like a sequel, except that, really, the sequel to Trac II was the Trac II Adjustable. This new release isn't adjustable, it's—Good News!—*disposable.* The whole thing.

When you already dominate the shaving market and you can't make whiskers grow any faster than they've been growing, you have to be pretty inventive to keep those sales and earnings climbing. So Gillette is in the business of periodically outdoing itself. Every so often the company develops a brilliant new advance in "shaving systems," as it calls its razors—but the old lines are kept in production, too. This gives Gillette an ever-widening swath of display space at the checkout counter, in a business where display space is the name of the game. Thus we have Gillette Blue Blades and Gillette Super Stainless, Gillette Thin Blades and Gillette Platinum Plus, but also the Gillette Techmatic, the Gillette Trac II, the Gillette Twinjector, the Gillette Trac II Adjustable, and now, backed by more than $2 million in print and TV advertising, Good News!!

The first exclamation mark is part of the product name; the second reflects my tremendous enthusiasm. Just what the world needs these days—more disposable products. According to Gillette, "It's the most exciting razor in years." Even if it *isn't* adjustable. Gillette is proud of "its many unique features," but, in fact, Good News! is identical to the Trac II—the same kind of shave, the same number of shaves per blade—except that the handle, made of even lighter polystyrene, is joined permanently to the shaving cartridge. So when the blade gets dull, the *whole razor* becomes useless and—Good News!—you can throw out the whole nonbiodegradable thing! Also, there is a clear plastic cap that fits over the shaving head to protect it between shaves. ("It looks simple," a man from Gillette told me, "but actually a hell of a lot of work went into that plastic cap. It's 'state of the art.' ")

It used to be that you'd go to the store and buy a slim nine-cartridge Trac II refill; then, when one cartridge went dull, you'd flip it into the wastebasket and slip on a new one. *Now* all you have to do is buy nine razors, pile them in the medicine cabinet as best you can, take the cardboard promo off one, take off the protective plastic cap, shave, replace the cap; then when the blade gets dull, just toss out the razor and pull out a new one (without having eight others fall out of the medicine cabinet at the same time).

The commercial genius here is not to be denied. Gillette has rewritten the textbook strategy of "giving away the razors to sell the blades" (or the cameras to sell the film or the film to sell the photoprocessing). Now they're *throwing* away the razors to sell the blades. Which is, depending on how you look at it, either really giving away the razors (one comes free with every blade) or a clever way to get us to pay for a new razor every time we switch blades. If you can't sell more blades, start selling more handles.

Granted, at its introductory 25-cent retail price, which is about what a Trac II cartridge alone costs, the handle would indeed appear to be "free." At a quarter, except for its environmental cost, Good News! is a bargain. But my source at Gillette—call him Slit Throat, or Cutthroat if you prefer—suggests that that price may not last forever.* Already, the

* Daisy, Gillette's disposable razor for women, has been on the market for a year now, at two for $1.19. It differs from Good News! in

single razor for a quarter is being phased out, right on schedule, in favor of a 50-cent twin pack. Can three for 98 be far
behind?

Actually, I don't much mind Gillette's attempts to worm its
way deeper into my budget. I am a loyal Trac II customer, and
would probably be buying Good News! too, if I weren't somehow troubled by the image of 10 million or 20 million of these
things being tossed into the garbage month after month, year
after nonbiodegradable, nonrecyclable year.

My source at Gillette says the company thought long and
hard about the environmental impact of Project 49 (as it was
called before the name was selected, winning out over such
contenders as "The Clean Machine" and "X-12"), and it decided the impact would not be significant. Like one more used
car a day on the vast junk heap Earth.

For one thing, he pointed out, people are not likely to dispose of these things along the highway, as they do beer cans.
For another, Gillette doesn't really expect Good News! to cap-
ture a major share of the market. (And yet it bills it as "the
most exciting razor in years," and plans to tout it between
innings on an awful lot of Monday night baseball games.) It
was introduced on the basis of market research that showed a
certain segment of the shaving public would respond well to
such a razor. Far be it from Gillette to argue with the demands
of the marketplace. Some of those polled liked the idea of a
disposable razor because of the buildup of dirt or slime that
apparently can form on razor handles after months of repeated
use; hence the name "The Clean Machine." Others liked it
because they found a one-piece razor "conceptually easier to
deal with." These are the people who have trouble chewing
gum and changing blades at the same time.

Anyway, one of the environmental justifications put forth by

---

that it is pink and has a heavier handle. But once the elaborate packaging is removed, it is essentially the same instrument you can buy
for a quarter. Gillette is apparently confident that women won't catch
on, or, if they do, that they won't give up the pink packaging to save
58 percent of the purchase price.

my source was that Good News! would not become a major factor in the market. But the history of disposable pens and disposable lighters—and Gillette sells both—leads one to suspect otherwise. (Bic is already bringing out a disposable razor, and Schick will undoubtedly follow suit.) Initial sales reports on Good News! are quite favorable—one instance, at least, in which no news would be better than good news.

July 1976

COINING IT
AT
FRANKLIN MINT

The fluorescent light, the electric yo-yo, rice that won't over-cook no matter how long it's left to boil—it takes but a small leap of imagination for the nonmarketing mind to see that the financial world has its "new products" as well, even though they are by nature intangible. Things like listed stock options (five years old and already a major share of Wall Street activity) . . . dual-purpose funds (one class of investors gets all the dividends; the other, all the capital gains) . . . variable-premium life insurance (flexibility at a price) . . . Treasury-bill futures . . . real estate investment trusts . . . diamond funds.

Some financial entrepreneurs are content putting together deals. But others—the retailers, aiming to improve life for people like you and me—lie awake dreaming of their own better mousetrip (a barely visible thread strung half an inch above the floor). Generally, the cleverness of new financial products lies less in the substance of the product being offered than in the offer itself. I happen to have two such financial products right here.

An outfit set up shop in 1977 to launch two mutual funds: The Bull Fund, which would aggressively invest in stocks and options, and The Bear Fund, which would aggressively *short* stocks, to profit if they went down. You would put your money in The Bull Fund if you thought the market was headed up and in The Bear Fund if you thought it was headed down. Just by picking up the phone, you could switch from one to the other.

A very clever idea.

Not only did this let you in on the fun—by allowing you to decide which way the market was going—it also got the fund managers off the hook. If the market zoomed, The Bull Fund would presumably zoom with it (even though The Bear Fund would take a beating). Or if the market fell apart, The Bear Fund would profit handsomely (even though The Bull Fund would get clobbered). So if you didn't make money, it was your own damned fault.

With a good deal of hoopla—as well as the relatively high management fee that such creativity can command—the two funds were launched in May of last year.

They *both* went down.

If the fund managers were embarrassed (at this writing, shares in The Bull Fund, originally issued at $15, have fallen to $12.83 and in The Bear Fund to $9.85), they did not show it in their first annual report. The front page of that report makes no mention of the declining value of the shares. Instead, there is a chart that shows how an investor who had called each of the turns in the market—switching back and forth between the funds with perfect timing—could theoretically have had a 48.8 percent gain versus a 2.7 percent decline in the Standard & Poor's index. Yes, the fund managers quickly stressed, such theoretical success would have been virtually impossible to achieve in practice, but they wanted to illustrate the possibilities.

Nowhere in the report do they illustrate what would have happened to the investor who guessed *wrong* at each of those turns.

In truth, I suspect these two funds were offered to the public in good faith and with genuine enthusiasm. (There was no sales fee charged, just the high management fee.) And no great harm was done. For one thing, $5,000 was set as the initial minimum investment, which would keep most amateurs out of the game. And even at that, only a couple of million dollars flowed into the funds. Most prospective investors probably recognized the futility in trying to call short-term swings in the market (few tasks are more futile); and those who did feel confident in their ability to call market turns probably felt equally confident to choose their own stocks.

More calculating, perhaps, and much more widely advertised, is a second new product offered to the public by The Franklin Mint in cooperation with American Express.

A million or more American Express cardholders received the enticing offer in the mail, along with a cover letter from American Express. Franklin Mint, the world's largest private mint, was offering you the chance—up until October 31—to buy a proof set of 25 unique sterling silver gambling coins, one for each of the world's most glamorous casinos—from the casino at Baden-Baden to Caesars Palace, in Las Vegas, to Nairobi's Casino de Paradise. In the midst of the current gambling craze, what better way could there be to get in on some of the glamour, romance, and excitement?

Not only was each coin to be made of silver, it would also have an average face value of $25 (or the approximate equivalent in marks, francs, et cetera); you could actually walk into a casino and redeem it. But, as the offer pointed out, it is unlikely you would want to do so, since "they are likely to be far more desirable as collector's treasures." The edition was to be *limited*, available *only* through The Franklin Mint, and would *never* be offered again.

And to make this set of $25 gambling tokens—yours for just $35 each—affordable, you would not be billed for the full $875 plus tax at once. Rather, the tokens would be mailed to you once a month. You would be billed for each token in advance.

If Meyer Rothschild himself were still selling "old coins, rare coins," in Frankfurt, he couldn't have made them sound more attractive than these brand-new limited edition sterling silver $25-face-value gambling tokens.

Nowhere in the brochure or the ads was there any mention of how much the tokens would weigh. How *much* sterling silver? Might an unsophisticated buyer assume $25 worth? I called The Franklin Mint and after a little hesitation—the "collector services representative" knew everything about the offer but this—was told that the entire set of coins would weigh about sixteen troy ounces, $86 worth at current prices. Yours for only $875 plus tax.

Indeed, this has been a problem with many of the other billion dollars' worth of "instant collectibles" The Franklin Mint has sold to the public over the last eight or ten years. The items are often beautiful—the packaging always is—but how much of a premium over intrinsic value is that design work worth? One way to find out is to try to sell existing Franklin Mint creations. When people have tried, they have generally been disappointed.

Perera Fifth Avenue, a world-renowned coin-trading firm, makes a market in 600 different Franklin Mint issues. Only 25 of those currently fetch a price equal to or exceeding the issue price at Perera; the vast majority go for 40 percent to 60 percent less.

But this is where the real cleverness comes with regard to the casino coins. Perhaps sensitive to the growing public awareness that as investments, anyway, Franklin Mint items have proved abysmal, the mint dreamed up these, with their $25 face value. The implication being that you were not being sold silver at some ten times its intrinsic value but, rather, a marvelous set of rare coins at only a rather modest premium over their redemption value.

Sure. Buy a $400 airplane ticket, fly to Baden-Baden, and you will indeed be able to redeem one of your set of 25 coins for $25. Then fly to Nairobi to redeem a second, to Las Vegas for a third, and so on.

So, practically speaking, the $25 "floor" that these ads suggested as the minimum value for the tokens was little more than a brilliant marketing idea.

As for the collector's value of these tokens—based on their beauty and rarity—that is, of course, harder to assess. I asked the collector services representative at Franklin Mint how many subscribers the exclusive limited edition would in fact be limited to. There was a surprised stutter at the other end of the phone. "Why, to however many people order by October thirty-first, when the offer expires." It was limited to whoever wanted to buy it.

And the amazing thing—to this philistine, anyway—is that people *did* buy it. Personally, I would rather buy fifteen shares of AT&T, frame the certificate (which is approximately the same size as the case of gambling tokens), and watch it throw off $70 in dividends each year.

A Franklin Mint spokesman explains that only about 15 percent of their customers give "possible price appreciation" as their reason for buying Franklin Mint offerings. Which is good, he says, because he agrees with me: Collectibles, by and large, do *not* make good investments, except as "investments in pleasure." He is quite sure that Franklin Mint ads do not give any opposite impression. Perhaps he should read the ads again.

I have an extraordinary hypothesis with regard to financial new-product development. Namely that financial research and development, such as it is, is not conducted in search of ways to make investors richer faster safer—as in the case of the consumer's whiter brighter wash or the instant cup of soup —but rather primarily to make the sellers richer faster.

I'll grant that almost *any* new-product development, financial or otherwise, is primarily profit motivated—and I am all for profits and innovation. But if there is a difference between the soap researchers and the financial entrepreneurs, it may be this: With a new soap or a new soup, if the product isn't really so great, it will get bought just once—one sale per customer—and that's not enough appreciably to impoverish the buyer or enrich the seller. With a financial product, however, once may be enough.

November 1978

IN DAYS OF OLD
WHEN SLAVES WERE SOLD
AND
TRAVEL PRE-VEHICULAR

The title: *Opportunities for Industry and the Safe Investment of Capital; or, 1000 Chances to Make Money.* How could I resist? Written by "a retired merchant" and published by J. B. Lippincott & Co., this remarkable volume—the gift of a generous reader—is a full 416 pages, handsomely bound, beautifully written, and just $1.25 per copy. Unfortunately, it has been out of print for 120 years.

Today it's no trick to get rich. Any number of el-sleazo books tell you how to do it. There are, for example, *The Poor Man's Guide to Riches* ("Take a rolled-up newspaper and begin hitting the back of a chair violently, screaming, 'I want MONEY!' "); *The Lazy Man's Way to Riches* (Think positively and take out mail-order ads for get-rich-quick books); and *How to Live Like a Millionaire on an Ordinary Income* (Go into debt and become a consummate phony). Or you could just pyramid real estate *(How to Wake Up the Financial Genius Inside You!).* Or, "to prosper during the coming bad years," you could buy gold.

It was not always so easy. You didn't just get off the boat from the Old Country in 1859, flip open a matchbook, and settle down to earning $500 a week in your spare time. People walked around in those days muttering such homespuns as "Neither a borrower nor a lender be" (today: Borrow to the hilt) or, if they were a touch more highfalutin, *"Nullum bonum sine opere"* (Nothing good comes without work)—an old-fashioned notion if ever there was one.

Today you can buy a Sir Speedy® Instant Printing franchise or learn to resole sneakers; you can open up a Sum Tan® Tanning Salon ("the leader in America's booming tanning industry") or, with $50,000 and the right qualifications, a Mr. Dunderbak's Bavarian Pantry. Opportunities abound. (I myself was so taken with "the world's largest egg roll," not to mention the world's tastiest teriyaki sauce, that I actually wrote away for a Takee Outee® application.) And yet there are lessons to be learned from the past. The streets may not all have been paved with gold, or paved at all, in 1859—there may not have been tuxedos to rent ("13,000,000 Men Will Rent a Tuxedo in 1979," announces a firm with 141 franchisees that is looking for more) or federal tax returns to prepare ("A $15,000 investment will provide you an opportunity to participate . . .")—but, the Panic of 1857 notwithstanding, there was hope.

Can anyone forget the Panic of 1857? The anonymous author of *Opportunities for Industry and Capital*—A. R. Merchant, I'll call him—describes it as a "financial tornado . . . eclipsing the cyclones of the Mauritius and the simoom of Arabia in power of destruction, utterly prostrating houses whose foundations, it was supposed, were laid upon boulders of gold, and teaching a new generation the old lesson of the uncertainty of fortune."

There had been a boom (the prerequisite for any self-respecting crash), grounded in part in the 1849 California gold rush and consequent expansion of the money supply. Milton Friedman, had he been alive, could have explained it all very clearly. But, with the collapse of the New York branch of an Ohio bank, ebullience quickly turned to panic, and panic spread around the world. "How destructive an agent fear may be, is not by any means a modern discovery," Merchant noted in 1859. And yet, he counseled, "It is probable that we are at the commencement of an era when fortunes will be acquired with a rapidity unknown, save in rare instances, in past times." Profit margins, he predicted, would be less—competition would see to that—but in the aggregate those profits would be enormous. "For the last half century the world has been 'putting up its machinery'—its railways, steamships, telegraphs and lightning presses—and is now, we may say, for the first time, ready to do business."

One could make the same sort of case today. Things look bad. But we have in the last half-century laid a technological base that could, in theory anyway, make for an era of prosperity heretofore unknown. Unfortunately, Merchant's readers would have to wait out one of the bloodiest wars in history before his predictions could begin to bear them fruit; just as today it is hard to feel confident that things will get better without first getting worse.

I want you to know that as I have been typing this, with the finger of just one hand, I have been smashing a rolled-up *Wall Street Journal* over the back of an old chair, shouting—insofar as one can think, type, and shout at the same time—shouting sporadically, in other words, "I want MONEY!!" And I intend to keep smashing and shouting as I lay out for you 1,000 chances to make a little. Some, like trafficking in slaves, may require adaptation to current U.S. tax law; but many remain applicable virtually without modification.

• *Inside Information.* Speculating in securities "with the advantage of early information," as Merchant puts it, has always been good, and it has never hurt to spread a little early *mis*information just prior to making your move.

• *Dealing Drugs.* Two high roads to profit in the mid–nineteenth century, as today, were drugs and monopolies. Imagine combining both! Reports Merchant: "[T]he East India Company, until recently abrogated, [was] the most gigantic monopoly for private emolument in the world. Its shipments of Opium to China alone, in the years 1848–9, were 57,918 chests, which, at $600 per chest, amounted to $34,750,800. Who can calculate what an amount of misery was produced by one single year's trade!"

• *Breeding Slaves.* Another source of colossal profit, although no more to Merchant's liking than opium, was the traffic in slaves. Even assuming the loss of a million of them in transit, Merchant figured the profits from this trade over the preceding fifty years at some three quarters of a billion dollars. It would be fascinating to know which of today's landed gentry trace their wealth back not to the robber barons—awkward enough—but to the great slave traders.

The slave trade was substantially diminished by the time *Opportunities* was written, but still was estimated to ship 30,000 Africans annually to Cuba and "the Brazils." The *New York Herald* budgeted the typical shipment of 400 slaves at $133,050 profit, after all expenses, gratuities, and commissions.

• *Real Estate.* "In cities, some very large fortunes have been made by the rise, in value, of town lots. Nicholas Longworth, of Cincinnati, has made a fortune of several millions by the rise of property, a portion of which he was compelled to take from debtors against his inclinations." (It was his *other* inclinations that compelled him.)

Merchant speaks of struggling cabbage gardeners near New York whose "small farms became as valuable as dukedoms."

• *Trading in Furs.* John Jacob Astor got his start this way, we are told, having been given the notion to do so by a fellow passenger aboard a vessel trapped by ice in Chesapeake Bay. (A future John Jacob Astor would get his *finish* in even icier waters, aboard a vessel called the *Titanic.*)

• *Peddling Pencils.* You may have heard of the stereo salesman who styles himself "Crazy Eddie." Or of the ad agency executive who, according to legend, got turned down by a prospective client, returned the next day—up the elevator and into the reception area—with a horse painted blue. "A horse of a different color." He made his point (whatever his point was) and, supposedly, got the account. If you want to make money, you've got to stand out from the crowd. You've got to be noticed. Merchant describes a Parisian pencil peddler who would stand on his cart dressed in gold-embroidered green velvet, rings all over his fingers, with a man he employed to blow a trumpet from time to time. "Why do I rig myself up in this ludicrous costume?" he would ask the crowds that gathered. "I will tell you candidly: because by going about in this dress I sell a great many pencils, and if I stayed at home in a warehouse coat I should sell very few." At two sous apiece he sold enough to accumulate a fortune estimated at 400,000 francs.

• *Rock Concerts.* Barnum sent a singer named Jenny Lind on a 95-concert tour, paying her an incredible $2,000 a night, and through the magic of his advertising managed to clear for himself $712,161.34. That it was the magic of his advertising rather than the magic of Jenny Lind that turned the trick is suggested by Barnum's equal success in attracting people, so Merchant tells us, to just about anything, "no matter how unattractive the subject of his speculation—whether an old woman, a mermaid, a dwarf, or a woolly horse."

• *Advertise.* There is no substitute for it. "Even those who say they never advertise," Merchant argues, "generally falsify their assertions by putting a sign over the store-door behind which they sit, waiting for customers, sometimes until hope deferred maketh the heart sick, or the Sheriff ousts them. . . . But the largest fortunes have been made by those who, without neglecting other auxiliaries, have placed their reliance principally on Printer's ink as an agent of advertising." A professor was reportedly spending $150,000 a year advertising his pills. A doctor in Philadelphia annually printed and gave away some 2.6 million "almanacs," in eight languages, the better to sell *his* nostrums. Merchant quotes *Freedley's Practical Treatise on Business:* "Put on the appearance of business, and generally the *reality* will follow." Recently, three immigrant brothers with nothing to speak of borrowed $3 million to advertise the snug-fitting blue jeans they had designed. They chose expensive spots on classy shows to make it look as if they were a large and established outfit. And they employed sexy topless models—green velvet suits and trumpeters—to be sure their ads would be noticed. At last count, they were shipping $3.5 million worth of goods *a month.*

• *Invent Something.* A good substitute for the coffee bean

would be a hit, Merchant felt, and he suggested that asparagus might contain the key. (Alternate route: "Dig up the roots of the dandelion, wash them well, but do not scrape them; dry them; cut them into the size of peas, and then roast in an earthen pot, or coffee roaster of any kind. The secret of good coffee is to have it fresh roasted and fresh ground." And, of course, to start out with top quality dandelions.) Aluminum, "a recently-discovered shining white metal," could probably be used for something. Artificial milk, which had the advantage of staying good for years, could be made, Merchant advised, of egg yolks ("yelks"), gum acacia, honey, and salad oil. Add water and stir. As for artificial ice, this could be a *very* big business. A machine had been invented for making ice not long before Merchant sat down to write, he says, but it cost too much to turn a profit.

Other things the world was wanting: some new kind of leather that would "combine the durability of calf-skin, the water-proof qualities of India Rubber, and the appearance of Patent Leather" (Corfam®!); a "substitute for Alcoholic Burning Fluids" (the first oil well was drilled that same year, in Pennsylvania); an economical process to adapt oil from coal (yes, and hurry!); a substitute for tobacco ("It is no exaggeration to say, that there are thousands of persons whose trembling nerves are anxiously awaiting the announcement of the discovery of a substitute for Tobacco, which shall possess its agreeable properties with none of its injurious effects"—this a century before the Surgeon General's report); "a new Drink, pleasant, wholesome, and exhilarating, without being intoxicating" (Coca-Cola?); "an efficient Apparatus for extinguishing Fires"; "a cheap substance that will effectually expel Musquitoes from rooms";* "a new plant combining the strengthening qualities of animal flesh with the healthfulness of vegetables" (the beefsteak tomato?); and, while you're at it,

---

* Merchant had already found the answer for roaches: "Strew the floor of that part of the house infested by [cockroaches] with green cucumber peelings cut not very thin. . . . A repetition of fresh peel for a few nights will effectually clear the house."

"a means of preventing Gas Lights from flickering"; "a Cooler, for keeping parlors or rooms cool in warm weather"; and "a substitute for Pen and Ink, combining both in one instrument" (the Bic Banana).

To which I would append: a typewriter that may be operated verbally (leaving both hands free to smash newspapers over chairs); an automobile that would consume as its fuel pollutants from the air (leaving as its residue an accretion of auric oxide); and, of course, an affordable self-making bed.

Other Mercantile suggestions: camel breeding ("The Camel has been found well-adapted for traversing the plains of Texas and the far West"); sardines ("the whole Southern coast is said to abound in that small but valuable fish"); oysters ("These, and Ice and Granite are among the great natural products of America"); mules ("Requiring far less food than the horse to keep him in good condition, yet capable of more constant labor, the mule, *as soon as the best mode of managing him is understood* [italics mine], will probably supersede the horse in team, draught and all slow and heavy work"); and finally, one of my favorite little money-making schemes—a climate-controlled city, in which streets were warmed from below by "carrying the smoke of all the chimneys into drains." I think the Disney people are working on it.

Opportunities includes also a formula for removing freckles, another for curing drunkenness, and a particularly appealing recipe for "Blackberry Diarrhea Cordial." And secrets such as "How to tell a Kicking Horse," "How to subdue a Kicking Horse," and (for that particularly recalcitrant Kicking Horse) how to turn horses into chicken feed.

Not that Merchant is without skepticism. Breeding camels for Texas transport is one thing; but growing orange and lemon trees in Florida? "Those who have attempted [such] cultivation," he warns, "have not as yet realized the results which are so prophetically depictured. At all events, it is always well, and we here repeat the admonition, to 'look before you leap.' "

In contrasting some of the modern and ancient schemes for making money—today you can make a bundle, ads say, installing peepholes in front doors; then you could invent rubber—it's easy to feel that the grandest opportunities are gone. This is hardly the case. It is the difficulties and discomforts more than the opportunities that are gone. And today many of the opportunities come packaged, instructions and all.

What is needed is what has always been needed: ingenuity, a little bit of seed money, and a great deal of hard work. An advanced knowledge of semiconductor technology doesn't hurt, either. It takes longer to get to the edge of technological progress than it did in Merchant's day. And yet the opportunities that are now gone—automobiles and flying machines having already become established realities, as Merchant predicted they would—simply serve as the tools with which to realize the next set of opportunities.

As for obtaining seed capital, Merchant surprisingly omits any mention of banging newspapers on the backs of chairs, or even taking out a Small Business Administration loan, favoring, rather, a steadfast resolve to spend a little less each week than one earns. He describes the wealthy New York realtor who, by contriving to save 50 cents a day from his bricklayer's wages, saved a full $180 his first year in America, building from there.

"Such considerations as these are full of consolation to the aspiring and of encouragement to the very poor. None need despair, and moreover, none need be dishonest. It is possible to accumulate capital, aye, to get the first thousand dollars from an income not exceeding the most moderate earnings or wages. And let it be inscribed on the lintel of every dwelling —on the desks in every counting house—on the pericardium of every heart—*It is better to live on ten cents a day than to do a wrong for the sake of money.*"

June 1980

"THE MOST ORIGINAL AND EXCITING MOTION PICTURE EVENT OF ALL TIME"

TIMES SQUARE—Night.
The first plan was to have a stuntman dressed as Kong scale the Allied Chemical Tower and drop the ball that ushers in the New Year. With the proper advance notice to the networks, it could be a million dollars of free publicity.

The problem was, a man in an ape suit looks awfully puny against the Allied Tower. So Paramount's publicity pros opted instead for the news ticker that runs in a belt of light around the mezzanine of the building. With ample notice to the networks, and for a mere $2,000—the cost of reprogramming the computer that feeds in the news—they arranged to have the following news item printed out every eight minutes from six o'clock on, and to be the last message to cross the tape in 1975: PARAMOUNT PICTURES AND DINO DE LAURENTIIS WISH ALL AMERICA A HAPPY KING KONG NEW YEAR.

Smart. But who ever heard of promoting a movie—and advertising it in double-page spreads—a full year before release? Even before the start of its monstrous 26-week shooting schedule?

One scents an ulterior motive.

LOS ANGELES—Day.
Fade in on a roomful of lawyers. The senior partner of a 70-man Century City law firm, Arthur Groman, is taking the

sworn deposition of the chairman of the board of MCA/Universal, Lew Wasserman. These are very big guns we are talking about. A court stenographer transcribes every word:

GROMAN: Did you ever see *Godzilla?*

WASSERMAN: Yes.

G: Did you ever see *Godzilla and King Kong?*

W: Yes.

You have no idea how many grown men and women have been working on, and battling over, the remaking of *King Kong.* Lawyers, artists, publicists, blacks in ape suits, Vietnamese refugees to be passed off as Indonesians, court stenographers, extras from Watts to be passed off as aborigines, movie magnates, tire magnates, an optometrist, more lawyers, a part–American Indian Jew who speaks fluent Italian . . .

Next to Ted Kennedy's appearance on the Howard Cosell show in November, perhaps the silliest—and very possibly the biggest—thing that has been going on in the entertainment business in recent months has been the battle between Paramount and Universal over *King Kong.*

It cost RKO $650,000 to make the original film in 1933. The Dino De Laurentiis/Paramount Pictures remake is budgeted at $16 million, "and I be very happy it comes in at-a budget," De Laurenttis says. The recently aborted Universal remake—which Universal still threatens to make someday but probably won't—was budgeted at another $10 million or so. Neither figure includes legal fees. Some movies don't gross what these two have been racking up in legal fees. The suits and countersuits between Universal, De Laurentiis, and RKO make the Rin Tin Tin copyright action against *Won Ton Ton, the Dog Who Saved Hollywood* seem like a friendly nip on the ankle. Tinsel Town has been temporarily transformed into Deposition City. (Beverly Hills: the city with a brokerage office on every corner, where the cars that look like Ford Granadas turn out to be Cadillac Sevilles, home of the pink-and-green Beverly Hills Hotel.)

It began this way, in December 1974: Michael Eisner of ABC is watching a rerun of *King Kong* on TV—and he suddenly has an idea. A short while later, he and his wife are dining with Sid and Lorraine Sheinberg. Sheinberg, Columbia Law '58, is the 41-year-old *very* smart president of MCA. How about a remake of *King Kong*, Eisner suggests. He is offering the idea gratis, just because he would love to see it done. Sheinberg stares blankly, which Eisner takes as a sign of lack of interest. It is not lack of interest, but Eisner doesn't know this—so a few days later he makes the same suggestion to his friend Barry Diller, 34-year-old *very* smart, newly installed chairman of Paramount Pictures. Zoom in on Diller's blond-peach-fuzz face: *tremendous enthusiasm.*

Diller enlists De Laurentiis; Sheinberg recruits a producer —Hunt Stromberg, Jr.—for Universal. And so, each unaware of the other's activity, the two entertainment giants begin to move along parallel courses.

(Not everyone agrees it began this way. De Laurentiis insists *King Kong* was his idea. His daughter, Francesca, had a *Kong* poster up in her bedroom, he says, and every morning when he went in to wake her, he would see it and think about doing a new *King Kong*. Then, he says, he and Diller were talking and Barry said they should do a monster movie and Dino said, "King-a- Kong!")

THE HARVARD CLUB OF NEW YORK—Day.
It is shortly past noon, April 15, 1975. Arnold Shane, of MCA/ Universal, and Daniel O'Shea, of RKO General, are having lunch. O'Shea, in semiretirement for the last fifteen years, receives a commission for negotiating sales of the properties in RKO's library. Since by far the most valuable of these is *King Kong*, O'Shea refers to himself as "the zoo keeper." He has long been negotiating RKO's deals, but hasn't the authority to close them or to sign any papers.

Shane, Stanford Law '54, has been sent by Universal to find out what O'Shea, Harvard Law '30, wants for the rights to *King Kong*.

De Laurentiis and his executive vice president, Fred Sidewater, the part–American Indian Jew who speaks fluent Italian, have also been in New York negotiating with O'Shea. Each party is aware that there is "another bidder"; neither party knows who. One meets with O'Shea in the morning, the other that same afternoon.

(Fortunately, in this drama it is easy to keep the players straight. All those with D's in their names—Diller, De Laurentiis, Bluhdorn, and Sidewater—are on one team. The Sh's —Sheinberg and Shane, and even, slurring it, Wasserman, Stromberg, and Universal—are on the other. The O-apostrophes—O'Neil and O'Shea—are caught in the middle. RKO'Neil, RKO'Shea.)

Anyway, here are Shane and O'Shea at the Harvard Club. Shane has brought a memo summarizing the points of the MCA offer: $200,000 cash plus 5 percent of the net profit. As Shane tells it, these terms have already been accepted, and they are just meeting to firm up details. He hands O'Shea the memo and O'Shea proceeds to read it. "He was putting his finger under each line as he was reading," Shane says, and "moving his head back and forth." They discussed the memo paragraph by paragraph, agreed to a few minor modifications, and then O'Shea put it down and said, "That's fine. We have a deal." Only he wouldn't sign it.

O'Shea's recollection of the Harvard Club meeting: "I did not make any agreement, written or oral . . . never told him we had an agreement, nor words to that effect . . ."

Somehow, though, Universal—which didn't get into this game just yesterday—became persuaded that they had the go-ahead. Dino, meanwhile, was offering $200,000 plus 3 percent of the *gross*—and *10* percent of the gross once the picture had recouped two and a half times its cost. *That* deal RKO officially accepted and eventually signed.

Comes the first week in May, and Dino and Universal discover that they are *both* claiming to have bought exclusive rights to remake *King Kong*, both gearing up for production.

The race is on; lawyers begin gathering like storm clouds.

By the end of May, Dino et al. are already being sued. In the six weeks since making an oral agreement at the Harvard Club, Universal charges, it has expended lots of time and money, including $19.38 in labor for a screening of the original *King Kong*. In recompense, it demands $25 million.

The affair is now "in litigation." A tight shroud of secrecy falls over the case. Half a year passes.

Despite the shroud of secrecy, huge ads begin appearing for the De Laurentiis picture, with Kong astride the World Trade Center under the headline THERE STILL IS ONLY ONE KING KONG. (As an afterthought, Paramount's publicity people throw in a line in small print at the bottom—not even a coupon—offering a free full-color poster reproduction of the ad. Sixty thousand Kong fans respond, including the executive editor of the *Georgetown Law Weekly*, the chairman of the Department of Newborn Medicine at Saint Francis Hospital, and a representative of the embassy of the Republic of China.)

De Laurentiis is attempting to assert himself, get the jump on Universal, and make it clear to any prospective juror that *should* Universal somehow be allowed to remake *King Kong*, he will lose a potential *fortune*. In December, De Laurentiis countersues for $90 million.

The Universal strategy seems to be to lie low, litigious— and menacing. Exuberance versus stony silence. It is a multi-million-dollar game of chicken, because everyone agrees it would be insanity to have *two* remakes of *King Kong* coming out at the same time. But who will back down?

A story appears in *Variety:* "Justified or not," it begins, "Dino De Laurentiis has created a strong—and sometimes angry—impression among minority actors here that he is looking for an 'ape-like' black actor to play the title role in *King Kong*. Whatever the intent, it's undisputed that a number of black males were summoned to De Laurentiis's studio last week where they were introduced to Dino's son, Federico, and asked to jump around and hop." Several weeks later, *Time* attempts to set the record straight: "Originally, De Laurentiis planned to use a man in an ape suit for the close-ups of

Kong. [But because of the uproar] now he will use a $2-million, 40-foot mechanical ape—throughout." *Wrong.* In addition to the mechanical Kong, he is using *three* black men in ape suits, complete with huge brown contact lenses. Three, because each is adept at a different kind of apelike movement.

Clearly, the time has come to dispatch a financial reporter from New York.

ON LOCATION

It is 84 degrees and sunny in Beverly Hills, and one or two shriveled Christmas trees have yet to be carted away. Happy King Kong New Year. I am sitting at the counter of the Beverly Hills Hotel coffee shop, reading the De Laurentiis *King Kong* screenplay, by Lorenzo Semple, Jr., wondering whether a $16 million-plus production budget can be supported by lines like "You goddamn chauvinist pig ape, what are you waiting for? If you're gonna eat me, EAT ME!" (The Fay Wray character, "Dwan," quickly relents: "I didn't mean that!—I swear I didn't! Sometimes I get too physical, it's a sign of insecurity, you know? Like when you knock over trees?") Barbra Streisand was interested in the Fay Wray role, but she couldn't start shooting until May. With Universal in pursuit, De Laurentiis couldn't afford to wait for her. Goldie Hawn was briefly considered but nixed. It was decided instead to take Jessica Lange, a New York model, and make her a star. She has never acted before.

I am at a party given by an owner of Roots Shoes, whose house looks down on Los Angeles as from Olympus. A shuttle limousine has been engaged to ferry guests from their cars up to the house, where parking is limited. I'm told this house was previously owned by an elderly couple who one day mistook the accelerator for the brake while backing out—and into the valley below. They survived, miraculously, but decided to sell the house. Houses are the subject of much conversation here, and they are expensive. Dino just bought one on *eleven acres* in beautiful Beverly Hills. I am asking people at this party

whether they know anything about *King Kong;* they are asking
me how one company, let alone two, could be so fired up
about remaking the classic in the first place. Surely not based
on the performance of the *Auntie Mame* and *Lost Horizon*
remakes, they observe dryly.

But consider Kong:

KONG'S CHEST. It covers the screen, a heaving mass like a
football field in December mud, growth clinging to it,
branches and weeds and clods of earth. . . . Powerful and
black and terrifying and unseeable. Incomprehensible.

KONG'S FACE. A simian colossus. Wells for eye sockets, nos-
trils set in the skull like howitzers, ears that flare from the
head like trees, and a mouth like a volcano, mandibles that
come down like granite towers and a jaw like a Himalayan
cliff. But it is the eyes that give him away, eyes that see, eyes
that feel. . . . With all the massive other-worldliness of this
creature, it is his eyes that are the great anomaly—like those
of a sensitive, retarded, oversized boy, every giant who has
ever lived in fiction from Lennie in *Of Mice and Men* to Gul-
liver.

I am reading Universal's script by the hotel pool, wondering
whether Universal will be able to bring to life the magnificent
images that Bo Goldman has written for them. (They have
been experimenting with a man in an ape suit running
through a miniature forest. This much I know.) All Universal
has let slip is that Joe Sargent, who directed *The Taking of
Pelham One Two Three,* will direct *The Legend of King Kong,*
as they are calling theirs, and that Sensurround ("the vibration
that made *Earthquake* so unpleasant"—*Time*) will be used to
enhance Kong's roars, his Manhattan rampage, and his final
Empire State Building battle. (Universal's script follows the
original very, very closely.)

I have come to think of this pool as Nat Cohen's. I don't
know for sure who Nat Cohen is, but I do know he is a much
sought after man. "Nat Cohen, telephone please. Mr. Nat
Cohen, telephone. Mr. Cohen. Mr. Nat Cohen, telephone. Mr.
Cohen." The operators at the Beverly Hills Hotel send his

name out over the pool loudspeakers with a special relish (as they do later in the day for a "Miss Suzy Creamcheese"). He is paged constantly, a half-dozen times for each call. There are only fifteen or twenty others by the pool ("Mrs. Ustinov. Mrs. Ustinov, please"), including, at one point, a Stephen Cohen, whose name I may be misspelling, and Sam Cohn, the super-agent, whose name I would not dare misspell. It was as if half the world were a man named Cohen, and the other half were trying to reach him.

I am at the pool so much because I am waiting for the first day's shooting on the De Laurentiis picture. With Dino I have been allowed to see everything.

The original *Kong* was done with eighteen-inch miniatures. De Laurentiis is building a hydraulic computerized forty-foot version. After shooting in the studio, the big Kong will be shipped to New York and, De Laurentiis says, lifted by heli-copter to the top of the World Trade Center for shooting there.

Construction is beginning on a $1 million primitive wall, 400 feet long and 75 feet high, for Kong to burst through (only to be doused in 1,000 gallons of "chloroform"). A Navy ocean-ographic vessel has been rented as a prop—$250,000 for three weeks in and around San Pedro harbor. Ten crew members are already on location in Hawaii—an interior location acces-sible only by helicopter, four of which have been chartered for the shooting; ten people are in New York plotting Kong's demise; and the current problem is to find the supertanker in which Kong is supposedly transported from Skull Island to Shea Stadium by the environmentally ruthless oil company. (Remember, this is the 1976 version.) Even at $35,000 a day, supertankers are hard to come by on the West Coast. If only his friend Onassis were still alive, De Laurentiis moans.

Three days later, they are ready to start shooting. De Lau-rentiis hops into his chauffeured Rolls-Royce for the drive to San Pedro.

AERIAL VIEW OF TRAFFIC BELOW—Dusk.
Personalized license plates are the Beverly Hills ego equiva-lent of Spanish Harlem subway graffiti. A brown Mercury: NO

KIDZ. Another brown Mercury, with the driver on the phone: HYDRIL. A Jaguar XJ6: UA (United Artists). A silver Mercedes 450 SE: EX CMA (the former talent agency). Also: JEFF B, RUSTY P, HARVARD, CAN WE, OOLLOO, GENRE, PITHY, and a light blue Rolls-Royce with white hardtop: ESTEST. My favorite, on a big silver Buick: T AND E.

Directing all this traffic from up in radio KGIL's single-engine Cessna is—the camera pans up from his hands on the controls to his face—Francis Gary Powers.

Dino is up to his elbows in *King Kong*. Unlike most of his movies, he is producing this one himself. It is, he admits, "the biggest picture I have never make."

A hundred union technicians mill around the set, waiting. Finally a shot. More milling, waiting. Take two. It goes this way, and will continue, painstaking bit by painstaking bit, for about half a year. The payroll runs nearly $300,000 a week.

We leave the set for dinner. What is the best Italian restaurant in New York? I ask, never quite sure Dino knows who I am or what I am doing sitting across from him. "The best Italian restaurant New York is-a my apartment," he says. His apartment is on Central Park South. He has, too, his home in Beverly Hills, one in Monte Carlo, one in Italy (where he left behind a failing production studio to come to the United States), and one at the Gulf + Western resort in the Dominican Republic.

The only things I learned about Dino at dinner that I had not already read elsewhere were: (a) he began thinking in English about a year ago; (b) he has five people in his office working to translate virtually everything he reads—*overnight*—into Italian. *Ragtime* he read in Italian the day after the manuscript arrived in English. He bought it the following day. Later, when there is less of a rush, he may read it in English.

MEANWHILE, AT UNIVERSAL. . .

No one at Universal will talk with me about *King Kong*. The public relations woman assigned to me has never even seen the original *King Kong*, let alone have any poop on the new one. Producer Hunt Stromberg, Jr., reached at home in bed with the flu—he hasn't been ducking my calls, he really *has* the flu—is awfully nice, but answers all my questions with "All I can say, according to the lawyers, is that we are proceeding with the picture."

Well, they are proceeding with their lawsuits, anyway. There are two of them, one filed in state court, the other, later, in federal court. To the layman, they seem a bit contradictory. The first one says: RKO made the deal with *us*, not De Laurentiis, so *we* have the rights to make the movie, not him (never mind that he has the signed contract). The second one says: Rights? Who needs rights? *King Kong* is in the public domain and we are proceeding with our picture on that basis.

So why should Universal bother to remake *King Kong?* If the courts decide that Universal, not De Laurentiis, owns the rights, they can let De Laurentiis make it and then sue for all his profits. If the courts decide Universal does *not* have the right to make the picture, it would look pretty silly to have spent $10 million to make it. And even if the outcome were that *both* studios could go ahead with their films, how much profit would Universal stand to make competing against De Laurentiis and the original *Kong?*

The rational thing for MCA to do is not to make this picture. It becomes partly a question of getting the best possible settlement (what would Dino and Paramount give to be done with all this?), and partly a question of saving face.

On January 29, a settlement is announced: the suits between the two movie companies will be dropped (but not against RKO). De Laurentiis will make his movie; Universal, if it makes one at all, will wait at least eighteen months. The financial settlement is kept secret but is highly favorable to Universal.

Paramount says it will open De Laurentiis's *King Kong* in 1,000 theaters across the country at Christmas. It will be billed as: "The most original and exciting motion picture event of all time."

February 1976

VI
Mergers
and
Impositions

THE DAY
THEY
COULDN'T FILL
THE *FORTUNE* 500

The largest merger proposed in the nation's history [General Electric's $2 billion acquisition of Utah International] will not be challenged by the Justice Department.

—*The New York Times*
October 2, 1976

NEW YORK, March 3, 1998—It wasn't such an awesome decision, really, and it had to be made, so Carol J. Loomis,* formerly one of *Fortune*'s most gifted writers and now, in 1998, its managing editor, made the obvious choice: They would *still* call it "the *Fortune* 500," even though this year there would be only 479 companies on it.

The day had finally come.

In prior years it had been possible to fudge a little: In 1991 the list had been broadened to include firms based outside the United States; in 1995 nonindustrial companies had been added to the list, where previously they had been accorded their own lists.

But now there was nothing for it, unless you wanted to include some of the Soviet bloc or Chinese state enterprises, a step which *Fortune*—every bit as much a capitalist tool as

* Carol Loomis, an editor of *Fortune*, was not consulted in the preparation of this story.

Forbes—simply would not take. (Not that the communist firms were really so different from the many *non*communist giants that were government-owned.)

First on *Fortune*'s list again this year, it would surprise no one, would be Citicorp, with worldwide assets, expressed in American dollars, of $1.2 trillion.* Over the past 22 years, Citicorp assets had grown at a more or less steady 15 percent, right on target. Buried somewhere in that total were this writer's automobile loan (and 17 million others, worldwide), his mortgage (the lines between savings and commercial banks having long since been erased), and a vast computer network that, with others like it at the seven rival global megabanks, had largely eliminated the use of checks and significantly lessened the use of cash. The same Citibank computer network handled this writer's brokerage transactions and travel arrangements, prepared his taxes, reminded him of upcoming birthdays and holidays, clipped his municipal-bond coupons, evaluated his creditworthiness, and would doubtless have scrambled or unscrambled his eggs for him, as it did his bank statement, had he been of a mind to sign up for the service.

The remarkable thing was that Citicorp had managed to expand so dramatically, swallowing so many other banks and financial institutions in the process, and yet still keep its payroll down to the 50,000 or so who were needed to man the infant operation back in the mid-1970s. Where once there had been fifteen clerical people at a work station, now there was a thumbnail-size silicon chip. Tellers now were mostly electronic. Mail boys had been replaced by robots—beginning as long ago as 1975. The entire margin department of what had once been the brokerage firm of Harris, Upham & Company, files and all, was now contained in a Citibank computer cell the size of a pack of Salems. Almost all of the *people* on the payroll in 1998 were officers. Several hundred were in the $250,000-plus compensation range.

---

* *Fortune* had switched from sales to assets in making its rankings when nonindustrial companies were added to the list.

Second on *Fortune*'s list this year would be Aramco, with stockholders on six continents but more than 80 percent of its shares in the hands of the Saudi royal family—which itself had spread lavishly over six continents. Once a largely American-owned oil operation, the global energy combine had most recently acquired a million square miles of Brazilian interior —640 million acres!—which Brazil, desperate to outbid Japan for an assured long-term source of energy, had reluctantly bartered. Valuing this land at $100 an acre, Saudi Aramco had in one falcon swoop added $64 billion to its asset base, putting it, too, over the trillion-dollar mark.

There followed the predictable list of megabanks, multinational energy combines, conglomerates, IBM, and AT&T in much the same order as in 1997. But it wasn't the rankings so much as the process of growth itself that had started Loomis ruminating.

In a way she couldn't complain. Her bank service was excellent; her phone service—miraculous (it now cost only 35 cents for the first minute to call from New York to Tokyo, although the rates to Westchester and Long Island were still somewhat higher). Her hamburgers were uniformly nutritious and quality-controlled, her brokerage commissions were cheaper than they once had been, and many of the companies she dealt with, although subsidiaries of one or another giant, were left largely on their own so long as they produced adequate profits.

And yet she was troubled. Somehow it struck her wrong— and had as long ago as 1976—that Marquis Who's Who, the snob-appeal company, was just another arm of ITT; that Dannon Yogurt had sold out to multibillion-dollar Beatrice Foods; that Halston was part of Norton Simon; that Welcome Wagon was part of Gillette; that Simon & Schuster was part of Gulf + Western; that *Indiana Farmer* magazine was one of the American Broadcasting Companies. What had really killed her was when, years later, L. L. Bean had been merged into Spencer Gifts, a division of entertainment octopus MCA.

The day *The New Yorker*, too, went to MCA—MCA had long been looking for a profitable magazine to acquire—had been even more depressing. Loomis had canceled her plans for a weekend out in Long Island's sludge-free zone and just moped around her apartment.

This relentless conglomeration troubled *Fortune*'s managing editor, but she couldn't say for sure that, on balance, it had been a bad thing. As for the executives who had built and now directed these giants, she considered most of them brilliant, ethical, tremendously hardworking men and women. They had played by the rules—and won.

Part of the problem, Loomis reflected, was just that—competition. Competition in industry was not like competition in an athletic league. In an athletic league, teams are of equal size and get to start out with a clean slate at the beginning of each new season, no matter how badly they have been clobbered. In a competitive economy, the strong tend to get stronger and the weak tend, over the long run, to go out of business.

The brokerage industry in the 1970s was just one example. In the spirit of free enterprise, the U.S. government had stepped into the securities industry to require price competition. As a result, commissions were cut, weak firms were liquidated or merged into stronger ones, and what had been a highly fragmented, largely inefficient industry became by the end of the decade a handful of efficient firms. (Their absorption in the following decade into still larger financial concerns simply completed the process.)

The same thing happened with the airlines in 1979, when the government lifted its price and route regulation, only there had been fewer companies in the industry to begin with.

And it happened throughout the economy generally when the government began cracking down in earnest on what the courts had come to define as "tacit price fixing." The crackdown—at first—was hailed with great enthusiasm by all but the tacit price fixers themselves. It was given much of the credit for slowing inflation to a crawl—but then most of the blame for plunging the country, and with it the rest of the world, into depression. The Econolypse of '81, it was called, although it actually stretched well into 1986. Truly aggressive competition had led to truly horrendous bankruptcies, which in turn led to a self-fulfilling lack of confidence in the future.

Vigorous competition was a requisite for a healthy economy, Loomis reflected, but *winners* posed a bit of a problem.*

It wasn't only competition, by any means, that had led to a world of 479 giant enterprises. It was largely the process of conglomeration—of old family managements selling out for estate reasons; of young entrepreneurs selling out to cash in big; of financially straitened companies merging into solid ones (particularly during the Econolypse); of acquisitive managers spying opportunities for synergy (at best) or for easy growth (at least); and of empire builders collecting assets as Midas once collected money.

My God, she thought, just look at what had happened! In the last three decades, small-town banks by the thousands had become BankAmerica branches (81,000 in all on six continents). Luncheonettes and family delicatessens had folded in droves under competitive pressure from McDonald's and McDeli's (two of eleven McCorp Corp. subsidiaries), from Jack-in-the-Box (a Ralston Purina subsidiary), and from Burger King (a Pillsbury subsidiary). Local groceries had given way

---

*She recalled a ditty Malcolm Forbes had spotted which illustrated the problem neatly:
You're gouging on your prices if
You charge more than the rest.
But it's unfair competition
If you think you can charge less.
A second point that we would make
To help avoid confusion:
Don't try to charge the same amount—
That would be collusion!
You must compete. But not too much,
For if you do, you see,
Then the market would be yours—
And that's monopoly!

—*R. W. Grant,* Tom Smith and His
Incredible Bread Machine

to Grand Unions or to 7-Elevens. (Along with Gristedes and many others, the 7-Eleven chain was even in 1976 an arm of Southland Corporation. Grand Union was a branch of the British-based Cavenham empire. Abroad, Southland and Cavenham were partners.)

Small proprietorships had become branches of subsidiaries of divisions of subsidiaries of conglomerates. And this was before taking any notice of the interlocking directorships *between* the sprawling giants.

What some called diversification, Loomis had as long ago as the mid-1970s thought of as corporate dilettantism. General Tire operated radio and TV stations and an airline (Frontier) and bottled Pepsi-Cola; General Electric was acquiring Utah International, a California-based mining conglomerate with major interests in Australia; General Motors grew coffee in Brazil; General Mills owned Parker Brothers; Parker Pen owned Manpower; Manpower operated service stations under contract to Shell; Greyhound, once a bus line, was in the meat-packing and computer-leasing businesses; LTV, the steelmaker and aerospace firm, was a major factor in meat packing, too; and Esmark, the largest meat packer of them all, was making dental supplies and panty hose and drilling for oil in the North Sea.

In 22 years the pace of conglomeration had, if anything, picked up. Take publishing. By 1976 many small newspapers had been consolidated into chains, such as Britain's Thomson Organization (148 newspapers and 138 magazines); most airline magazines had been consolidated into a single publishing company, East/West Network; and a company called Professional Sports Publications was putting out programs—once highly local affairs—for no fewer than 27 pro teams. But in 1983 all three of these—the Thomson chain, East/West, and Professional Sports—were picked up in rapid succession by publishing behemoth McGraw-Hill.

Rival publishing giant Macmillan, meanwhile, after a brush with bankruptcy in 1982, had been acquired by Mobil/Marcor, the oil-and-retailing giant, and had, with this new backing, gone on to acquire MCA, Morton Salt, and Motown Records. Analysts began to wonder whether strategic planners at Mobil/Marcor/Macmillan had decided, in a moment of corporate whimsy, to go after only *M*'s—when without warning the company turned around and acquired Belgium.*

Carol Loomis closed her eyes. All she could see were corporate logos, corporate slogans, corporate letterheads. Then she had a vision of a Gulf Stream IV zooming across the sky at supersonic speed with Harold Geneen, still deferring retirement, waving from the window. Geneen, whose ITT would be nineteenth on this year's list, with assets of $122 billion, was one of the original, and most adroit, conglomerateurs. Charlie Bluhdorn was another, and he, too, had not let up. A vigorous 72, he had in the past eight years added to Gulf + Western, among others: Perdue Farms, the Lefrak Organization, Federated Department Stores (which included, as of 1976, Rich's, Bloomingdale's, I. Magnin, Burdine's, Bullock's, and Filene's, and had subsequently added Abercrombie & Fitch, Franklin Simon, and Zayre, Bally Manufacturing, and the E. & J. Gallo Winery). All had gone kicking and screaming to Gulf + Western, which the average man on the street still mistook for some kind of far-flung railroad. Financiers marveled at how Bluhdorn, cursed as always with a pitifully low stock market multiple, had managed to pull off these acquisitions, but pull them off he had.

The antitrust division of the Justice Department, which enjoyed a confidence rating of 8 percent of the public even in 1976, could not begin to cope with the conglomeration of the world economy. Its big effort of the late 1970s and early '80s, the crackdown on tacit price fixing, valiant though it was, had brought on the Econolypse and, with it, a spate of colossal desperation mergers. (It was the Econolypse that finally ce-

---

* Why not? The Belgians were a practical people, and Mobil's terms had been good. If countries could own companies (as, for example, Britain owned British Steel or Iran owned the Iranian National Oil Company), why couldn't companies own countries?

mented Chrysler to Volkswagen, for example.) To the extent Justice *was* able to keep firms from acquiring related concerns, it merely forced them to go outside their fields of legitimate expertise in search of growth.

Beyond that, lawyers in the Justice Department were ridiculously outnumbered and undercompensated vis-à-vis their corporate counterparts. And much of the conglomeration had been achieved abroad, where U.S. antitrust regulations did not apply. A favorite merger haven, particularly after Mobil acquired it, was Belgium. Just as U.S. firms had once favored Delaware as their state of incorporation, so now multinational firms tended, for technical purposes anyway, to be headquartered in Belgium.

As for other regulators, well, they had gradually been made to see private industry's point of view. For example, there had been the marathon bargaining session late into the night of March 3, 1983, when the bankers agreed, for their part, not to foreclose on the cities, and the President agreed, for his, to see to it that the banks be allowed to cross state lines. ("The President is still the President," opined one dismayed columnist, "but Citibank's Walter Wriston, apparently, is chairman of the board.")

Conglomeration, competition, automation, economies of scale, corporate elephantiasis . . . in 1964 there were 1.2 million egg farms in the United States (statistics like this stuck in Loomis's head; she didn't know why), and by 1976 the ranks had been thinned to 200,000, of which 4,000 accounted for 90 percent of production. By 1997, seven major producers accounted for 98 percent of total production, and all but one were subsidiaries of larger firms.

It was all damnably efficient, damnably rational, and Loomis found it damnably depressing.

She turned her attention back to the list. There *were* more than 479 companies in the world, she knew she would have to explain in her preface. There were still tens of thousands of firms that ranged from one-man shops up to what once would have been considered a fairly good-sized company. But the gap between these and the 479 giants was enormous. It would have looked silly to put even a company with $248 million in assets on the list, when the next largest, United Immortality (hospitals, nursing homes, artificial organs, blood banks, sperm banks, vitamins, pharmaceuticals, and health foods)—number 479—had assets of nearly $7 billion.

There were still small companies, and any man or woman with enough gumption and modest backing could still try to build his or her own business. But as the giant corporate sector of the world economy had ballooned, the independent entrepreneurial sector had shrunk nearly to nothing as a proportion of the whole.

Loomis had worried over this problem on and off for 30 years and had never come up with much of an answer, except perhaps to think of what the Chinese were doing. (The Chinese, in the mid-1970s, were stressing local economic self-sufficiency, even at the expense of efficiency and economies of scale.) Lots of people had worried about this problem, but nobody had come up with much of an answer. The problem was so abstract and corporate momentum so overwhelming that no one had done much of anything at all—and this was the result. And Carol Loomis was not even sure that it was bad. But it troubled.her.*

December 1976

---

* Three weeks after this story appeared in *New York* magazine, *New York* magazine was itself without warning acquired by a multinational giant.

EPILOGUE
Can America
Find Happiness
at 55 M.P.H.?

In the past five years, from the fall of 1969 to the fall of 1974, the market value of all the companies on the New York Stock Exchange, adjusted for inflation, has dropped more than 80 percent. The market value of companies on the American Exchange is down more than 90 percent. (In England, adjusted for inflation, the *Financial Times* Index is back to where it was in 1935.) And real per capita income lately has been going backward, not forward.

There is some comfort in the thought that if we're going to have a 1929-style stock market crash it may in fact already be over. Netting out the deflation of the early 1930s and the inflation of the early 1970s, the current plunge approaches the magnitude of the former one. But even if it turns out that the worst of the damage to the stock market has already been done, the dire economic scenarios that *underlie* these depressionlike stock values have yet to work themselves through. Life in this country is still nearly as rich, in material terms, as it has ever been. "Look up, America, see what we've got," exhorts Coca-Cola, "let in the sunny side of living."

That constructive message struck a responsive chord in the summer of 1974, but two other songs have become themes of the summer as well. (Feel free to sing along.) "Good things, GOOD THINGS, don't last for-e-ver," runs the first—and the suntanned throng on the discotheque floor belts out the words en masse—but "Where do we go from here?" runs the second—"Please tell me, Where do we go from HERE???"

Devastated stock prices, among other things, suggest we may not be going exactly where we'd like to be going from here. Forty-six percent of us, according to Gallup's latest poll, think we are headed for the Second Great Depression (G.D. II). Some sophisticated financial observers agree. I think it is unlikely, particularly if we, and other countries, cooperate in making the sacrifices necessary to avert it. But I am convinced that as a nation we are going to have to learn to live happily with less affluent visions dancing in our heads. We will still be a nation, I trust, where anybody has the opportunity to acquire an air-conditioned house with a pool, two big cars, and a snowmobile—but no longer a nation where *everybody*, given time, might hope to do so. Many individuals will still see their living standards rise as they climb the rungs of the economic ladder and as their savings mount; but the ladder itself will no longer rise. It may even slip back a few feet into the mud. It may be that we will be doing exceptionally well over the next couple of decades just to keep our average standard of living constant, where once it would have been unthinkable not to expect more/bigger/faster almost every year. If this is so, it would make better sense to lower our expectations somewhat than to keep them high and be disappointed year after year. (Mind you, I personally still expect to be fabulously rich one of these days, but I have scaled down my definition of "fabulously rich" and stretched out my definition of "one of these days.")

"Labor is determined to keep wages rising faster than inflation," reports *Business Week*. But consider some of the factors that stand in the way of an ever more affluent society. Chiefly, our good life has been built on three things: cheap resources, cheap labor, and technology.

Resources. The summer before I entered college, in 1964, we prospective freshmen were asked to read *The Challenge*

of Man's Future by Harrison Brown. Written in 1953, no less.
On the cover were quotes from Albert Einstein, William O.
Douglas, and a Nobel prize winner named H. J. Muller, who
said, "If we choose to remain ignorant of the facts in this great
book, we choose a fool's paradise." *The Challenge of Man's
Future,* like *The Limits to Growth* nineteen years later,
merely extended man's various growth curves out into the
future, compared them with estimates of the earth's finite supply of resources, and found that the future would end right
around the turn of the millennium, give or take a century or
two. Even in 1953, Harrison Brown was talking about "coal
gassification" and "breeder reactors" as ways to extend our
energy supply.

So, really, this is an old story—ecology, the population ex-
plosion, etc.—and I apologize for that. But when General Motors decides to hold up plans to switch more heavily from big
cars to small cars, and when oil companies consider reintrod-
ucing trading stamps to goose up gasoline sales, to take just
two examples from recent news reports, it seems that the same
old story, with variations, is likely to be repeated over and
over and over again for quite some time.

Admittedly, most of us and most governments have enough
trouble trying to get next week to turn out right, let alone
worry about twenty years hence. Slow-motion crises, the
media know, are much less salable than easily photographed
disasters. But it does seem as though in the next century, if
not the next few decades, Homo sapiens will have to put up
or shut up, after millions of years of evolution. Things will
either get very sticky indeed (with another 12 billion new
faces coming on stream by the time our children are reaching
retirement, at present birth rates, and with nuclear devices
already in some very hungry hands), or else perhaps we will
find ways of taking control of our future and of learning to live
within the limits of a finite planet.

Now, it is true that as nations develop, birth rates tend to go
down, and that in America we have finally reached the "replacement rate," at which, on average, each parent brings into

the world one child. (Contrary to the widespread misconception, this does *not* mean zero population growth, because parents do not pass away immediately after childbirth. There are more people being born than dying each day by a wide margin. Not until 2040, if the replacement rate is maintained, will the U.S. population stabilize—at 320 million.)

But the ranks of those with high expectations for material comfort are growing even faster than the population as a whole. Television, among other things, is for the first time beginning to wave America's tempting automobile/appliance/luxury/leisure life-style in the faces of hundreds of millions of people who might, in the last century, have been content to live a simpler life. And while I would be hard pressed to argue that we should keep our affluence a secret, I am equally hard pressed to see any way to fulfill the desires and expectations that more and more people are beginning to have.

Consider: in ten days America's 200 million people consume as much energy as India's 600 million people consume in a year. If India, a "developing nation" (nuclear-equipped, no less), really developed along the lines we have, then their energy consumption would have to increase a hundredfold. Yet our 5 percent of the world's population already consumes 45 percent of the world's energy production—so for India's needs alone, world production would have to double. And then what about China? Indonesia? Ecuador? Our own coal supplies, which are estimated to hold us for the next 300 years, would last only 75 years if we met India's needs as well.

Indeed, if industrialization is what's needed to slow the population growth in underdeveloped countries, we may be in big trouble. It just doesn't seem feasible that the earth will be able to support development of these nations—at least not along the lines we ourselves have developed. To bring the rest of the world up to our present standard of living would require in the first place the production and support of nearly 2 billion new automobiles. Not to mention a quadrupling of the world's grain production.

In short, the age of cheap resources is over. And that simply has to pinch the American standard of living.

Cheap Labor. Well, let's see. We freed the slaves. The flow of those fabulously industrious European immigrant laborers has slowed to a trickle (and they've joined unions). The Depression-trained workers—who as any foreman knows really put in a day's work for a day's pay—are retiring. We have all but eliminated hunger as an incentive to productivity, what with our unemployment and welfare programs. The Europeans and Japanese are no longer willing to work for peanuts. Cesar Chavez has organized the grape pickers. Two million military men are now paid civilianlike, rather than slavelike, wages. Sanitationmen are demanding, and getting, as much pay as architects. Women are demanding equal pay for equal work. There's the minimum wage. And indirect labor costs now include massive pension and medical plans, as well as the costs of safer and less noisy working conditions.

And all of these developments are good, of course. But crushingly expensive.

Most importantly, the productivity gains that were the foundation of our steady improvement in the standard of living have ceased—indeed, gone into reverse—at least temporarily. Where can you raise capital these days to improve productivity? And, of what capital *is* available, a good proportion must go to cleaning up the accumulated pollution of the last generation and to assuring that we don't leave the next generation with an even bigger mess.

The obvious result of all this is that you can't hire a pro football player for anywhere near as little as you used to, let alone a sleep-in maid. But the less obvious result is that as major portions of the underpinnings of our economy come due for renewal, the cost of renewing them is staggering. Buildings and water pipes and railroad lines and West Side Highways that were built with a high proportion of cheap labor must now be renewed with labor that demands the good life.

The thing I used to love about going to Europe when I was

in college was the play money. A friend and I spent a week in
Tossá in 1967 and shared a modern room with bath for $4 a
night each, which included a good breakfast and an excellent
dinner. We were financial giants in a Spanish Lilliput. (Even
their cars were tiny.) What power! What luxury! And, I supposed, but couldn't quite figure out how, what exploitation! It
struck me that something was very much out of balance. And
things out of balance have a way of swinging back into balance.

We are having to share the good life with hundreds of millions of people who once worked for us for next to nothing.

Technology. The *deus ex machina,* of course, though it
seems to be coming a little late for the starving children of
Africa and Asia, is technology.

The earth was formed 4.6 billion years ago, give or take.
(Time enough, Believe It Or Not, for you to spend a full year
in bed with every man, woman, and child and still have 600
million years left to write the great American novel.) Nothing
much happened in the first 4.599 billion years. In the next
million years man invented his arms and legs and caves. In
the 100,000 years that followed, he invented language, tools,
the wheel, fire, primitive warfare, and agriculture. Five thousand years later he had invented recorded history, pyramids,
pornography, chariots, and the Dark Ages. Five hundred
more: gunpowder, printing, the steam engine, and the Industrial Revolution. And in the last *one hundred* years he has
invented—everything. Electricity and oil wells (power), automobiles and airplanes (transportation), telephones and television (communications), the computer, the laser, the light
bulb (twinight doubleheaders), and nuclear energy (world an-
nihilation).

On the one hand, if we could accomplish all this in the last
hundred years, surely we can accomplish *anything* in the next
hundred. On the other hand, it might be said with equal fair-
ness that this blistering and accelerating pace of development
just might blister us all off the face of the earth. But in any

case, to say that the "energy shortage" was really an oil-company-induced hoax, and that technology will rescue us from our growth curves as it "always has," may be a little shortsighted, because by "always" what people are referring to is the last hundred years or so, out of 4.6 billion.

Now, I grant you that curves are gradual things and that only an abrupt, unnatural act like the Arab oil embargo helps to bring the general trend into focus. The world will certainly not end tomorrow. We will continue to have our upticks, and are in no imminent physical peril. But that makes the situation all the more insidious, as it makes the problem harder to keep in mind. It also makes it harder to convince the poorer segments of society of the need for lowering their expectations. Understandably, they have a lot of catching up to do before wanting to sit back and take a long-term global perspective on things.

Somehow, though, the message must be gotten across. Two messages, really. One is this "mega-economic" message, if you will, concerning the long term—that we will have to learn to live happily with less. The other message is much more immediate. It seems that this country and the rest of the industrialized world is teetering on the edge of bankruptcy and depression. We are overextended. We have borrowed too much from the future in an effort to meet these tremendous expectations of ours. Too much fly-now/pay-later (it's later); too much personal, corporate, and government debt. As *Fortune* put it in its August [1974] editorial: "Despite all the recent professions of puzzlement concerning the U.S. economy, there is no mystery about what is basically wrong with it. The economy is suffering from an excess of claims. The claims upon the output of society add up to more than the output. . . . Government says yes too much, promises too much, and tries to provide too much for too many."

In large measure, the world is at the brink because of the new cost of energy. Oil is by far the most important commodity in world trade—$135 billion worth in 1973 compared with

$5 billion for second-place sugar. If you think of each country as a separate, competitive business enterprise, you will see that the oil-producing nations are beating hell out of the oil-consuming nations.

Why are interest rates so high? Largely because of foreign borrowing to pay for oil. Why are stocks so low? Largely because of high interest rates. Why is the housing/construction industry already in its own private little depression? Oil. Why is inflation so high? In large part because of food and oil. And food? In large part because of fertilizer, which in large part . . .

American wealth in massive amounts is being transferred from our pockets through the oil companies and the utilities to the oil producers. The profits that Exxon and Con Ed siphon off along the way, though they may look large, are nothing at all compared with what the Arabs and others are taking. (Per capita income in Abu Dhabi is up to around $47,000 a year.)

Now it happens that by driving smaller cars slower, you save an awful lot of oil. In doing so, you slow the outflow of American wealth and you relieve considerable pressure on the precariously strained international financial situation. You may even help to lower the price, as there is a fine line between glut and shortage, although the crude oil producers, aware of this, are busily cutting production back apace. Furthermore, by driving smaller cars slower you conserve a precious world resource, you still get where you're going (and isn't that the main idea?), and, as a special introductory offer, you save tens of thousands of lives. (That in turn should lower auto insurance costs and lessen the need for expensive safety equipment.)

Do you know how boring it is to drive at 55 miles an hour? As one who sports speeding tickets from Maine to Georgia, and for whom 70 to 80 has always been the ideal cruising speed on all but dirt roads, I tell you that 55 miles an hour is very boring. But not nearly so boring as a depression.

To me, the following measures under the circumstances seem absolutely irresistible:

1. The national 55-mile-per-hour speed limit should be

willingly observed—and strictly enforced. Emergency vehicles would of course be exempted; and trucks and buses, perhaps, in the interest of the economy, might be allowed a 60- or 65-mile-per-hour speed limit.

If everyone is driving 55 miles per hour, it becomes somewhat less frustrating. At least you are going as fast as everyone else. I have found also that driving at 55 in the fast lane, or at least in the middle lane, affords a certain perverse satisfaction by way of compensation. I strongly recommend it as a way of gently reminding others that we are going down the drain to the Kuwaitis.

One might even try driving with the windows open. The noise and the rush of air makes 55 seem more like 70. And the need to use the fuel-hungry air conditioner is thus eliminated.

2. Everyone should go for a tune-up. Apparently, a well-tuned engine can save a lot of gas.

3. People should learn how to drive. One automobile club found that gasoline efficiency could be increased by as much as 44 percent if driving habits were improved over a typical stop-and-go commuter route. The A.A.A. makes suggestions like this: Avoid excessive warm-ups when starting a cold engine. It may be necessary on cold mornings to depress the accelerator once to set the automatic choke—and added pumping will only waste gas.*

* Other tips from the A.A.A.:
Don't rev up the engine and then quickly shut it off, thinking you've primed it to restart. Actually, you've dumped raw gasoline into the cylinder walls where it may wash away the protective oil film and increase engine wear when you restart. It's also a waste of fuel.

Look well ahead to spot slowdowns and red lights. Pace yourself to reach them when they turn green. A car uses much fuel when accelerating quickly from a complete stop. Keep a good space in front of you so you can adjust your speed gradually without closing the gap on the car ahead. If stops are necessary, release the accelerator early and brake gradually.

Smooth "footwork" is crucial to good gasoline mileage. You'll get the best fuel economy by smooth, steady accelerator pressure for

4. To encourage attention to such details, and the purchase of smaller cars—which is by far the best way to save fuel—a dollar-a-gallon gasoline tax should be imposed. This would bring the cost of our gas up to the level that has prevailed in Europe for years. The bulk of the tax should be divided up equally among American taxpayers in the form of income tax cuts. This would put most of the money back into consumers' pockets and increase the incentive to earn and invest money —improve productivity—while serving to cut back significantly on our gasoline consumption. President Ford's 10-cent-a-gallon excise tax was the right idea, only much too small to do the job.

5. Any corporate purchasing agent who buys or leases a fleet of large cars should be shot. He is unnecessarily dipping into the common pool of oil—yours and mine—and, to add insult to injury, he is passing the cost of the big cars on to the consumer in the form of higher prices. Large corporate cars and limousines must become symbols not of prestige but of corporate irresponsibility.

6. Likewise private cars. If the image of big-car-as-status-symbol can be changed, it may not be so painful to ride around in compacts.

7. And rental companies, which relentlessly favor big cars even though most of their customers are single passengers, should make subcompacts and compacts their standard

---

cruising conditions. Gradual acceleration and braking are also helpful. Hard acceleration pours more fuel into the engine for more power, but the fuel is incompletely burned and mileage suffers.

When approaching a hill, build up speed early to avoid fuel-robbing hard acceleration on the upgrade.

A.A.A. tests have shown that when air conditioning is not in use, fuel economy improves by 5 to 14 percent or more. Air conditioning also adds weight—about 100 pounds—to a car, increasing fuel consumption even more.

Top quality radial tires usually will result in a 5 to 10 percent fuel saving. Steel-belted radials are generally even better than fabric-belted radials in this respect.

models—at reduced prices, of course. They should offer bigger cars only to the people who demand them. And corporate expense-account policy should prohibit rental of the large cars unless they are needed to carry several passengers. (Corporate budget cutters would love such a rule, if only it did not put them at a disadvantage with their employees relative to the perquisites offered by other companies.)

8. Analogous steps—incentives and disincentives—should be devised to cut the fat out of our use of electricity, air conditioning, and heating.

This is hardship? This is suffering? Really, the wonder—and the rush of relief—comes in recognizing just how much fat this country has to lose before it really hurts. Indeed, it may prove to be less a matter of reducing expectations than simply of shifting them. Smaller cars but, someday soon, video discs, wall-sized TV's and crystal-clear digital recordings. Fewer human servants (who can afford servants?), but the prospect of astounding electronic ones: telephones that forward calls and redial busy numbers, home computers and word processors, programmable microwave ovens, robots to eliminate the dullest assembly-line jobs, machines that will read aloud to the blind. Increasingly expensive and less lavishly heated and cooled houses—but improved health care, increased longevity,* cleaner air, and (my personal favorite) two dozen television channels to choose from. The economic ladder may not sink into the mud, after all—just tilt in a somewhat different, less energy and resource intensive, direction.

Finally, I offer two thoughts. First, it is said that Americans eat too much. We would actually be healthier if we ate less, particularly less high-priced beef. Second is this quotation from a book called *Stone Age Economics* by Marshall Sahlins:

By the common understanding, an affluent society is one in which all the people's material wants are easily satisfied.

* In the 1970's the average American lifespan increased three full years, from 70 to 73!

...[But] there are two possible courses to affluence. Wants may be "easily satisfied" either by producing much or desiring little. The familiar conception, the Galbraithean way, makes assumptions peculiarly appropriate to market economies: that man's wants are great, not to say infinite, whereas his means are limited, although improvable: thus, the gap between means and ends can be narrowed by industrial productivity. . . . But there is also a Zen road to affluence, departing from premises somewhat different from our own: that human material wants are finite and few, and technical means unchanging but on the whole adequate. Adopting the Zen strategy, a people can enjoy an unparalleled material plenty—with a low standard of living.

Well, this kid is not about to adopt a Zen strategy. But he has found life in a New York floor-through apartment surprisingly bearable without air conditioning this summer; and a little spaghetti hasn't killed him either.

September 1974

APPENDIX
THE DECADE
AT A GLANCE
(And Other
Sad Details)

APPENDIX
THE DECADE
AT A GLANCE
(And Other
Sad Details)

THE DECADE AT A GLANCE

	OPEN	CLOSE
VALUE OF $1	$1	54¢
DOW JONES INDUSTRIALS	800	838
IBM (price)	73	64⅜
(dividend)	80¢	$3.44
AVON (price)	85½	39⅜
(dividend)	90¢	$2.80
ATT (price)	49⅜	52⅛
(dividend)	$2.60	$5
TELEDYNE (price)	36⅛	134
(dividend)	—	—
AVG. DAILY NYSE VOLUME	11.6 mil.	32 mil. shares
GOLD	$35/oz.	$524.50/oz.
SILVER	$1.80/oz.	$34.45/oz.
OIL (Saudi crude)	$1.80/bbl.	$24/bbl.
(daily U.S. imports)	3.4 mil. bbl.	8.1 mil. bbl.
SUGAR (5-lb. bag)	65¢	$1.29
HAMBURGER		
(lean ground chuck)	66¢/lb.	$1.89/lb.
(Big Mac)	49¢	95¢
(billions served)	6	30
LETTUCE	30¢/hd.	59¢/hd.
MERCEDES 450 SL	$9,254	$31,589
CHAUFFEUR (excl. overtime)	$9,000	$13,000

THE DECADE AT A GLANCE

	OPEN	CLOSE
NEW HOME	$35,500	$74,000
HOME MORTGAGE	8¼%	13%
PRIME RATE	8½%	15%
SIX-MONTH TREASURIES	6.5%	12.5%
WORKERS EMPLOYED	81 mil.	100 mil.
WORKERS UNEMPLOYED	4 mil.	6 mil.
PER CAPITA INCOME	$3,893	$8,800 (est.)
"DISPOSABLE" INCOME	$692 bil.	$1.7 tril. (est.)
GNP (Actual)	$982 bil.	$2.4 tril. (est.)
GNP (in 1970 dollars)	$982 bil.	$1.3 tril. (est.)
GERMAN MARK	25¢	58¢
PRO FOOTBALL TEAMS	20	28
OPERATING STEEL MILLS	148	154
SHOPPING MALLS	12,170	19,201
CABLE TV—HOMES	4.5 mil.	15.2 mil.
REGISTERED MOTOR VEHICLES	105 mil.	154 mil.
FEDERAL BUDGET	$197 bil.	$547 bil. (est.)
NATIONAL DEBT	$370 bil.	$845 bil. (est.)
CONSUMER DEBT (excl. mortgages)	$101 bil.	$310 bil. (est.)
COMPUTERS (U.S.)	65,000	300,000
100,000 CALCULATIONS	5¢	¼¢
COAST-TO-COAST CALL	75¢	21¢
FIRST-CLASS STAMP	6¢	15¢
CREDIT CARDS	450 mil.	579 mil.
OBJECTS IN ORBIT	1,845	4,555
LAWYERS	355,242	464,851
STOCKBROKERS	50,787	50,466
FEDERAL EMPLOYEES	2.9 mil.	2.9 mil.
LOCAL GOV'T EMPLOYEES	10.1 mil.	12.7 mil. (est.)
ALL-TIME MOVIE GROSS (N. Amer. rentals)	$72 mil. (*Sound of Music*)	$176 mil. (*Star Wars*)
ALL-TIME PAPERBACK SALE	$410,000 (*The Godfather*)	$3.2 mil. (*Princess Daisy*)
CHIEF EXECUTIVE SALARY (Incl. bonus; excl. fringes, options)		
IBM	$150,000	$484,000
GM	$250,000	$475,000
Citicorp	$272,000	$416,000

THE DECADE AT A GLANCE

	OPEN	CLOSE
Safeway	$155,000	$313,000
Exxon	$440,000	$768,000
PRISON POPULATION	196,429	306,602 ('78)
MENTAL INSTITUTION		
POPULATION ('68/'78)	532,406	189,927
U.S. POPULATION	203 mil.	222 mil.
WORLD POPULATION	3.6 bil.	4.5 bil.

COMMON STOCKS

DOW JONES INDUSTRIALS
The 1970's

OPEN	HIGH	LOW	CLOSE
800	1051	577	838
	1973	1974	

NEW YORK STOCK EXCHANGE
Annual total volume, billions of shares

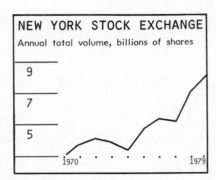

9

7

5

1970 • • • • • • • 1979

DOW JONES AVERAGE
Yearly high and low, 30 industrials

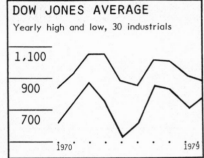

1,100

900

700

1970 • • • • • • • 1979

VALUE LINE INDUSTRIALS
Index: June 30, 1961 = 100

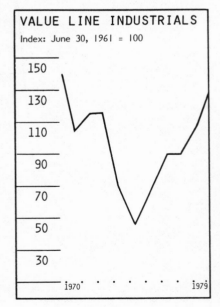

150

130

110

90

70

50

30

1970 • • • • • • • 1979

Value Line's industrial average is broader than the stodgy Dow, and more likely to reflect the typical investor's experience. From a high of 140 at the beginning of the decade (and a peak of 200 at the start of 1969), the index plunged to below 50 at the midpoint of the decade (the loss only slightly mitigated by dividends). A crash! But investors who bought at the bottom tripled their money (including dividends) in five short years.

COMMODITIES

In the 1960's the name of the game had been "earnings." In the 1970's it became "assets." Real estate was good; land could only appreciate; and anything that came from *under* the land—minerals, hydrocarbons, diamonds, silver, gold—well, that was best of all. (Water, it was said, would be the hot commodity of the 1980's.)

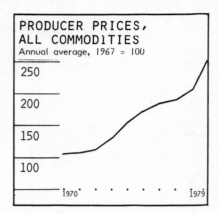

**PRODUCER PRICES,
ALL COMMODITIES**
Annual average, 1967 = 100

250

200

150

100

1970 · · · · · · · 1979

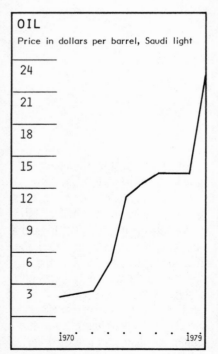

OIL
Price in dollars per barrel, Saudi light

24

21

18

15

12

9

6

3

1970 · · · · · · · 1979

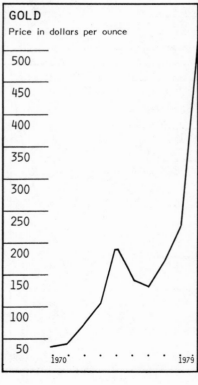

GOLD
Price in dollars per ounce

500

450

400

350

300

250

200

150

100

50

1970 · · · · · · · 1979

INFLATION

By assuming people bought the same mix of things at the end of the decade as they did in 1972—*and* by assuming they bought new homes and took out new mortgages every month—the Consumer Price Index badly *overstated* inflation in the latter part of the decade. And so helped to fuel it. The C.P.I. put 1979 inflation at 13 percent. By better measures it was "only" 10 percent.

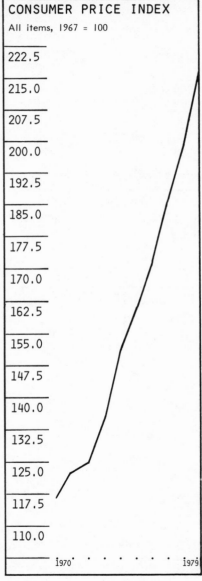

CONSUMER PRICE INDEX

All items, 1967 = 100

222.5

215.0

207.5

200.0

192.5

185.0

177.5

170.0

162.5

155.0

147.5

140.0

132.5

125.0

117.5

110.0

i970 · · · · · · i979

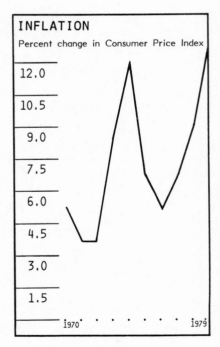

INFLATION

Percent change in Consumer Price Index

12.0

10.5

9.0

7.5

6.0

4.5

3.0

1.5

i970 · · · · · · i979

THE ECONOMY

PRODUCTIVITY

Output per hour, 1967 = 100

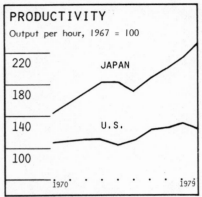

220

JAPAN

180

140

U.S.

100

1970 · · · · · · · 1979

For manufacturing jobs only. Non-manufacturing productivity was even worse.

EMPLOYMENT

Millions of workers

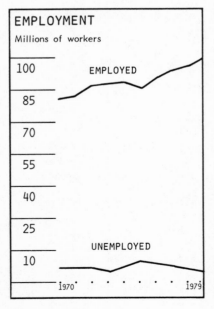

100   EMPLOYED

85

70

55

40

25

UNEMPLOYED

10

1970 · · · · · · · 1979

GROSS NATIONAL PRODUCT

Trillions of dollars

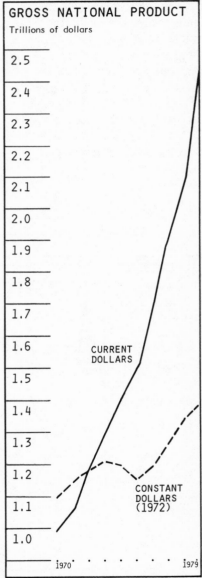

2.5

2.4

2.3

2.2

2.1

2.0

1.9

1.8

1.7

1.6   CURRENT
       DOLLARS

1.5

1.4

1.3

1.2

1.1   CONSTANT
       DOLLARS
       (1972)

1.0

1970 · · · · · · · 1979

HOUSING

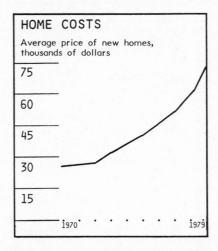

HOME COSTS
Average price of new homes, thousands of dollars

75
60
45
30
15

1970 · · · · · · · 1979

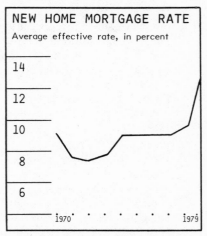

NEW HOME MORTGAGE RATE
Average effective rate, in percent

14
12
10
8
6

1970 · · · · · · · 1979

INTEREST

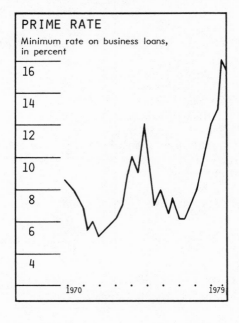

PRIME RATE
Minimum rate on business loans, in percent

16
14
12
10
8
6
4

1970 · · · · · · · 1979

EVENTS TO REMEMBER
(or Forget)

1970

Jan. 5—UMW's Joseph Yablonski slain.
Jan. 8—Gold in London falls below official $35 U.S. price.
May 8—Hard hats bust Wall Street antiwar rally.
June 21—Penn Central fails.
Nov. 9—De Gaulle dies.
Dec. 15—GNP hits $1 trillion.

1971

Jan. 12—*All in the Family* debuts.
Feb. 4—Rolls-Royce: bankrupt.
Mar. 24—Senate shoots down SST.
May—Swordfish scare.
June 13—"Pentagon Papers."
June 30—Banker dies of Bon Vivant vichyssoise.
July 1—U.S. Postal Service launched, service to improve
  dramatically.
Aug. 15—Nixon freezes wages, prices; cuts dollar's tie to gold.
Oct. 19—*Look* folds.

1972

Jan. 9—Howard Hughes telephone news conference: "The book's a
  hoax."
Feb. 21—Nixon meets Mao.
May 15—Wallace is shot.
June 14—EPA bans DDT.
June 17—Watergate break-in.
July 1—*Ms.* born.
July 8—$750 million Russian wheat deal heralded.
July 25—Eagleton nominated.
July 31—Quits.
Nov. 1—Esso: Exxon.
Nov. 14—Dow closes over 1,000, first time ever.
Dec. 29—*Life* folds.

1973

Jan. 27—Draft ends.
Mar. 29—Last GI's leave Vietnam.
Oct. 10—Agnew resigns; no contest.

Oct. 19—Arabs embargo oil.
Nov. 17—"I am not a crook."
Dec. 28—Kohoutek's comet!

1974

Mar. 7—First streakers reported.
Mar. 18—Oil embargo ends.
Apr. 2—Academy Awards streaked.
Apr.—Toilet paper panic.
Aug. 9—Nixon out.
Sept. 8—Pardoned unconditionally.
Sept. 8—Largest bank failure in U.S. history (Franklin National).

1975

Jan. 1—Mitchell, Haldeman, Ehrlichman: "guilty"; literary agents mob courtroom.
May—Unemployment exceeds 9 percent, highest since 1941.
Oct. 2—W. T. Grant, second largest bankruptcy in U.S. history.

1976

U.S. beef consumption peaks at 128.5 pounds per capita.
Jan. 30—Record 38.5 million shares trade on New York Exchange.
July 4—Happy birthday, America.
July 9—Queen Elizabeth visits Bloomingdale's.
July 20—Viking I on Mars.
July 28—Worst quake in 400 years kills 655,000 Chinese.
Sept. 16—RCA chief canned; paid tax but failed to file.

1977

Mar. 27—Tenerife: 747s collide on runway, 581 dead.
Apr. 18—"Moral equivalent of war."
May 24—Concorde begins U.S. flights.
July 13—New York City blacked out, looted.
Aug. 2—Disease fells Legionnaires.
Oct. 8—Mao embalmed.

1978

Jan. 17—Gary Gilmore executed, first in ten years. He asked for it.
Mar. 2—Charlie Chaplin stolen.
Apr. 18—Panama Canal treaty voted.
June 6—Proposition 13 passes; cuts California property taxes 57 percent.

June 9—Pinto recalled.

June 20—Alaska pipeline open.

July 28—Gold breaks $200; obviously poised for fall.

Sept. 25—*Life* unfolds.

Nov. 1—Fed bumps discount rate full point to save dollar; Dow jumps 35.

Nov. 18—Jonestown massacre.

Dec. 15—Cleveland defaults.

1979

Jan. 1—Mandatory retirement raised to 70.

Feb. 1—Khomeini arrives in Iran; Deng Xiaoping arrives in Atlanta.

Mar. 26—Israeli-Egyptian peace pact.

Mar. 26—$10 million Los Angeles computer thief sentenced to eight years.

Mar. 28—Three Mile Island.

May 3—Margaret Thatcher elected.

May 21—Murderer of San Francisco mayor, supervisor, sentenced to seven years, eight months.

June 7—Carter approves 8,800 concrete MX missile shelters.

June 12—Man flies English Channel.

July 11—Skylab falls; much ado.

July 15—Carter: "Crisis of confidence."

July 18—Gold breaks $300. Crash imminent.

July 19—Supertankers collide off Tobago.

July 25—Test-tube tot.

Aug. 17—U.S. balloonists cross Atlantic.

Sept. 25—Five-year snail darter delay ends; dam approved.

Oct. 2—Gold breaks $400. Unquestionably the top.

Oct. 4—Pope in Iowa.

Oct. 6/8—Fed bumps discount rate full point to save dollar; Dow plunges in panic selling.

Oct. 10—81.6 million shares trade on New York Stock Exchange.

Dec. 27—Gold pierces $500. Tippy, tippy absolute top.

ABOUT THE AUTHOR

Andrew Tobias, a graduate of Harvard College and Harvard Business School, is the author of two best-selling books, *Fire and Ice* and *The Only Investment Guide You'll Ever Need.* Mr. Tobias is a contributing editor of *Esquire* Magazine. At present he is at work on a book about the insurance industry.